# ROGER
# MARIS

Also by Maury Allen

Sweet Lou
Mr. October: The Reggie Jackson Story
Damn Yankee: Billy Martin
Where Have You Gone, Joe DiMaggio?
You Could Look It Up
Bo: Pitching and Wooing
Now Wait a Minute, Casey
The Record Breakers
Joe Namath's Sportin' Life
The Incredible Mets
Reprieve From Hell
Baseball's 100

# ROGER MARIS

## a man for all seasons

# MAURY ALLEN

**DↃIF**

DONALD I. FINE, INC.
New York

796. 357
A
C-1

*For Janet, Jennifer and Ted*

*Love is never having to say
I'll be home late because
the game ran long.*

# Acknowledgments

This book was born twenty five years ago, on September 20, 1961, as Roger Maris thrilled a kid reporter with a performance my literary hero, Ernest Hemingway, would have called, "Grace under pressure." The idea germinated for many years, floated in and out of my brain, rose and fell for many reasons over many summer seasons around the game I love. As Roger's health failed in 1985, I knew time was an enemy.

Roger was gone but the idea lived on. When Donald Fine called my agent, Julian Bach, and asked if I would be interested in doing a biography in time to mark the silver anniversary of that golden summer of '61, I knew he was a publisher with taste and timing.

This work could not have happened without the kindness of the Maris family, the generosity of old pal Julie Isaacson, the patience and poise of those old Yankee teammates of Roger's, the loyalty of friends, and the professionalism of many of my newspaper colleagues. There was much help from baseball pals of Roger's from

Cleveland, Kansas City and St. Louis, as well as New York. The old clippings helped as did Jim Ogle's book on Roger. But this is a work built on the memory of so many. I thank them all.

Don Fine made this book happen. Editor Rick Horgan made it happen much more smoothly. Julian Bach made it happen under a schedule I thought impossible to meet. They are all superstars in their own leagues.

# 1

## the 61 in '61

THE world was younger then. John F. Kennedy, the dashing young President, exuded optimism as he faced global problems. The Reds had widened a razed strip between East and West Berlin and the city was being separated by ugly barbed wire. The president of South Vietnam, Ngo Dinh Diem, was quoted in the New York *Times* as saying the struggle in his country "has grown from guerrilla action to real war." Adlai Stevenson, the United States representative to the United Nations, had reported hopes that the Soviets had softened their stand on a nuclear test ban. In Madrid, Generalissimo Francisco Franco celebrated twenty-five years of power in Spain. In Cairo, Gamel Abdel Nasser cut Egypt's ties to Jordan and Turkey over Syria's withdrawal from the United Arab Republic.

None of that seemed to matter much on that Sunday morning, October 1, 1961, in the Bronx, New York, or Grand Forks or Fargo, North Dakota, or Hibbing, Minnesota, or Detroit or Boston or Kansas City or Cleveland or any one of a dozen cities where baseball was being discussed or played that early fall day.

Roger and Pat Maris awoke early, as was their custom, in room 324 of the Loew's Midtown Hotel in Manhattan, enjoyed a leisurely room service breakfast and walked three blocks in the bright sun to St. Patrick's Cathedral for the eight o'clock Mass.

In Lenox Hill Hospital, in room 411, Mickey Mantle restlessly drank a glass of orange juice and sipped a cup of hot tea. He was still in much pain from the abscess in his right hip. Fluid drained into a large gauze pad as he shifted with some difficulty to his left side while he perused the morning sports pages. He saw that Maris had not hit a home run in four days. He was stuck on 60 homers, tied for the all-time single season record with Babe Ruth, and now had his final chance. The Yankees were playing the Boston Red Sox at Yankee Stadium. Bill Stafford was listed as the starting pitcher for New York. The Red Sox starter was listed as either Gene Conley, the tall basketball player, or Tracy Stallard, a rookie right-hander. The game would not start for some five hours, but Mantle asked the floor nurse to move his television set closer to the bed. He did not want to miss a pitch.

In Lake Success, Long Island, Whitey and Joan Ford ate breakfast with their three small children. Ford enjoyed Sunday day games. The drive to the ballpark was easier because of less traffic, and he almost always got home in time to throw a ball around in the back yard with the kids. Since he was not scheduled to pitch this day, he would leave his house early and spend time in the Yankee clubhouse getting on the other players. His routine differed only slightly—as it would on Tuesday, when he opened the 1961 World Series against the Cincinnati Reds—arriving later on days he was scheduled to pitch. On those days he hated the dead time before games. He would arrive an hour later than usual, dress quickly, get his arm rubbed by trainer Gus Mauch, put on his uniform and go out to pitch, most of the time, another brilliant Yankee victory. He was 25-4 that season and an almost certain bet for the Cy Young award, the most prestigious pitching award in baseball.

Manager Ralph Houk, finishing his first season as the Yankee field boss, was glad it would soon be over. He could forget the pressures of the home run chase and concentrate on winning baseball games. It had been tough on Maris, tough on Mantle, but almost as tough on him. He got sick of all those fan letters telling him he was mishandling Roger and Mickey. He drove easily from his Saddle River, New Jersey, home to the Stadium. He was most pleased it was a sunny morning. There would be no controversy about playing the game if it rained. Ralph hated controversy.

Yogi Berra drove to the Stadium from his sprawling home in Montclair, New Jersey. Bob Turley walked the two blocks up the hill from his room in the Concourse Plaza Hotel. Clete Boyer and rookie Tom Tresh took a quick cab ride together from the Stadium Motor Lodge. Bobby Richardson picked up Tony Kubek at his New Jersey home and they drove in together. Moose Skowron told his wife Cookie he would take her out to dinner that night no matter what time the game ended. He was so glad the season was over. Arlene Howard drove her husband, Elston, across the George Washington Bridge from Teaneck, dropped him at the Stadium and returned home. John and Nancy Blanchard drove to the Stadium together. She would visit friends after dropping him off and return to the Stadium for the game. Hector Lopez rode the subway to the Stadium, got off at 161st Street, signed a few autographs on the street for a couple of kids and walked into the ballpark.

Tracy Stallard and Gene Conley, good buddies and pitching partners on the Red Sox, shared a small table in the coffee shop of the Roosevelt Hotel. One of them was supposed to pitch. Neither knew who it was. They kidded about walking Maris four times. The team bus had already left for the ballpark, and the two pitchers shared a cab to the Stadium. Stallard remembers remarking about the beautiful day. He secretly hoped he would be selected to start. Pitching against the Yankees always brought out the best in him.

Maris sat at his locker now in the far left corner of the Yankee clubhouse. He puffed on a cigarette, and clubhouse man Pete Sheehy brought him a cup of coffee. He wore a T-shirt with the large number 9 stenciled at the collar and a pair of undershorts with the name MARIS printed on the waistband in indelible pencil.

"He was trying to look calm," says Whitey Ford. "He failed."

On March 15, 1985, with his life span down to 245 days as an insidious cancer traveled through his system, Maris sat behind the large desk in his office at the Maris Distributing Company in Gainesville, Florida. The crewcut was familiar. He talked easily. He smiled rarely. He did not seem to be in any pain. He wore a white shirt, open at the collar, tan slacks and dark shoes. I asked him what he remembered most from that October 1, 1961. His mouth turned down, his eyes stared straight ahead and he leaned back in his swivel chair. His voice was firm.

"I remember that if I hit a home run that day, if I got number 61, if I did anything else as a Yankee it wouldn't matter to a lot of people. No matter what I did, Mickey Mantle *was* the New York Yankees."

The Yankees went about their business as routinely as possible on that final day of the regular 1961 season. It had been an exciting year with the Maris-Mantle home run chase, the magnificent season of Ford, the .348 batting of Howard, the incredible defense of the entire team. But it had been filled with stress. From late June onward, the pressures on Maris and Mantle, called the M and M Boys in the press, had been excruciating. Houk had done his best to diffuse it. Now, with this final game, it would be over....

Maris had his complete uniform on now. He sat on his locker stool entertaining catcher John Blanchard with his skills at the labyrinth game he played daily. It was a wooden board game with steel balls moving this way and that along a narrow path. The object of the game was to keep the balls from falling through holes. Maris could keep those balls moving thirty, forty, fifty times without falling through the holes. No other Yankee could ever get past ten. "I would watch him through the mesh screen between our lockers," Blanchard says. "I felt like I was at a confessional."

Down the Stadium hallway, some one hundred yards from the Yankee clubhouse, the Boston Red Sox dressed for their final game of another lackluster sixth-place season in the first year of the American League's expansion to ten teams. Rookie Carl Yastrzemski, a kid from Long Island, worked the clubhouse scrounging up a few more complimentary tickets for his family and friends coming in from Southampton, Long Island, to see him play at the Stadium. Third baseman Frank Malzone reminded Yastrzemski that he, Malzone, lived in the Bronx and would outbid him for tickets. "Just kidding, kid," Malzone said. "You can even have mine."

Stallard and Conley arrived together. They walked to their lockers. Because they arrived later than the team but still well ahead of the prescribed time ordered by manager Pinky Higgins, they were kidded about having a long night in New York. "Short night," corrected Stallard. "Long cab ride."

"Expensive," said Conley.

Pitching coach Sal Maglie walked toward them. He had a new baseball in his hand. He bent down and dropped it into Stallard's right shoe. It was his ritualistic way of informing the starting pitcher he would begin the game. "Good luck," said the guy the old New York Giants knew as the Barber.

**TRACY STALLARD** is forty-nine years old, still a handsome man with thick black hair and wicked gray eyes. He pitched for the Red Sox, Mets and Cardinals before ending his career in Mexico. He is in the strip coal mining business in Coeburn, Virginia.

**STALLARD:** "Gene and I knew one of us would pitch. We wished each other good luck a lot the night before and again over breakfast. I was really happy when Sal gave me the ball. I don't know what Maris was feeling but I didn't feel any particular tension. I didn't think much about his home run record. I wanted to win because it was the last day of the season and I wanted to go back to Virginia leaving a good impression with the club. Maris didn't particularly concern me. I had faced him a couple of times before and got him out. It was that entire lineup

that concerned me. Mantle, Berra, Howard, Skowron, Lopez, all of them. There was not an easy batter in that group.
On the Yankees of 1961 there was not a single batter to
pitch around. No sir, that was one tough team."

Houk sat in his office writing out the lineup card. With
Mantle out, he batted Berra in the fourth spot. Boy, would
he be glad when he would no longer need to answer that
question again about Mickey batting behind Roger. He put
down Richardson, Kubek, Maris, Berra, Blanchard, Howard, Skowron, Boyer and Stafford.

**RALPH HOUK** is sixty-seven years old, lives in retirement
in Pompano Beach, Florida, tries to catch every fish in
the Atlantic Ocean and enjoys a good cigar every chance
he gets. He had a distinguished World War II record, an
undistinguished playing record as a backup catcher on
the Yankees, a successful managerial career in New York,
Detroit and Boston. He retired after the 1984 season.

**HOUK:** "It got so I was answering that question about the
lineup every day. People think all we did that year was
concern ourselves with the home run race. Sure it was
thrilling, certainly the most thrilling individual effort I
had ever witnessed. But more importantly we won. People
forget we had a tough pennant race. We weren't in first
place for good until the middle of July. We didn't bust the
race open until we won thirteen games in a row in September. I started going with Roger third and Mickey fourth,
instead of Roger fourth the way Casey [Stengel] had it the
year before, because I wanted Mickey hitting right-handed
against left-handed pitching between Roger and Yogi. Then
we started winning and I wasn't about to change the lineup

around after that. Once they started hitting home runs, we were drawing big crowds. If you want to continue working in baseball, you don't fool with a lineup drawing big crowds."

Shortly before two o'clock, public address announcer Bob Sheppard began announcing the lineup to the modest crowd in the huge Stadium. He announced the names of Richardson at second base and Kubek at shortstop.... "Number 9, Roger Maris, center field," he said with that marvelously modulated voice. There was a murmur in the crowd, some smattering of applause and a great deal of movement in the seats behind the right-field fence.

In Lenox Hill Hospital Yankee outfielder Bob Cerv, recovering from knee surgery, was wheeled into Mantle's room to watch the game on television. The two Yankee outfielders had shared a two-bedroom apartment on Van Wyck Boulevard in Forest Hills, overlooking the famous West Side Tennis Club, that summer with Maris. It was Mickey's idea to take some of the pressure off Roger and to dispel those rumors that the two sluggers were feuding. Mickey had a catch-all gag line all season. He would walk up to Roger, make a mad face and shout, "I hate your guts." It meant some other item of gossip, suggesting a bitter feud, had appeared in print. Then the three roommates would read the item and break up. Mantle and Cerv watched as Stafford retired the Red Sox in order in the first inning. Richardson and Kubek went out, and Sheppard intoned,... "batting third, the center fielder, number 9, Roger Maris." Mantle looked at Cerv and laughed. "Roger, I hate your guts."

In the stands behind home plate Pat Maris sat with good friends Julie and Selma Isaacson. Julie Isaacson was a former minor league ballplayer who had a tryout with Brooklyn before the war years. He had gotten involved in his father's labor union activities and had by now risen to the leadership of the Novelty and Toy Makers Union. He had befriended Irv Noren, a former Yankee, who led him to Cerv, who led him to Maris when Roger joined the Yankees in 1960. "I picked him up at the airport when he joined the Yankees for the first time," Isaacson says. "He had that crewcut, real short, wore an old sweater and a pair of sneakers. I told him, 'Raj, you're with the Yankees now. You can't dress like that. Go out and buy yourself some clothes.' The next day he came to the park with a new sports jacket, new trousers and the same old sneakers. This was just a good country kid. What did he know from New York?"

In the dugout Houk leaned on one foot, reached down for some pebbles, shuffled them in his hand for a while and then scattered them in front of him. Blanchard moved nervously from one end of the dugout, where he had been sitting, to the empty seat in the middle. Boyer leaned forward and nearly fell off the bench. Richardson sat with his arms crossed. In the bullpen, coach Jim Hegan stood up against the small railing by the stands. Pitcher Bob Turley crept over toward the right-field stands. Pitcher Luis Arroyo leaned back on the bench, closed his eyes and took some sun.

Stallard, working easily on the mound, threw a high fastball for ball one. "I wasn't going to walk him if I could help it," Stallard remembers thinking. His next pitch was a little down and on the outside part of the plate. Maris was a split second late in reacting and couldn't get the fat part of his 35-inch, 33-ounce Louisville Slugger bat with his name inscribed on top of it into the ball. He hit a soft fly into left field and after a couple of quick steps rookie left fielder Carl Yastrzemski caught the ball smoothly. Roger had barely reached first base. He turned quickly to his right, jogged with his head down toward the Yankee dugout, flipped his batting helmet to coach Wally Moses, collected his glove from Blanchard and turned back toward center field. "I had hit a lot of homers that year, 21, including four in a row," says Blanchard, "and I remember thinking if Roger doesn't get it maybe I can switch one of mine to him."

Stallard and Stafford, tuning up for his Series start, kept the game scoreless into the fourth. The Red Sox went down in order in the top of the inning. The crowd began moving around again in the right-field stands. A Sacramento, California, restaurant owner named Sam Gordon had announced he would award $5,000 to any fan who caught the sixty-first home run and presented it to him. He was a sports fan who wanted to mount the ball in his establishment. He thought $5,000 was cheap enough for that kind of publicity.

"When the inning started I jogged down to the bullpen," says Whitey Ford. "I was starting the Tuesday Series opener but I wanted to throw about fifteen minutes. I got out there just as Roger came up. Jim Hegan had a ball and his big glove and he wanted to get going. 'Not yet.' I didn't want to miss this. The pitcher warming up in the Yankee bullpen had his back to the plate and was behind the fence. It would be impossible to see the ball land from there. 'After Roger,' I told Jim. Suddenly a strange memory had flashed into my mind. When Don Larsen pitched his perfect game in 1956 I was in the bullpen. Larsen didn't have a lot of stamina, and Casey was afraid he would lose it. Sometimes he could lose it quick, and the score was only 2-0. I threw every inning from the sixth inning on. I missed most of the Perfect Game. When he struck out Dale Mitchell for the last out I was probably busting off a curve in the bullpen. I missed that. I didn't want to miss this."

Maris walked to the plate and the crowd gave him a friendly hand. There were 23,154 people in the stands. The Yankees considered this disappointing on a day when history might be made. A lot of people thought history would not be made. A lot more didn't want history to be made. They were loyal to the memory of Babe Ruth or they were emotionally tied to Mickey Mantle. Maris ground his right front foot into some little holes in the dirt around home plate.

"We had similar stances," Tony Kubek says. "I used to dig those holes the first time up and Roger would get his front foot into the same spot. One time he was in a small slump. 'Hey, Tony, are you still lining up the holes the same way?' I convinced him I was, he got a base hit the next time up and that was the end of the slump."

Maris was dug in now in the fourth inning, those strong, muscular arms pumping that bat back and forth, back and forth as he loosened up for a swing at Stallard's fastball. His batting helmet was pulled down tight over his fore-head. His legs were spread about eighteen inches apart at the plate, and his uniform leg bagged at the knees to give him some play as he followed through on his swing. Stallard looked in at catcher Russ Nixon and saw the sign for a curve ball. "I didn't want to hang it so I made sure I gave it a good pull back," Stallard says. The pitch was a little high and a little off the plate to the left. Plate umpire Bill Kinnamon called it a ball. Maris moved one foot out of the box as Stallard fiddled with the ball on the mound.

Houk moved some pebbles in front of the dugout. Blanchard took a deep sigh and pounded his fist into his glove.

In the broadcasting booth, above home plate, statistician Bill Kane pushed some home run figures in front of Phil Rizzuto. The former Yankee shortstop, in his fifth year as a play-by-play broadcaster, was good at calling the game but a little shaky without printed information. Pat Maris inched forward on her hard Stadium seat. Bob Turley, sitting on the right end of the Yankee bullpen bench, got up. "I moved to the left side of the bullpen," the side closest to the right-field stands. "If it went in there I wanted to see it. If it came into the bullpen I wanted to catch it. I wanted to be the guy to give it to Roger," he says.

Now Stallard threw his second pitch, this time a fastball, to Maris in the fourth inning. Kinnamon turned from the plate, held his fists clenched at the side in the traditional sign that the pitch was called a ball, and looked over his right shoulder into the Yankee dugout. Several players were sitting on the bench tapping their feet on the wooden dugout floor. The crowd had started booing Stallard. "I heard it but I didn't get concerned over it. I wasn't trying to walk anybody in a 0-0 game. Heck, Yogi was the next hitter and he could hit one out as easily as Roger could," Stallard says.

The bat was high over Roger's left ear now. Stallard kicked his left foot forward and brought his right arm through as he had hundreds of times before. The white ball whistled to the plate. Nixon had his big catcher's mitt in front of him and his right hand, or meat hand, behind his back. He could feel Kinnamon's hand on the small of his back as the umpire bore down to get a good, close look at the pitch. "I saw the pitch was going to get a lot of the plate," Stallard remembers. "It wasn't quite down enough and outside enough where I wanted it. I watched him swing, hit it flush and I knew it was out there a long way."

Now Maris was standing at home plate, the bat still in his right hand, his head tilted upward, his left hand resting against his left thigh, his right knee slightly cocked, his left toe leaning forward and the heel off the ground. There was the impact of silence as the ball raced for the stands. Then it hit with a thump, about ten rows deep, some ten feet from the Yankee bullpen, maybe 365 feet from home plate, and the crowd let out a giant collective sustained roar.

"I was staring out there as the ball went in," says Turley. "I saw a guy lift his suit jacket and try to catch it in the jacket. He stopped it and then it fell down off the jacket and this other guy, a little guy with dark, wavy hair, pulled it off the jacket and held it up in the air."

Maris finally started running now, holding on tightly to his batting helmet halfway to first, rounding the base with his head down, breaking into a smile around second when Boston shortstop Pumpsie Green winked at him and smiled, reaching third as Malzone said, "Nice goin'," rounding third and being applauded and congratulated surprisingly by coach Frank Crosetti, who played with Ruth and considered home runs a divine Yankee right, jogging toward home when a young fan who had bolted from the stands pumped his hand and followed him toward the plate before security guards interrupted his home run echo journey.

"I couldn't even think as I went around the bases," Maris would say later. "I was all fogged out."

Berra, carrying three bats on his shoulder, pumped Roger's right hand and patted him on the back as he ran by on the way to the dugout. The crowd was standing, yelling his name, clapping their hands together, sharing his historic baseball moment: the only man to ever hit 61 homers, more than Babe Ruth in a single season, more than Mickey Mantle who had ended his own bid at 54 in a hospital bed, more than Jimmy Foxx and Hank Greenberg, who had come up just short of Ruth with 58. He had done it in Yankee game 162 in baseball's first ever expanded season and Ford Frick, the commissioner, had ruled a "distinctive mark" would be necessary in the record book to note the feat. "Distinctive mark" or not, no one would come within striking range in the quarter of a century following that October day. Only Willie Mays and George Foster would even hit as many as 52 in the next twenty-five years.

Now Maris was moving to the edge of the dugout and his teammates were lined up outside the top step, shaking Maris's hands, rubbing his bare head, patting his back, shouting a jumbled collection of congratulations. He tried to move into the dugout, a wide grin on his face, but Lopez, Skowron and Blanchard would have none of it. They stood between Maris and the top step, pushing him forward as they blocked his path to privacy. He held his batting helmet in his hand and waved vigorously to the fans behind the Yankee dugout and to the fans behind third and to the fans scattered through the old ballpark, the House That Ruth Built, soaking in that esteem, that admiration, that thanks from each of them who had paid $3.50 for a box seat and 75 cents for a bleacher seat to participate in this happening.

"When he hit it I wanted to be part of the celebration with him, we all did," says Turley, "and I jumped down into the runway to get to the dugout. As I did I bumped my head on the concrete and almost knocked myself cold.

I was woozy but I struggled through it and made it to the dugout as he was coming back from his last bow."

The young man who had caught the baseball, Sal Durante, a nineteen-year-old from Brooklyn, was escorted by Stadium cops to the Yankee clubhouse. While the inning continued, photographers were summoned to record the historic rite. Maris had been collecting most of his home run baseballs all that season, but Durante wanted that $5,000. There would be a photo, a trip to Sacramento later for both of them, the $5,000 for Durante (who would soon marry), and the final delivery of the baseball much later, by Sam Gordon, back to Maris and finally to the Hall of Fame at Cooperstown.

Maris was back on the bench now, his baseball bat resting at his feet, his eyes fixed on the field as the game continued, his cap pushed back on his head, a grin creeping out from the corners of his mouth.

"After everyone settled down I sat there on the bench and I let out a deep sigh," Tony Kubek remembers. "We had all gone through it with Roger and Mickey and in a way it was as much a relief for us to have it over as it was for Roger. I looked over at him and for an instant his eyes were closed and I could see him breathing deeply. I think he just let loose a deep, deep sigh and all the air came out of his balloon. So much pressure had built up, so much tension over these past weeks. It was incredible. I think that Roger's feeling wasn't as much excitement over doing what nobody in baseball had ever done. It was just relief, plain old-fashioned relief. He could relax now. He could be just another guy at the ballpark."

After Roger hit the historic home run and circled the bases and accepted the applause of the crowd, the noise continued.

"I stood out there on the mound and I wanted to pitch,"

says Tracy Stallard. "It was still a 1-0 game and I wanted to win it. Yogi was at the plate but he never seemed to get into the box. The crowd wouldn't settle down and the noise continued and Yogi kept fidgeting with his bat and walking around the batter's box. I don't know how long it took for him to get back in there. For me it seemed like an hour."

Maris batted twice more in that final game of the 1961 season. In the sixth inning he ran the count to 3-2 and Stallard struck him out on a high fastball. In the eighth inning, with Stallard removed from the game for a pinch hitter, left-hander Chet Nichols faced Maris. Maris got under a fastball and popped it up to second baseman Chuck Schilling.

There would be no 62 home runs.

"There was a strange feeling in the ballpark all day," says Clete Boyer. "There was surprising quiet until Roger hit it and even more quiet afterward. Roger was never one to show his emotions and even though he was obviously happy and smiling a lot when he hit it, there was an edge of sadness to the entire day. The ruling by Commissioner Frick about the 60 homers in 154 games or else it didn't count took so much joy away from the feat. That was the game that was filled with tension. There was so much pressure that night, so much tension I could hardly breathe. Roger wanted that one badly. When it came down to the last day of the season, 60 homers or 61 homers didn't seem all that different. Roger was never one to discuss those kinds of things but I always had the feeling he was hurt, and hurt badly, by that ruling. It just gave us all, especially Roger, some feeling of emptiness about the final homer, as if it were more of an exhibition kind of thing, like a spring training homer. It was more than any man had ever hit but despite the crowd reaction, despite how much Roger enjoyed it, despite all the press, the entire day was a letdown, a disappointment. That's always been my feeling."

During that season, during the next season, in many of the years following, whenever that sensitive subject would come up, Maris would answer with some edge to his voice and that touch of brutal honesty so typical of his character.

"A season's a season," he would say. "I don't make the schedule."

The game was over now. The home run had given the Yankees a 1-0 victory, the first 1-0 game Maris had ever won with a homer. It also gave him the league's runs-batted-in title with 142—as well as the home run title, of course—and the lead in runs scored at 132, in a tie with Mantle.

**MICKEY MANTLE** is fifty-four years old, still blond and strong with that Oklahoma drawl dripping from his lips. He was the most popular Yankee of his time and a team legend, equal in fan esteem and historic lore to Babe Ruth and Joe DiMaggio. He makes his home in Dallas but travels extensively to golf tournaments, charity banquets and a variety of public appearances. He represents an insurance company, a cable television company and a casino hotel in Atlantic City. He retired after the 1968 season with aching shoulders, bad legs and a slowing bat, but his fame has only grown. His fame is not confined to a Hall of Fame plaque at Cooperstown. He may well be one of a half dozen most recognizable faces in America.

**MANTLE:** "I was sitting on the edge of my hospital bed when Roger hit the home run. I watched it closely on television and I got goosebumps all over my body. Sure,

I wished it was me, but I had been sick for a couple of weeks and the excitement of the race wore off. I wasn't in it any more and I wanted Roger to do it. He was my teammate, my friend and a guy I admired very much. We used to kid a lot about being tied for home runs on the last day of the season. I told him if he hit a home run and I was at the plate when he came home I'd hit him with the bat, he'd fall down and the home run wouldn't count. He would laugh and say if he was on base and I hit one he would run in the other direction and pass me and I'd be declared out. We had a lot of fun all year going back and forth with that stuff. In late August when we were tied at 45 home runs I thought I would beat him. I really didn't think either of us would hit 60 or 61. Every time I thought we had a lot of home runs somebody would come up and remind me that Babe Ruth hit 17 in the month of September. By that time of the year the bat feels like a dead weight sometimes and your whole body is weak.

"I can't hardly believe that Roger is gone now. He was never a big drinker like Whitey and Billy and me. It seemed every time we got together it was a drinking contest. Roger would have a few and then he'd quit. He was a good family man and took good care of himself and it just seems so strange that he went first. I still can't believe it. I still see him in my dreams. We were competitive as players, of course, and each of us wanted to win that title that year, but we got along real good. We lived together, we kidded around a lot, we enjoyed our time out there. Roger was a hell of a player, a Hall of Famer for sure in my book. He was a terrific outfielder, a great base runner, a marvelous slider. He studied the game. He always concentrated. I would be out there looking at the stands or catching the eye of some pretty girl or thinking about my last strikeout and Roger was out there remembering the count on the hitter or moving with the pitch.

"Let's face it, the home run year took a lot out of him. But it was some feat. Ted Williams was my hero and I was a little upset when Ralph moved me down to fourth in the order and moved Roger up to third. I always liked hitting third because Williams and Stan Musial, my other hero, hit third and I was lucky there. People say Roger got the edge that year because he didn't receive one intentional walk in front of me. Hell, he still had to hit 61 baseballs out of the park. He had to do that himself. Williams once said that hitting a baseball is the hardest thing to do in sports. I have always believed that. That's why what Roger did that year, hitting 61 home runs, doing it under that incredible pressure—knowing a lot of people didn't want him to do it because they wanted me to do it or Babe Ruth to keep the record—was simply the greatest single feat in the history of sports. I believe that. I'll argue that with anybody. I can still see that home run of his go into the seats and I still get chills thinking about it. Even now, even this very minute."

The Yankees came up the ramp from the dugout to the clubhouse. They were hollering and slapping hands and reaching out for Maris. When the last player was inside, the doors were closed for a minute and Maris asked Pete Sheehy for a beer. He sat in front of his locker, lit up a cigarette and sat down on the stool. Manager Ralph Houk saw that Maris was composed now, and the ritual had to be played out. "Let 'em in," he shouted. The door was opened. Some fifty or sixty members of the press lunged toward Maris.

"I was next to Roger but I knew I couldn't dress there

that day," says Blanchard. "I grabbed my clothes before they came in and put them in Hector Lopez's locker down the side. I went in for my shower and when I came out fifteen minutes later Roger was being crushed against the back of his locker."

"Okay, fellows, shoot," Maris said.

The questions began about the pressures, the satisfaction of the home run, the pitch Stallard threw, the location, the meaning, the emotion of the moment. Maris was patient and direct. He answered every query. He answered a lot of the same questions over and over. He never raised his voice. He was doing his job, serving the Yankees in a public relations performance. It had been that way most of the summer. There were times when he was short-tempered, sometimes gruff, often curt. It was part of his stoic, private, shy personality. Most of his anger, especially on the field, was directed at himself. He was, as the ballplayers say, a red ass, an angry young man under certain circumstances. This day was not one of them.

The game had ended shortly after four o'clock. It was now well past five. The press had thinned to a final few. Maris started walking toward the shower.

"I walked over," says Whitey Ford, "and I was finally able to get to him to congratulate him. Sometimes I wondered if he would survive that summer."

Maris left the Stadium between a phalanx of cops outside the gate, climbed into his car with his wife Pat, and Selma and Julie Isaacson. They drove downtown to Joe Marsh's Spindletop restaurant. They were joined by New York *Post* sports columnist Milton Gross. "Maris had a shrimp cocktail, a steak medium, a mixed salad with French dressing, a baked potato, two glasses of wine, a sliver of cheese cake, two cups of coffee and three cigarettes," Gross reported.

The dinner was pleasant and warm. Maris revealed the tension when he said, "I haven't unwound yet. I'm just beginning to unwind. A lot of it is still a little hazy."

Maris told a story about a radio reporter asking him, "As you were running around the bases, were you thinking of Mickey Mantle?" He thought that was the strangest question of the day, the one most fraught with wicked innuendo. Then he continued. "Last winter I was home and kidding with my daughter, Susan. She's four. I asked her who's the best baseball player in the world. 'Mickey Mantle,' she says. I got a laugh out of that."

Shortly before the dinner was over, a teenage girl spotted Maris near her table and gently asked for an autograph on a menu.

"Would you put the date on it, too, please?"

"The date? What is today's date."

"The date," said Isaacson, "is the one you did what nobody else ever did."

Maris was leaving now, and he asked Isaacson to drive him to Lenox Hill Hospital before he returned to the hotel.

"I want to see Cerv and Mickey over there," he said.

They drove across the quiet Manhattan streets, the last traces of daylight fading behind the tall buildings, and Maris remained quiet. They reached the hospital. Maris went in alone while the others waited. He took the elevator to Mickey's fourth floor room. Mantle was watching television. He looked up, a surprised grin on his face. Then he said, "I hate your guts."

The M and M Boys, Roger Maris and Mickey Mantle, who had combined to make 1961 the most electrifying year in baseball history, laughed together uproariously.

# 2

## fargo

**THE** pallbearers, all dressed in dark suits without over-coats in the sixteen-below-zero temperature, stood rigid under a small canopy. An icy wind cut across the frozen earth of Holy Cross Cemetery. These middle-aged men, baseball players who had excelled in the summer of their time—Mickey Mantle, Whitey Ford, Mike Shannon, Bill Skowron, Clete Boyer, Whitey Herzog, Bob Allison—and the local friends, George Surprise, Dick Savageau, Robert Wood, Don Gooselaw, and New York buddy Julie Isaacson, struggled for breath on that frigid afternoon of December 19, 1985. A light snow fell on the glistening casket holding the remains of Roger Maris. Bishop James S. Sullivan of St. Mary's Cathedral clutched a bible as he waited for the family—Roger's father, his brother, his wife, his six children—to assemble across the grave. He intoned a few words, called for God's mercy, recited a gentle prayer and recognized the struggles of the living in ending the service quickly. The family moved to waiting cars and the middle-aged men thought, perhaps, of a sweeter, sof-

ter, warmer time. Factory smoke from the sugar beet pro-
cessing plant spewed into the afternoon sky.

The cars rolled back to town now or out to the airport,
across the rock-hard land, with a foot of snow piled high
across the edges of the road, the sugar beet fields, the
potato farms, the winter wheat and barley fields fading
now beyond the city streets.

These fields of North Dakota's Red River Valley, so rich
and lush and bountiful in summer, were imbedded deep
in the character of the man whose life had now been
celebrated in sadness.

The upper Midwest had beckoned to new immigrants
from Germany and Austria who found the cold winters
and vast, open lands of North and South Dakota as much
like home as one could find in the developing lands of
the Great Plains. It was here, across the border in Minnesota, that Roger Maris's grandfather first settled when
he came to these shores as a teenager from Austria in 1900.
He was soon settled in Hibbing, then a mining town, and
opened a bar with his brothers to serve the needs of the
miners who escaped from the hollows of the earth each
day to the warmth of a lager. He met and married the
pretty daughter of another local Austrian immigrant family, and their son, Rudolph, was born of that marriage in
1910.

**RUDY MARIS SR.** is seventy-five years old, a retired supervisor of the Great Northern Railroad who lives alone
in a condominium in Gainesville, Florida. He has been
divorced from Roger Maris's mother for twenty-five years.
"Why jump in a fire again?" he says, when asked if he
ever considered remarrying.

**RUDY MARIS:** "I always had a fascination with trains when I was a boy. They would come through Hibbing and I would run out of the house and chase them all the way out of town. I went to school in Hibbing and played a lot of sports. I just loved sports. I was a real good hockey player and almost tried out with the Boston Bruins in 1932 but I had just married Roger's mother then, Connie Sturbitz, and I hadn't skated for a while and my legs were out of shape. I always played hockey as long as we lived there. Hibbing had one of the first indoor rinks in that part of the country. The ponds and lakes froze real early and stayed frozen real late into the spring so you had all the hockey time you wanted. I was a pretty good baseball player, too, and I was good at football, only my mother didn't want me to play football. Too dangerous, you know.

"I worked as a mechanic on the passenger cars and the boxcars and whatever rolling stock the railroad had and enjoyed it a lot. Then I got promoted to a supervisor and they asked me to move to Grand Forks, and then I got promoted again to a bigger job and went to Fargo. That was a fine place to live. I may go back up there, still. I just can't stand the heat down here in Florida. I could leave any time I want. All I own is a 1983 Buick, a couple of suitcases and a few clothes. That's all I need. I just enjoy relaxing after all those years of hard work and watching television and talking to my friends. I always got along with people. Roger was that way, too, if he knew you. He could be stubborn and tough to get along with at times, but he liked people, liked to play around with them when he was a kid. Not my older boy, Rudy. He was always a loner. Still is, now. They were both great athletes, but Roger seemed to get along better with his teammates.

"They are only fifteen months apart, Roger and Rudy, and if I had known they would have turned out that good

I probably would have had a few more kids. Maybe that's why both Roger and Rudy had large families. Rudy was always a good student, very smart, and now he runs the beer business Roger had down here and his kids are doing great. Two of them are in law school and will probably practice around here. A couple of Roger's kids are in the business but mostly the boys like to play golf and chase women. I think it hurt Roger that none of them was ever interested in baseball. I can understand that. Roger's first boy, Roger Jr., was playing baseball once in the Little League and some kid yelled at him, 'You think you're as good as your father, but you ain't.' That really upset him and he ran home. When Roger told me about that, I said that's one thing that probably isn't very smart, naming your boy after yourself. I did it with my older son, Rudy, but I wasn't a famous baseball player."

Roger Eugene Maras was born in Hibbing, Minnesota, on September 10, 1934. Baseball record books always listed his hometown as Fargo and the spelling of his last name as Maris.

"Roger just felt like Fargo was his hometown because he grew up there," says his father. "I think people in Hibbing resented that. Some of the newspapers wrote about it when he died. I have a sister who lives there in Hibbing and she said some people made a big fuss about that. As far as the name was concerned, it had always been spelled with the second 'a' until Roger got into professional ball. Then he listed it as Maris because some of the kids he had played with had started kidding him by calling him mare-ass and that sort of upset him. So to avoid any problems he just switched it when he got old enough. The rest of us did, too, but there are a lot of people around the country who spell their names M-a-r-a-s and they all seemed to write letters and call Roger when he was playing ball, claiming he was a relative of theirs. I never could understand that. Why do some people want to be associated with someone who is famous even if they don't know him?"

When Roger was five the family moved from Hibbing to Grand Forks, some seventy-eight miles west of Fargo, the town that would become most identified with Maris's earliest athletic exploits. The Maris family lived at 624 Fifth Avenue in Grand Forks, a low-slung, small, middle-class apartment building with twelve separate apartments. One of his neighbors was Don Gooselaw.


**DON GOOSELAW** is fifty-two years old, a handsome, wavy-haired man with a ruddy complexion, a quick smile and a dapper appearance. He is the divorced father of three grown daughters, owns and operates a beauty school in Fargo now, and remained good friends with Maris throughout his life.

**GOOSELAW:** "My father was a barber and Roger and Rudy would come in for haircuts. Roger always wore that tight, blond crewcut, always as far back as I can remember. We were real good friends as small kids, played on the streets together, played in each other's homes, spent a lot of our free time together. Roger went to a different school, Washington School, and I went to the Catholic School, St. Vincent, and we played against each other in grade school. Roger and Rudy both were terrific football players and we played against each other in high school in football and basketball. There were no school baseball teams because it was too cold in the spring to play baseball, but we played with and against each other in the American Legion baseball program. Roger was one of the first guys from around here to be elected to the North Dakota American Legion Hall of Fame.

"There weren't as many homes and the neighborhoods weren't as built up as they are today, so we played a lot of games in the local lots around the neighborhood. When we were say eight, ten, twelve years old there were always games in those lots, using somebody's beat up baseball or football and just having a great time. Roger was kind of skinny then and he was a good athlete, but he wasn't somebody that you fussed over or noticed especially, or said, 'Hey, that guy will hit 61 homers some day.' Nothing like that. He was just another guy playing in the empty lots in those days."

The Maris family moved to 1510 13th Avenue South in Fargo shortly before the Maris boys were to enter high school. Both were fine athletes by then and they began considering the possibility of making sports their life's work. They had shown their skills at every sport they tried.

"A lot of people didn't know this about Roger, but he was also a track man," says his father. "He could really run. One time this guy who had been the state dash champion was around in the summer time, and the kids got to talking, and somebody said that Roger could run faster than this guy. Maybe Roger was fifteen, sixteen then, but he didn't care about just running for the sake of running. 'Loser buys a steak dinner.' The guy agreed, and Roger and this guy had a race over 100 yards, and Roger beat him with a rush. This track guy just didn't think that could happen, and he began pestering Roger to run the race again. He was a ten-second dash man, and now he had been beaten by Roger who had never run in a big meet, and that hurt his ego. He said he would throw in a steak dinner for Rudy if Roger could beat him again. Roger just took off again and beat him, this time by a bigger margin, and the two of them got that steak dinner."

The boys entered Fargo High and the elder son had an exceptional season as a sophomore football player. Roger and Rudy looked forward to playing together in the same backfield the next year. A new coach took over in Fargo when Rudy was a junior and Roger a sophomore. He didn't like the Maris brothers and used Rudy—or Bud, as he was called by the family—as a part-time player on the varsity. He demoted Roger to the B squad. The dream of playing together in the same backfield seemed unattainable until Roger and Rudy hatched a plan. They would transfer to the Catholic High School in town, Bishop Shanley, sit out a year as required by the rules, and play together in Rudy's senior year. Roger Maris would do things his own way. It would be something he would later grow famous—or infamous—for as a professional player.

"We hadn't told anyone our plans except our parents," Maris wrote in his autobiography. "When the first semester ended we transferred to Bishop Shanley. We were ineligible to play until the following year but when the football season came around we were ready to go. Bud and I would be responsible for splitting the town in half when we switched schools."

The impact of this transfer, especially after the two Maris brothers led Shanley to a victory over the bigger, athletically stronger Fargo High, cannot be fully measured. It can only be understood in the light of the emphasis small towns throughout America, in that day and this, place on high school sports. Local athletes take on significance in their young lives that may have lasting—and often negative—consequences in later life. High school sports often lead to intense rivalries, emotions, conflicts and bitterness. In this case, it was even more so, since there was an extra dimension of conflict: the transfer from the secular high school to the Catholic high school, unleashing deeper emotions and greater animosity. Religious prejudice remains hidden in most small towns and communities, but it is a factor that can not lightly be dismissed in any honest analysis of American life. Fargo had some 50,000 people then (it has climbed to 60,000 now) and few families in Fargo in the early 1950s did not have a relative in one of the schools at any given time.

"Oddly enough the people in Fargo never forgave me," Roger wrote in 1962. "It is hard to believe but the same situation exists today. I have a lot of friends in Fargo, but I have just as many enemies. I went back there a couple of years ago for a banquet and didn't know what to expect. I would say it was still 50-50 ... even one of the television stations had an anti-Maris sportscaster."

(The only book on display in the small Roger Maris museum in the West Acres Shopping Center of Fargo is ROGER MARIS AT BAT by Roger Maris and Jim Ogle. Ogle was a sportswriter for the Newark *Star-Ledger* then, a close friend of Maris who now runs the Yankee alumni organization out of an office in Fort Lauderdale, Florida.)

Roger and Rudy would team for two touchdown passes thrown by Rudy and caught by Roger in their first victory over Fargo High in several years. It was one of the most significant early sports victories for Roger.

The triumphs occurred in the first year of new coach Sid Cichy's tenure at Bishop Shanley High. **SID CICHY** retired from coaching after more than 30 years and now runs a company in Fargo.

**SID CICHY:** "Roger was a wonderful athlete, very dedicated, very determined, but a free spirit. His honesty was the thing I remember most about him. One day we were running a ridiculous drill in practice. I was a young coach back then. The drill was dumb. We ran it too long. And then Roger, who was only a junior then, said something about it. Well, you don't want to hear that when you are a young, self-important coach. But he was right. I let them run it a little while longer before I called it off. I didn't want anybody to think it was Roger's idea and not mine.

"We ran out of the single wing then in football and nobody could stop him. On defense, he would come up from the secondary to cut down the ball carrier on one play and intercept a pass 25 yards downfield on the next play. As a blocking back, we'd run him in motion and then bring him back to crack block on the linebacker—it was legal then—and if you ever saw him hit, you'd know how the block got its name."

Roger ran 65 yards on a reverse to score against Valley City on the first play of a big game against an old foe. It was the play that led to victory and would start Shanley on its way to an undefeated season and the state Catholic high school championship.

Maris probably reached his greatest heights as a football player in a well-remembered game against Devil's Lake. Shanley traveled by bus to a tiny town near the Canadian border late in the fall season, icy winds howling across the small field, and only the brave parents, girlfriends and town politicians chanced the weather to witness the event. Devil's Lake was a small school with a winning tradition. Maris shattered it.

Roger Maris wore uniform number 37—the baseball number famed in New York because Casey Stengel wore it and both the Yankees and Mets have retired it—with

a red and white jersey and red helmet with a white stripe
as he took the field for that memorable event. Maris caught
the opening kickoff and ran it 73 yards for a touchdown.
Devil's Lake returned to score. They kicked off and Roger
caught the ball on the 26, got a block from Rudy at about
the 35, and scored his second straight touchdown. He
repeated that performance two more times: four touchdowns on four kickoffs as Shanley edged Devil's Lake in
a wild game.

Years later, Cichy says, "Their coach told me he was
hoping they wouldn't score at the end because he was
tired of watching Roger take the kickoffs in."

Several years ago *Sports Illustrated* magazine ran an
item in their Faces in the Crowd section about some young
high school player running three kicks back for touchdowns. They described it as a national record.

"I was still coaching then, and somebody on our team
showed it to me," Cichy says. "I read it and immediately
thought of Roger. I knew he had done it four times. I got
the local sports editor to look up the game and send me
a copy of the clipping. When I got it I sent it on to *Sports
Illustrated*. A few weeks later they ran a correction and
reported accurately that Roger had run back four kickoffs
for touchdowns at Shanley, and that was the national high
school record."

In 1952, when Roger was a high school senior, a shock
hit the Maris family. Rudy suffered from a polio attack.
The disease was a killer then, with the Salk and Sabin
discoveries still several years away.

"Rudy was eighteen and he was beginning to think about
sports as a professional career," Roger's father says. "Both
boys were good, I couldn't say who was better, but since
Rudy was older it seemed as if he would get the first
opportunity. I was all for it and we began talking to some

of those baseball scouts watching him play. Then the polio hit Rudy and it was a tough blow for all of us. He was sick a good long time, and when he got up out of bed he just didn't have that coordination any more. He could still play a little ball for fun, but you could see he would never be a professional in any sport. I think it was about four years before he was really back to normal. He fought that thing off, but for a good while there we were seriously concerned about him. Maybe that's why Rudy was so supportive of Roger's career and took such a big interest in it. He probably knew he could have had a lot of that, too, but for the polio."

There was much talk in 1952 around Fargo about the young man at Shanley, Roger Maris, who was making a big impact on the school football fields and an even bigger impact on the American Legion baseball program.

"I had been a pitcher and a pretty good hitter myself in high school," says Mr. Maris. "I knew Roger had the goods. I didn't know how far he could go but I wanted him to try as hard as he could. Playing sports was a big part of our lives, maybe the biggest for the boys. Pretty big for me, too. That's one of the reasons I became such a good dancer as I got older. I was in shape. I really enjoyed dancing. I only gave up country dances about a year or two ago."

Despite his athletic success, despite the attention of coaches, local sportswriters and even professional scouts by now, Roger remained loyal to his old friends, unimpressed by the fussing and quiet. Tom Wold was a high school classmate and friend.

**TOM WOLD** is the manager of the Holiday Inn in Fargo. He has housed many of the Maris friends through the years and was the headquarters for the players who came to Fargo the past few summers to play golf in the Roger Maris Golf Tournament, with proceeds going to the American Cancer Society.

**WOLD:** "If there is anything that typified Roger from his first day to his last it is that his personality never changed. He was a big baseball star and he would come back here, and we'd sit in the coffee shop and chat about the old days, and it was as if Roger had never left Fargo. He had been everywhere, been fussed over by a lot of important people. But as far as I was concerned, he would be the same solid guy I knew back in school."

In the spring of 1952 Roger Maris made a decision that would be the most significant of his life. He chose to ask Patricia Carvell to his senior prom. She would be Mrs. Roger Maris in four years.


**PAT MARIS** was born and raised in Fargo. Her family had much stronger ties to Fargo than the Maris family did. She is fifty years old, lives in Gainesville, Florida, is the mother of the six Maris children and grandmother of daughter Susan's two children. The children are Susan, 28, Roger Jr., 27, Kevin, 25, Randy, 24, Richard, 22, and Sandra, 20.

**PAT MARIS:** "Everything centered around the high school and the church in those days. There were only 250 students at Shanley High and everybody knew everybody else. I was only a freshman when Roger transferred over from Fargo High. You can't imagine what a fuss that made. I was sure glad he transferred. We lived on opposite sides of the town and may never have met if he didn't come to Shanley.

"The big social event was the Friday night dances in the gym or in the school cafeteria. You either went to the dance or you went to a movie. That's about all there was for young people to do. I think we started dating in my sophomore year, and the next year when I was a junior we were going together, and it was a foregone conclusion that we would some day marry even though we never really discussed it. Things like that just sort of happened then.

"The night of his senior prom was very exciting. The boys were all wearing dark suits. Nobody in this town could afford to rent a tuxedo. Roger borrowed his dad's beat-up old car and drove up to my house. I was peeking out the curtains, but maybe I acted as if I was real surprised when he showed up on time. He looked real cute and a little nervous. He had always been an athlete, a casual dresser in school, and the suit made him feel self-conscious. In his right hand he had a corsage in a box for me and I was really touched."

Pat Maris had always been the rock Roger could lean on, raising the children while he traveled in baseball, taking care of family problems, watching their finances carefully (Roger would only call home to Missouri once a week during the emotional 1961 season because their phone bills were so high) and softening the pressures on him. Richard Nixon had once spoken of his mother "being a saint." Many of the wives of professional baseball players hold equal claim to that standing because of their assigned chores in life as mother and father to growing youngsters while husbands are working in baseball. "All I wanted from him," one baseball wife once stated in a divorce proceeding, "was more of his time."

Roger had a girlfriend now in his senior year; he had some clear direction in his life's work, a close-knit family and a host of friends. The next few months would be vital.

"I think the first time we ever thought about professional ball for Roger was when a scout for the Chicago Cubs came around. He said he was interested in Roger and he said he was willing to pay our way to Chicago for a tryout," says Mr. Maris. "Roger had graduated from high school and was playing American Legion ball."

"I first saw Roger when he was twelve years old," says Sid Cichy. "He was a skinny kid but he had lots of ability. I was a college student at North Dakota State and I spent a good part of the summer with the Legion program and the junior program. Roger seemed better than the kids he was playing with. He was a fine baseball player, there was no doubt about that. What you don't know, especially with players from small towns, is how good they are compared to kids who've seen more and better competition. That was the question with Roger. North Dakota can't be considered a big baseball state the way California or Florida is. There isn't all that much time for baseball. I knew he was good. *How* good remained to be seen."

The Cubs called Mr. Maris and told him two tickets were on their way and they would see him and Roger in Chicago in a couple of days.

Maris worked out in Wrigley Field before manager Phil Cavaretta and a few scouts. He was unimpressive.

**MR. MARIS:** "I can't even remember the names of any of the players we talked to or the people we worked out for. The only name I remember was Harry Chiti. He was their catcher and he caught the batting practice and was real nice and friendly to Roger. He hit a few balls and that was it. We walked off the field and this guy in a suit comes up and says, 'Too small, we don't think he has much.'

That was it. He didn't even thank us for coming or anything. Lucky they had sent us a round trip ticket or we
would have never been able to get home."

Mr. Maris does remember that he had one last parting
shot for the Chicago executive in the dark suit.

"I could get hot in those days and I was pretty upset at
the shabby treatment, I guess. I just told that guy he would
be sorry. 'My son will play across town for the White Sox
some day and you'll be sorry you didn't sign him.' He
didn't say anything and we left. Roger never played for
the White Sox, but he did play against them a lot and did
real well. I wonder if that Cubs' scout ever noticed that."

Maris had received letters from close to fifty colleges
around the country. He was clearly an outstanding high
school football player and many colleges projected him
as a very big star. The school that showed the most interest
was the University of Oklahoma.

"That school was on top then, and Roger wasn't sure
he could play in that company. They invited him that
summer to come on out and take a look at the campus,
meet the head coach, Bud Wilkinson, and decide about
their program. He went out there alone. I didn't want to
butt in with that. Whatever decision he made about college would be fine with me. He spent a couple of weeks
out there and came home. I don't know whether he didn't
like it or just didn't like the idea of college. Anyway, he
decided against it. He said he wanted to go to work. I got
him a job in the railyards as a helper and that was it."

Maris would become a professional player in 1953, move
out of Fargo to Raytown, Missouri, in 1956, and return
occasionally for a public event or a visit with his or Pat's
family. Many of Pat's relatives still live in the Fargo area.
None of Roger's do.

"I moved out of there in 1971," says Mr. Maris. "I wanted to get down south to Gainesville where Roger was. Now I think I miss it and I just might go back up there. With Roger gone there isn't much holding me here.

"I guess I just don't get along with Pat and Roger's children the way I thought I would. Roger had this place out on a lake about fifteen miles from Gainesville, and I went out there one day to sweep the place up and spent a while there. A couple of days later Pat called me up and said I had left a mess there, something about a can of sardines on the table, and that riled her up. I don't know, Roger's kids are always there and I don't know how *they* leave the place. They have had it easy with Roger's fame and success and all that and maybe they don't work as hard as they should. I can't really put my finger on it. I guess I just don't want to get involved in that kind of thing at this stage of my life. I want to relax and fish and just enjoy myself and let everybody be. I sure do miss Roger and I guess I always will. In a lot of ways it doesn't really seem like he's gone. I think about him all the time, and my sister in Hibbing just sent me a bunch of clippings she had collected through the years about him and a scrapbook to put them in. I'll do that for a while. That will give me some pleasant memories. I was never one to push myself, to tell everybody Roger Maris was my son or anything like that. I just enjoyed having him with me and I wish he still was."

The funeral had ended now on that chill December day in 1985, and Roger Maris had been laid to rest in the flatlands of North Dakota. In a few hours the people of Fargo would return to their homes and they would brace for the onslaught of another severe winter. The temperatures would drop to 20 or 30 degrees below zero several times that winter, with the wind-chill factor measuring almost twice as much. None of the locals seemed to mind the severity of this wicked weather and enjoyed kidding with the visitors at this funeral about their inability to handle it.

Mickey Mantle and Whitey Ford had a couple of drinks at the bar of the Holiday Inn before it was time to be driven to the airport. They talked of years gone by, of the joys of their youth, of the baseball times and off-the-field times of Roger Maris. It was time to leave now and the wind ripped into Mantle's face. The Texas resident uttered an obscenity about the weather as tears seemed to form on his face from the cold or the wind or the passing of Roger Maris. He sat quietly in the limousine as the driver turned out of the parking lot of the huge hotel and headed for the airport. Ford stared out of the window.

"You know how much I hate these things, Whitey," Mickey finally said. "The last one I attended was my father's thirty-four years ago. The next one I attend will be my own."

"I go to them all the time," Ford said. "I have to make sure they are not mine."

Mantle didn't hear the little joke. He was staring out the window, watching the sugar beet fields whiz by as he prepared to leave his friend Roger Maris forever to the fields of Fargo.

Roger Maris, age nine, in front of his home in Grand Forks, North Dakota. *Credit: Wide World.*

Roger as a basketball player at Washington School, Grand Forks. *Credit: Wide World.*

Roger (front row, third from left) as a baseball player on Fargo, North Dakota's American Legion team. Brother Rudy is in the top row, second from left. *Credit: Wide World.*

Roger as a football player for Shanley High in Fargo. *Credit: Wide World.*

# 3

## play for pay

**CASEY STENGEL** had been named the manager of the New York Yankees for the 1949 season. The Cleveland Indians had won the pennant in 1948 under the leadership of owner Bill Veeck and player-manager Lou Boudreau. That upset Yankee owners Dan Topping and Del Webb enough to fire Bucky Harris. They told their general manager, George Weiss, to get a new man. Weiss had known Stengel since the early 1920s. The Ol' Perfessor had a reputation as a funny man and a spirited manager. Which was not at all consistent with the somber Yankee image.

"The feeling around the Yankees in those days," says Lee MacPhail, who was then farm director, "was that the Yankees had hired a clown."

Some clown. The Yankees won the pennant in 1949 and defeated Brooklyn in the World Series. They won again in 1950, 1951 and 1952. Cleveland had finished second to the Yankees in 1951 and 1952 and would certainly be a major threat in 1953. The Indians were drawing good crowds, had a successful franchise and would eventually overtake the Yankees in 1954 under new manager Al Lopez.

Few organizations were as aggressive in their scouting as the Yankees. They seemed to have scouts everywhere. Mickey Mantle had been signed in the back seat of scout Tom Greenwade's automobile in 1949 during a heavy rainstorm near a drenched baseball field in Commerce, Oklahoma. Now the Indians were challenging them. They were moving scouts all over the country and into Central and South America. If the Yankees wanted to stay on top of the American League, they had to resupply their big club with kids every year. The Indians understood that philosophy. They had some pretty good scouts themselves, including a man named Cy Slapnicka. He had gained much fame in 1936 when he discovered and signed a hard-throwing sixteen-year-old by the name of Robert William Andrew Feller. After Bob Feller attained instant fame with the Indians, Slapnicka became a scouting legend.

MacPhail once said, "You have to sign a hundred ball players to get one big leaguer. You probably have to scout a thousand others."

Roger Maris had destroyed American Legion pitching in 1952. His feats were talked about throughout the area of Fargo and Grand Forks. But he was probably better known as a football player, and so it was no surprise when he accepted Oklahoma football coach Bud Wilkinson's offer to look over the campus and consider a football scholarship at the most successful football college in the country.

"I think he liked football a lot but he understood that college was more than football," says buddy Don Gooselaw from Grand Forks. "Roger wasn't all that interested in school. He knew he would have to keep up his grades, and that is what really turned him away from football. If he could have gone immediately into professional football the way you can go into professional baseball, I think he might have gone that route."

The area scout, Jack O'Connor, and the head scout, Cy Slapnicka, had stayed in touch with the Maris family. They knew Roger had gone off to Oklahoma. They figured they had lost him. One day O'Connor got a call from one of his friends in Fargo.

"Maris is back home. I saw him yesterday afternoon. I don't think he'll go to Oklahoma. I think if you get out to the house you might be able to make a deal with him," the friend said.

O'Connor got on the phone to Slapnicka. He flew in from a scouting trip to Chicago. They called the Maris home, spoke to Roger's dad and arranged to come out to the house. They told Roger they were interested in signing him to a professional contract if he was interested in playing for the Cleveland Indians.

"How much?" asked Mr. Maris.

"I have no idea," said Slapnicka. "That's up to the front office. I can take you up to Cleveland, let them take a look at you and then we can make a deal."

Slapnicka contacted the Cleveland front office. General manager Hank Greenberg, Bill Veeck's trusted aide, had heard Maris's name several times. He was interested and told Slapnicka he could buy two first-class seats for Roger and his father and bring them to Cleveland. "Let's take a look at him and then we'll talk," Greenberg told his scout.

About a week after he had returned from Oklahoma, Roger Maris and his father boarded a two-engine plane in Fargo, switched to another flight in Chicago and arrived in Cleveland with Slapnicka. They took a cab to the ballpark, shook hands with Greenberg, and were led to the clubhouse. Maris was dressed in a Cleveland uniform as he walked out on the field to take some swings.

**HANK GREENBERG** is seventy-five years old, still a handsome, impressive figure of a man. After a Hall of Fame slugging career with Detroit and one season at Pittsburgh, he went to work for the Indians under Bill Veeck in 1948. He was the GM there until 1958, moved with Veeck to Chicago in 1959 and retired to Beverly Hills after the team was sold, where he now plays tennis daily and enjoys a peaceful retirement.

**GREENBERG:** "When the scouts brought him in with his father I watched him swing and catch some fly balls and I knew quickly he was a hell of a prospect. Nobody can ever know that a guy will be a home run hitter. He was only a kid, eighteen years old, and not as big or strong as he would get later. What impressed me was the fact that he could pull the ball. We worked him out against a couple of pitchers, a right-hander and a left-hander, and he was able to pull the ball hard. When they traded him after I left the Indians, I knew he would wind up with the Yankees. That was the ballpark that was made for him. Yankee Stadium was a dream park for left-handed pull hitters.

"After he hit we talked a while and I made him an offer. I think it was eight or nine thousand dollars, the going rate then for a kid out of high school. His father said Roger really wanted to be a football player. That was a negotiating ploy. I talked to the kid and I had talked to our scouts, and by then I think he had given up the idea of being a football player. He didn't seem like the kind of kid who had the patience for college. He just wanted to play ball.

That's something you can see right away. We raised our offer to $15,000 and then we made a deal.

"He was coming along real well with the Indians and I expected him to play in Cleveland a long time. I didn't know he would become the home run hitter he did. I sort of expected him to be another Enos Slaughter type—a good, solid player with a good bat, tough defense, a good arm, and a hard-nosed player. The Stadium made him. Then they traded him and I followed his career all the time, especially in that 1961 season. When I hit 58 homers in 1938, I lost out because we finished in Cleveland's big park. It was tough to hit a home run there. I didn't get a home run the last four days. The pressure was nothing like Roger went through. Ruth had hit 60 in 1927, and everybody expected he would hit 61 or 62 or 65 a year or two later. Then Jimmy Foxx hit 58 in 1932, only five years after Ruth, so there wasn't much of a fuss about it. I came along in 1938 and hit 58. This was only eleven years after the Babe and it was followed in the press but not to the degree it was with Roger. It was 1961, thirty-four years later, when Roger challenged Babe. That's what made it so dramatic. By then everybody in baseball seemed to accept that it wouldn't happen. It was like Ted Williams hitting .406 or Joe DiMaggio hitting in 56 straight games.

"I thought the thing that really hurt the season and hurt Roger was Frick's ruling about the 154 games. That was just damn stupid. What was the difference? Conditions always change in baseball—day ball to night ball, new towns, new teams, new parks. They don't make rulings every time something like that changes. Why that year? Why for 162 games? I think the fans accepted Roger's record as the best single-season record. That's it, no matter what the commissioner said. Nobody ever accused baseball people of being terribly smart. I went to meetings with these people behind closed doors. I know them. That's why they couldn't tolerate Bill Veeck. He wasn't their kind of owner. It's outrageous that Bill isn't in the Hall of Fame. When he died, some newspaper headline read, 'Bill Veeck, entertainer, dies.' All they talked about was the midget [Eddie Gaedel], as if that was the only thing he did. That was dumb. He was great for the game, a great baseball mind and innovator. It was the same way with Roger. People say all he ever did was hit 61 homers one year. All he ever did?

"I remember once that year being in New York in late August or early September and the home run race was really hot. I was eating dinner in Danny's Hideaway and Roger came in with some friends. I greeted him and I told him, 'Just keep swinging the bat and don't get upset with the press. Just play ball and roll along with it. We all have to put up with it.' He was just a quiet man. He found that difficult to deal with.

"The Mantle factor was part of the paradox. People rooted for Mickey and against Roger. Why? They were teammates. If you were a Yankee fan you should have been rooting for both of them. That was tough for Roger to handle. I guess I remember the 154th game more than most. I was invited by some television station to come to the game and help broadcast it. They thought having hit 58 homers—and Roger had 58 going in—I could relate to what he was doing. I really couldn't, because conditions had really changed by then. I was like a lot of people that year. I thought Mantle would do it if anybody did because he was a switch-hitter. That was an edge. It was very exciting, like a great horse race running all year, first one horse is in front and then another. Roger just proved he was tougher in the stretch."

*   *   *

The Indians had several clubs in their minor league season where they could start Maris out. He would only consider one town. He wanted to start his professional career at home. He asked the Indians to assign him to their farm club at Fargo-Morehead. On May 1, 1953, he played his first professional game at Barnett Field in Fargo.

"Roger was probably better known as a football player than a baseball player around here," says Don Gooselaw. "I think people were surprised when he suddenly showed up as a professional player at Fargo-Morehead. He had played Legion baseball, we had played against each other many times, but he really wasn't the best baseball player around. There were a lot of good young players around North Dakota in those days. I think he liked the idea of playing before the home folks. Nobody bothered him, nobody made a fuss over the fact he was now a professional, nobody changed their ways of thinking about him. We would watch him play, and then we might go downtown and have a beer or play a game of pool. We all wanted to play ball professionally and he was the only one of us to make it. We envied him, but he never let on he was better than we were or different in any way. I guess that was Roger's strength. If he was your friend, he was your friend always. That's all there was to it."

Maris was an instant hit with Fargo-Morehead. He got off fast in professional baseball and stayed strong all year. He played in 114 games, batted an impressive .325, hit left-handed pitching as well as right-handed pitching, slugged nine home runs, knocked in 80 runs and scored 74 runs. He played mostly center field and his arm was strong and accurate. He also had great running speed.

"Roger was one of those gifted athletes who had the ability to turn up his running speed a notch when he needed it," said Sid Cichy, his high school football coach.

"He would go into overdrive on the football field, and I think he could do that also in the outfield in baseball."

The Indians had finished a strong second to the Yankees again in 1953, and were getting the club set for a strong run at the Yankees in 1954. There was a lot of time spent on building the ball club, and Greenberg and his assistants concentrated on producing the team that would finally halt the Yankee pennant streak at five with the 1954 American League pennant.

At the same time, as in any successful baseball organization, they were looking ahead. They had to have that constant supply of players. They assigned Maris to their Keokuk club in the Three-Eye League, the league's name deriving from the fact that teams were situated in Iowa, Indiana and Illinois. But first Maris went to spring training with the Indians in Daytona Beach, Florida. One of the young Cleveland organization managers in that training camp was a man named Phil Seghi.


**PHIL SEGHI** was a minor league ball player who quit playing in his twenties to become a manager in the Cleveland system. He worked his way up through the Cleveland organization and later moved to Cincinnati as an assistant to Gabe Paul. He retired last year and now lives in Fullerton, California, where he smokes his pipe quietly each day, attacks enemy golf balls and scouts California players for his former Cleveland ball club.

**SEGHI:** "I was a young manager then and I saw a lot of ball players, but few with the talent Roger had. It didn't take very long to see he would be something special. He had a good year in 1953 and everybody knew he was moving up the organization ladder real quickly. One day

I was walking along the grounds near our lodging and I saw Roger was wearing street clothes and carrying a suitcase. We had been working out for a couple of weeks by then, and I couldn't imagine where he was going. I asked him, and he just said he was going home, going back to Fargo. He said if the Indians didn't want him, maybe somebody else would. If nobody wanted him he would just stay home and work in the railroads or something. I didn't have him as a player, but I knew most of the younger players from squad games and training sessions and I knew Roger pretty well by then. I knew he was a pretty headstrong young man, but I also knew he had a good year and the Indians wouldn't be too happy if he just took off like that.

"I asked him if we could just sit down and talk. He was pretty hot but he always liked me, I guess, and he said that he would but that I couldn't change his mind. We started talking and pretty soon he spelled out his problems, which seemed pretty big to him but were not really. I can't even remember the details, but it had something to do with some manager or coach down there trying to change his stance, and he resented it. He had hit .300 with good power in his first season and he didn't see how anybody could suddenly start telling him how to hit. Roger wasn't a guy that you could tell things to easily. He was one of those stubborn Dutchmen, and I knew better than to reason with him. I just told him how good he was and what he would miss. He had already shown he had power and the Cleveland club was always looking for guys who could drive the ball.

"Well, he began asking me about different things about the game and how I thought he could improve and what it was like for a young player in the Cleveland organization. Things like that. All of a sudden he just got up and started walking back to the lodging quarters and I knew he would be okay. He just liked playing ball too much to just jump up and take off. He needed some time to sit down and think about it.

"Well, pretty soon he was back to work. Roger was a free thinker, and those kind of guys are a little more difficult to handle in baseball. It is a pretty regimented business, especially in spring training when they tell you what time to get up and what time to go to sleep. He was a young kid and that has to be an adjustment.

"Of course he was an outstanding talent, as later developments showed, and I was glad he didn't walk away. What a loss that would have been. He was a grade A ballplayer and a grade A man. He had a strong, independent personality, but a lot of guys do, and they can't hit the ball the way Roger could."

When spring training ended Maris was assigned to Keokuk, Iowa, and had another strong year. He batted .315, smashed 32 homers, knocked in 111 runs, scored 105 and led the league in outfield putouts with 305, an indication of his speed and ability to cover ground. The reports were going back to the Cleveland offices weekly that this kid, who had turned twenty years old that September of 1954, was a comer. The Indians were on their way to the greatest American League season in history. The big club won 111 games, outdistancing the hated Yankees by eight games, and even surpassing the win total of the most famous and most successful baseball team in history, the 1927 Yankees of Babe Ruth, Lou Gehrig, and the rest of the famed Bronx Bombers. Not even a four-game World Series sweep at the hands of the New York Giants could diminish the pleasures in Cleveland over the ending of the Yankee streak. The organization was very strong, and Veeck and Green-

berg were hopeful there would be more pennants to follow. In this matter, they began paying more and more
attention to the performances of their younger players and
the glowing reports sent to Cleveland by their minor league
managers. No report was more glowing than the one sub-
mitted to the Indians at the end of 1954 by their manager
at Keokuk, Iowa, Jo Jo White. His prize possession on that
ball club was Roger Maris.

**JOYNER (JO JO) WHITE** is seventy-seven years old, a
former journeyman big league outfielder with the Tigers,
Philadelphia Athletics and Cincinnati Reds. He was a minor league manager for many years and later a big league
coach in Kansas City. He lives in retirement in Tacoma,
Washington, fishes, reads sports pages and enjoys the out-
doors.

**WHITE:** "Yes, sir, I'm real proud of being associated with
Roger Maris. I read a few times during those years that
he said I was the best manager he ever played for. That's
real nice, especially coming from a great player like him,
but I wouldn't know about that. I do know he was a whale
of a player for me. He could run, hit, field and throw, he
had power and he played dangerously hard. One time he
threw himself into a guy at second base and he nearly
tore his head off. But he was safe. Later on, when he was
playing with Kansas City and I was a coach there, he did
about the same thing. I went up to him after the game and
said, 'Roger, you're a big league star now. You don't have
to do that kind of thing any more.' He said, 'Jo Jo, that's
the only way I know how to play.' That was Roger.

"One time in Keokuk we were having this tough game
with the leading club in the league, and Roger was on

third base with one out. I was coaching down at third, managers did that in those days, and I got this clever idea that I could steal home with Roger. You see, I knew he had real good speed because I used to race him before the games with our other players. I don't think I ever had a guy who could beat him. Once in a while somebody would jump him and be ten or fifteen yards up on him. But all of a sudden, whoosh, here comes Roger and he takes that guy like he is standing right still. Anyway, this one game I want to win it real bad. I whisper in Roger's ear that I want him to steal on the next pitch. The hitter was our big first baseman, Joe Randozzo, and I gave him the take sign and sent Roger flying in. Well, something got messed up, I don't know what, and all of a sudden Roger is running home and the big first baseman swings that bat and here comes a line drive right at Roger's head. I mean it was right there. But he hit the ground and the ball shot over his head and went down the line like a bullet. Roger jumped up and you could see the blood rushing to his face, and he was real mad at me and he kept yelling, 'I told you so, I told you so,' like we had had a big discussion about the play when we hadn't.

"Another thing about Roger was, he had great morals. He was just a fine young man, no problem at all to manage. He was real serious about his work and you never had to go looking for him in one of them gin mills like you do with a lot of young players. He knew that he had come down there to attend to business, to play ball and to get up there to the big leagues as fast as he could. I recommended him and pushed him every chance I got. There wasn't anybody in the Cleveland organization from Bill Veeck and Hank Greenberg on down who didn't know that I liked Roger Maris.

"Nobody was making a lot of money in baseball in those

days, not like now, and most of the people played because that was what they wanted to do more than anything. I think Roger just enjoyed playing no matter what he made. My top salary as a player was $8500, and I got up to about $15,000 a year when I was coaching in the big leagues for Joe Gordon in Kansas City. I didn't complain about it. That's what I liked, baseball, and I knew I would never get rich doing it. I'll tell you what makes me mad. That's the pension setup. The modern players make a million dollars or two million, but they don't stop to think about the ones like me years ago that kept the game going for those owners, especially during the war years when there were no young kids around. What kind of a pension do I get? Maybe four or five hundred dollars a month because I coached at Kansas City. Otherwise I'd get nothing, because I stopped playing before 1946 when the whole thing started. These players are making millions, but they can't see it in their heart to come up with some money for the oldtimers so they could live a little easier.

"Anyway, that's nothing to do with Roger. Just say I was really fond of that boy and enjoyed having him with me. It was a shame what happened to him, but nobody can know about that. While he was here he was a good man, had a good family and could play that game of baseball pretty good, too."

In his third professional season Maris was assigned by the Cleveland organization to their double A farm club at Tulsa, Oklahoma. There was only one more major step to make before he would be in the big leagues, the Triple A farm club at Indianapolis. He was following that path taken by thousands of other players: moving up the minor league ladder, learning his trade, refining his skills, adjusting to playing baseball every day for six months, realizing that winning is more important than individual goals. It is baseball's eternal conflict: individual marks versus team success. Salaries have always been based on individual performance. Before the Players Association and free agency, ballplayers were told that the idea was to win. When a team didn't win, they weren't given individual raises no matter what their production. No better example was ever given than when Ralph Kiner hit 47 home runs for the last place 1950 Pittsburgh Pirates. "I went in to see [General Manager] Branch Rickey to negotiate my contract. I thought I had had a pretty good year. I expected a big raise," Kiner says.

Rickey and Kiner argued for some few minutes, and then Rickey made his final take-it-or-leave-it offer.

"We finished last with you," Rickey said. "We can finish last without you."

Managers also knew their chances of moving up depended strictly on winning games. Maris found that out in 1955 from the manager of his Tulsa club, Lambert Daniel (Dutch) Meyer, a journeyman with the Cubs, Tigers and Indians from 1937-1946.

The Tulsa club was involved in a tough early season game. The score was tied in the eighth inning, with one runner on first base and one out for the Dodger farm team at Forth Worth. Maris was playing right field. A batter hit a bullet toward the right field corner. Maris moved to his left, caught the ball on the first bounce, whirled and threw the ball toward the infield. He was a bit off balance and the throw sailed. It went past the shortstop who was acting as the cutoff man, past the third baseman and past several fans sitting in the stands behind third base. The ball had stayed high all the way in from the outfield and landed about six rows deep in the stands. The runner, moving to third, was sent home by the umpire and the second runner was awarded third base. He scored on a fly ball. Tulsa was beaten.

After the game, Meyer was livid. He yelled at Maris and ordered the young outfielder to report to the ball park an hour earlier the next night to work on his throwing. Maris didn't think he needed work on his throwing as the result of one errant toss. But he obliged the manager.

"We went out there the next night," Maris once said, "and he started hitting fly balls to me and making me throw to the cutoff man. I don't know how many he hit me, but it seemed like a hundred balls."

Meyer showed no signs of letting up on his twenty-year-old outfielder. Finally, Maris caught a ball and didn't throw it. He walked in to the infield.

"Where the hell are you going?" Meyer yelled. "I didn't tell you to leave."

"I'm through. I'm not blowing my arm out for you or anybody else," Maris said.

He continued into the clubhouse. Meyer continued yelling. Maris was hitting .233, his slowest start in three professional seasons, and Meyer was unconcerned about the youngster's future. He was concerned about winning.

"If you leave, you're gone," Meyer yelled.

Maris left. The next morning he was gone.

Meyer had called the Cleveland front office, told them about the incident and demanded they get Maris off his ball club. Meyer said Maris wasn't ready to play on that level. Maris went home to Fargo for a few days and finally reported to the Cleveland farm club in Reading, Pennsylvania. It left him with a bitter taste in his mouth.

Years later Tony Kubek would remember that Maris never did like throwing very hard in practice before a game. It might have had something to with that experience.

"Roger had a great arm, strong, accurate, as good as there was in the game," Kubek said. "Some guys just know their own arms."

Clete Boyer said Maris was the only right fielder he ever played with who could throw a ball shoulder high for a good tag from deep right field to third base. Maris won one Gold Glove in 1960 as the best right fielder in the league.

"I think he was always being compared to Al Kaline, who was a great right fielder and a wonderful guy. Kaline got the award every year," Boyer says. "It's like me playing third base in the American League during Brooks Robinson's peak years. Who is going to give the Gold Glove to me?"

Maris reported to Reading and immediately began hitting Eastern League pitching as he had hit every place he played, except for Tulsa. He batted .289 in 113 games, knocked in 78 runs, had 19 homers and scored 74 runs. More important, he had nine assists at Reading, a tribute to the strength and accuracy of his arm. He was also a happy ball player again. He was back with Jo Jo White.

"When he came back to me at Reading, he was a little confused," White says. "Those things happen with young ball players. They go out there in professional ball from high school and figure it will be easy. Once in a while it is, but most of the time it isn't. It's a big adjustment and some of them take a little longer to make it. I think Roger probably was playing a little over his head at Tulsa. Sometimes the organization takes a young boy and pushes him along just a little too quick. It takes some doing to find out what a boy can handle and what he can't handle."

White worked hard on restoring Maris's confidence. He spent long hours at the batting cage, encouraging him, changing nothing, reminding him how good he had been at Keokuk and the year before at Fargo-Morehead. The chipper older man and the dour youngster just seemed to hit it off. White was warm and kind and understanding with Maris. He was a sort of surrogate father for the young player as he groped his way through the jungles of professional baseball. They would often have dinner together in one of the small restaurants in Reading, or go to a movie or play cards together on the team bus during those long rides.

"We got real close. It was just one of those things. I liked the boy and I wanted to help him as best I could. I had been in the big leagues for a few years and I knew what it was like. I knew he had the talent. He soon came out of it and was winning ball games for me every which way. There was no doubt about it. When that Reading season was over I knew the Indians had something in this Maris boy. Yes sir, you could see he was going to be somebody."

# 4
## the road to cleveland

**THE** Yankees recovered from the shocking loss of the pennant in 1954 to the Indians by winning again in 1955. It was the sixth pennant in seven seasons for New York under the leadership of Casey Stengel. The Indians finished second again.

Bill Veeck and Hank Greenberg knew that the Indians would have to have an influx of young talent if they were to catch the Yankees in 1956. They kept their eyes on a young outfielder at Reading named Roger Maris.

"One of the things a good organization does," says Greenberg, "is show patience with young players. Roger had a big year at Reading but we decided he needed one more year at Triple A before we brought him up. It is always better to have a young player have that last good year in the minors rather than have a struggling first year in the majors. A good part of the game is confidence."

In his fourth year in professional baseball Maris went to spring training with the Indians, played in a few exhibition games, hit one spring home run and was shipped out to the minor league club at Indianapolis before the Indians broke camp. Maris had another strong season in the minors with the Indianapolis Indians in 1956. He batted .293, hit 17 homers, knocked in 75 runs, scored 77 runs and played brilliantly in the outfield. He was a phone call away from Cleveland.

The Yankees blew open the American League pennant race early and won by nine games. The best player in baseball in 1956 was Mickey Mantle. He won the Triple Crown with a league-leading .353 average, 52 homers and 130 RBIs.

**MANTLE:** "That was the year I finally played the way people said I would. When I came up as a kid I was expected to be a combination of Joe DiMaggio, Babe Ruth and Lou Gehrig. It didn't work out that way. I was overwhelmed by it all. I was just a kid from Oklahoma and I was scared. I was so scared my first year in 1951 that I never could even talk to DiMaggio. I would just look over at him and try to copy what he did on the field and in the clubhouse.

"After a couple of seasons the pressures really started to build. I guess I was disappointing to some of the fans because I wasn't doing what they expected. I was playing good ball but I was hurt a lot, and I wasn't winning any titles even though we were winning the pennant every year. The 1956 season changed all that. I finally had that big year and I really could play relaxed the rest of my career. I got a good raise that year, just about doubled my salary to about $60,000, and then in 1957 I hit .365. Ted Williams hit .388. George Weiss, the Yankee general manager, cut my salary. He said I didn't do as good as I had done in 1956. I hated that son of a bitch, I really did. I hit .365 and he cut me. Can you believe that?"

While Mantle was leading the Yankees to the pennant in 1956, Maris was showing the Indians he was ready to lead them to a pennant in the American League. There was no longer a reason to hold him back. In the spring of 1957, Maris was clearly marked for stardom in Cleveland. The Indians envisioned a power attack of exceptional left-handed and right-handed slugging—with Maris and a right-handed hitter who had slugged 21 homers as a popular Cleveland rookie in 1956. That young man was Rocco Domenico Colavito of the Bronx, New York. He had somehow escaped the Yankees.

**ROCKY COLAVITO** is fifty-three years old, a dark-haired, dark-eyed good-looking former Cleveland heartthrob who was responsible for depressing a great many Indian fans when he was traded away to Detroit for Harvey Kuenn in 1960. Colavito hit 371 homers in his career, some of them huge shots, and threw the ball from right field with more strength and accuracy than almost any player of his time. He played 14 years, worked as a batting coach and television sportscaster, and is between jobs now as he awaits another baseball offer at his home in Bernville, Pennsylvania.

**COLAVITO:** "Roger Maris was a friend of mine. We were very close. We knew each other even before he joined up on the Cleveland club. We had been to spring training together, two guys moving up the organizational ladder. We were both home run hitters, so we had that in common, and we both were being counted on to help the Indians win.

"Roger wasn't a very talkative guy but he always said

what was on his mind. Some people took it the wrong way. I always liked it. You always knew where you stood with Roger. I was a kid from New York, and when I got to the Indians I was pretty cocky. Some people said I was brash, too pushy, too much filled up with my own importance. Hell, that's the only way you can make it in this game. If you don't have confidence in yourself, nobody will have confidence in you.

"I'll tell you this. Roger had as much confidence in his ability as any player I ever saw. He may not have been as outspoken about it as I was, but he certainly had it. For a while Kerby Farrell, the manager, was platooning us in 1957 and neither of us liked that. Then he started playing both of us every day. I played right field and Roger played center field. That wasn't all that pleasing to Roger. He wanted to play right. If they played both of us, he had to play center. He had more speed.

"I always followed what he was doing in Reading and Indianapolis because I had gone the same route. I met my wife, Carmen, in Reading, and I often spent an off day there in 1955 when I was with Indianapolis again the next year for a while, but Hank Greenberg wanted me to go to San Diego. His good pal, Ralph Kiner, ran that ball club and Greenberg wanted to help him. He sent me there in 1956, I hit 12 home runs, and they brought me up. Then in 1957, Roger made the Cleveland ball club and we became friends.

"I was renting a home in Palma, Ohio, about twenty minutes from the ballpark and Roger rented a home a couple of blocks away. We carpooled to the ballpark every day and we became roommates on the road. We really got close. We spent a lot of time together socially, drinking beer, playing pool in my house, making home movies together. I have some real funny movies of Roger around the house. You wouldn't believe he was the same serious guy he was around the ballpark.

"One of the things you heard about Roger through the years was that he was aloof. He may have been that way with guys he didn't know, but he certainly wasn't that way around the guys he knew. He was easy to talk to, easy to get along with, a real straight shooter. See, Roger never changed through the years, he never put on airs. There was always a lot of camaraderie around that Cleveland ball club, and Roger was part of it.

"I had a few good home run years [Colavito hit 45 home runs in the Maris home run year of 1961] and I certainly admired what he did and knew how hard it was to do it. People talked about the lively ball that year and the expanded schedule and bad pitching and nonsense like that. If that was true, how come ten guys didn't hit 60 or 61 homers? What happened was a freak thing, a big home run year because a lot of hitters were at their peaks and were swinging for the long ball.

"As the years went on and the furor around Roger tended to diminish that feat and disparage him as a player, I thought more and more of the two years I played with him and the years I played against him. He was an outstanding, complete ballplayer. His true worth to his team was overshadowed by the home run year. He could do everything a ballplayer is supposed to do on the field. He could play the outfield as well as anybody. He was a very good hitter, not just a home run hitter. He never made a bad throw in all the time I saw him play and his head was always in the game.

"Roger was a tough player, very determined to excel, and very strong-minded. If he made up his mind to do something his way, that was just his way. He was not a wishy-washy guy, which was one of the things I liked about him. He gave loyalty as a friend and he expected loyalty in return. I think some of the things he said in New York put him in hot water with a lot of people, but Roger just couldn't be a politician. He couldn't say one thing to one guy and another thing to another guy. If he felt strongly about something, he said it and that was it.

"I'm not saying this because he is gone. I said it all along and I believe it. Roger Maris was as honest and stand-up a person as I have ever known. As for his baseball ability, he belongs in the Hall of Fame. He was the most underrated ballplayer of my time."

Al Lopez had moved on from Cleveland to become the manager of the Chicago White Sox in 1957. A rookie manager named Major Kerby Farrell, a longtime minor league skipper, was named to handle the club. He was a gentle, soft spoken fellow from Leapwood, Tennessee. Farrell, who died in 1975, had the difficult task of rebuilding the aging Cleveland club, winners in 1954 but slipping back by 1957. Third baseman Al Rosen had retired. Pitchers Bob Feller and Hal Newhouser had retired. Early Wynn, Mike Garcia and Bob Lemon were past their peaks.

**BOB LEMON** is sixty-six years old, a Hall of Fame pitcher for the Indians, a former coach, big league manager and now a scout with the Yankees. He led New York to the miracle pennant in 1978 when Bucky Dent hit the famous home run in the playoff game at Fenway Park. He lives in Long Beach, California, enjoys a game of golf, likes to fish and is one of the most likeable people around baseball. Lemon enjoys nothing more than a couple of cold beers and a lot of baseball talk on a summer day.

**LEMON:** "I had started with Cleveland in 1941 and I would play one more season in 1958 after Maris joined us. The Cleveland club had always been a tightly knit team. We didn't have any cliques. No matter how well or how poorly a player was doing, he was just the same to us. It wasn't the kind of team where a guy had to play three or four years before somebody would say hello. We didn't have the kind of high-salaried guys that the Yankees had. One of the things you recognized if you played in Cleveland was that you wouldn't make the same money a guy did in New York. It also helped to win every year like they did.

"We had seen him a couple of times in spring training before 1957, a good, solid-built kid, obviously a heck of a prospect. Then he made the ball club in 1957, and when we came north to open the season we stayed in the old Auditorium Hotel downtown, a couple of blocks from the ballpark. Players walked to the park most of the time and when I came down opening day, Roger was in the lobby and I walked up to him and asked if he was getting ready to go to the park. He said he was, and I told him I'd walk with him. I could see that he was real nervous and I certainly remembered what that was like. We still had some time before we had to be in the park, so I told him I would buy him a beer. We sat and talked at the bar for fifteen or twenty minutes and I told him that he was a good ballplayer or the Indians wouldn't have brought him up. I reminded him that he had done real well in the minor leagues and it wasn't that much harder up here. I think that relaxed him.

"The Cleveland club was close and we all seemed to get along real well. Roger fit right in right away. We didn't have a division on that club between rookies and veterans the way they did on some other clubs. If you were a member of our ball club, you were just one of the guys. That was all there was to it. There was one other important thing to remember about those days in baseball in 1957 and 1958. We traveled by train and that led to a lot more fraternal feeling. We sat together in groups of five or six, played cards, ate together, shared some laughs. On airplanes today they get on, get into their seats, put on the seat belts and fall asleep. It doesn't lead to a lot of conversation about baseball or anything else among the players.

"Roger had a good, athletic body and you could see that he was strong enough to play the game. He did all the fundamentals correctly, and I think the consensus was that he would be a very successful player. Nobody could guess he would be a big home run guy, even though he pulled the ball. He didn't hit that many balls in the air then. I think he got better at that when he went to New York.

"He was a first year man and didn't make much of a fuss around the club. My roommate and pal was Jim Hegan, and we sort of looked over him that year. Hegan was with the Yankees in 1961 when Roger had the big home run year. I was the pitching coach at Philadelphia and we had an off day in the last weekend of the season, Friday night I think. Lee Walls, one of our outfielders, knew Roger from the minor leagues and we decided to drive up together from Philadelphia to see one of those last games. It was real exciting just to see how far Roger had come. He had 60 homers by then and you could feel the excitement in the ballpark. I don't think he got a home run that night we were there, but he certainly took some good rips. He had a very good swing and was a tough man to strike out for a home run hitter. He wasn't one of those guys who would just swing from his ass and not know what he was doing. Roger had a good sense of the game, where the ball was, what pitch to hit, who would be the pitcher, just the little things that make a guy a good all-around hitter.

"When he first came up I thought he'd be a little like Minnie Minoso, a guy who would make contact, hit for average and hit a few homers. I never expected him to hit 61. We stayed friends through the years. I would see him at a golf tournament, get on him about his crewcut, call him 'Meat,' like I do everybody I like [for meathead], and have a few laughs. To me Roger Maris stayed the same all the years I knew him—a good player, a good guy and somebody who never blew his own horn."

The Yankees had another big season in 1957. Mantle hit .365 and had to accept a pay cut. Yogi Berra had 24 homers. Don Larsen, who had pitched a perfect World Series game in 1956 against the Brooklyn Dodgers, was pitching well with his no-windup style. Tom Sturdivant would end up with his best season at 16-6. Whitey Ford would win only 11 games in an injury-filled year, but the bullpen and the Yankee depth would be the difference.

For the Indians under Farrell, Vic Wertz would have a strong season with 28 homers and 105 RBIs, Gene Woodling would hit .321, and Colavito would slug 25 homers in his second season with the Indians.

"Roger played center field and I played right most of the time, and we learned each other's moves in the outfield," Colavito says. "It was fun playing next to him. You knew that any ball that came out that way would be caught. Roger was a take-charge outfielder."

Early Wynn, who would wind up his career with 300 victories, won 14 games to lead the staff in victories at the age of 37. (He also lost 17, to lead the staff in that department as well.) Mike Garcia won 12, relievers Don Mossi and Ray Narleski won 11 each, and Lemon won only 6 games and lost 11. His heavy fastball was lightening up, and the batters were finally getting even for all those tough years. His ERA was 4.60, and the end for Lemon would be a season away.

Cleveland felt it would be strong in pitching while the rest of the young players, led by Colavito and Maris, matured. Their best pitcher was an overwhelming left-hander by the name of Herb Score. He was a handsome devil, only 23 years old that spring, with wavy brown hair and dark eyes. He stood 6-2 and weighed a solid 185 pounds. Score had come out of Long Island, New York, and won 16 games in his rookie season and 20 games in 1956, his second season.

"There was no question he was on the road toward becoming one of the finest left-handers in the history of baseball," says Al Lopez, his manager in his first two seasons. "He could throw hard, he had a marvelous curve ball, he could change up and he had good control for a left-hander."

Score had walked only 129 batters in 249 innings in 1956. He struck out 263 to lead the league for the second straight season. (That feat would go unequalled until a young man by the name of Dwight Gooden would lead the National League in strikeouts in his first two seasons for the Mets, with 276 strikeouts in 1984 and 268 in 1985.) Score was the fair-haired boy of all baseball—a crowd pleaser, a guaranteed draw at the box office, and the pitcher the Indians were counting on to lead them back to a pennant. It all ended on a May day in Cleveland. Shortstop Gil McDougald of the New York Yankees rifled a line drive straight back at Score on the mound. He could not get his glove up in time and the baseball tore into his right eye.

Score was bleeding profusely when he was carried from the field. No player who witnessed the event, including center fielder Roger Maris of the Indians, would ever forget it. The blow had a devastating effect on Score, who would attempt to rescue his career over the next five years without success, and on McDougald, who played three more years and quit prematurely at the age of 32.

The injury cast a pall over the Indian clubhouse for weeks. Sportswriters kept writing about it, questioning the players and reporting on Score's progress as he struggled to regain the sight in that eye. He recovered completely, but was never much of a pitcher after that—for physical or for psychological reasons.

"I've been around the game a long time," said Yogi Berra, who was waiting to bat next. "You always know something like that can happen but you don't really believe it until it does. It was the most sickening thing I ever saw, and I saw a lot of bad injuries in baseball."

Many observers of the game believe one of the factors that separates talented—if unsuccessful—players from star players is their control of the aspect of fear. Batters get hit on the head with the ball. Hitters must learn to control that. Pitchers, in the extreme such as Score, get hit with baseballs. They must free their minds of any possibility of injury if they are to pitch with the proper motion and pitch smoothly and without fear. Pain and injury are a part of baseball. Each player must know how much pain he can deal with and how much will damage his performance. The people who know most about the pain ballplayers deal with are the trainers. They see it every day. Even the team doctors—called in only when pain becomes serious—do not have the closeness to the players that trainers do, regarding pain. Joe Soares was the Yankee assistant trainer for many years under head trainer Gus Mauch. Mauch passed away five years ago.

**JOE SOARES** learned his trade in the minors and worked with Gus Mauch, one of the most respected trainers in sports, for many years. Soares lives in retirement in Santa Maria, California.

**SOARES:** "The thing you have to know about pain with ballplayers is that some can take more than others. It's sort of built into them. Some players get a hangnail and they are in the trainer's room and really hurting. It may seem like a little thing, but it's a lot to them. Some players just don't tolerate pain as well as, say, Mickey Mantle did. He [Maris] had a lot of hamstring pulls while I was there. I'd pack his leg in ice until the discoloration would go down, and then I'd start him with the heat treatment. We had a massage that helped them, and they all enjoyed soaking in that whirlpool. I think around 1962, 1963, after the big home run year, Roger had a couple of bad hamstring pulls and Ralph Houk wanted him to play, and Roger just couldn't make it. That's the way he was. He knew his body better than anybody else—the manager, the trainer, anybody. If he didn't want to play there was no way to make him play.

"He was quite a boy and I liked him a lot. He was always friendly to me and he enjoyed kidding around in the trainer's room with the other players. I think in that 1961 season he spent a good part of his time in there. He was one of the most clean-living fellows I had ever known, and I was really happy he got that record. I won't ever forget that day. He hit that ball into the stands—off Tracy

Stallard, I think it was—ran around the bases real shy, no waving or jumping up like they do today, and came to the dugout. The players had all jumped out to shake his head. Gus [Mauch] jumped out, too. I wouldn't do that. I was only the assistant trainer. My job was to stay in the dugout unless I was sent out for an injury. Roger gave us a lot of thrills that year. I felt real bad about what happened to him."

The loss of Score put more pressure on the Cleveland pitching staff. They just weren't up to it and, as the Yankees began running away with the pennant, the Indians began slipping down in the standings. They would finish in sixth place. As the season wore on, with no hope for a pennant, Cleveland concentrated on bringing along their younger players. Maris and Colavito were playing every day now, and the Indians sensed that they would have a solid one-two batting punch for many years to come. Maris was getting some notice around the league.

Maris hit a home run in Yankee Stadium off right-handed pitcher Bob Grim. The ball was pulled deep into the right field seats, some 385 feet away from home plate and close to the foul line. The Yankees had won the game and manager Casey Stengel was in an ebullient mood. He talked of this and that, throwing in some of his favorite double talk—known as "Stengelese" to sportswriters—and then paused suddenly and faced a couple of the Cleveland scribes who were in his office.

"What about the kid in center field, you don't think he has power. He hits a ball pretty good for a young man and why wouldn't you like to have him if you could," Stengel said.

When the Cleveland sportswriters asked a New York sportswriter for a translation, it came out something like this: Stengel had seen Maris for the first time and liked his actions at bat. He pulled a good fastball by Grim and he deposited it deep into the right-field seats. That always impressed Stengel, who won two World Series games for the Giants against the Yankees with homers in 1923. Stengel enjoyed beating Babe Ruth's team that day. He had lost to Ruth's team when the Babe pitched for Boston against Stengel's Brooklyn team in the 1916 World Series. He also knew that Ruth had hit many of his 714 career homers close to that very spot where young Maris had now delivered his first Stadium homer. Stengel, ever alert for talent, especially left-handed power hitters, took note of young Maris. When he said, "Why wouldn't you like to have him if you could," he wasn't referring to the Indians. He was referring to the Yankees. He would like to have him if he could.

Later that night Stengel had dinner with his boss, Yankee general manager George Weiss. He would tell a reporter about it the next day. He told the reporter about a lot of other things before he finally got around to it. But when he did, the Ol' Perfessor winked at the sportswriter and said, "That kid in center, Maris, I like him. I told George to buy him."

It wouldn't be all that easy. But Stengel had made the first move toward acquiring Maris for Yankee Stadium. He saw the potential in his swing, his power and the quickness of his bat. He also recognized that the blond-haired, crewcut youngster from North Dakota, who now was twenty-two years old and a fully developed six-feet-even and 200 pounds, was the perfect player for Yankee Stadium. Stengel had been around professional baseball since 1910. He had seen them all. He often remarked at the incredible skills of Babe Ruth, the player he considered by far the best in the game's history. He had first seen

Ruth in the World Series in 1916. Perhaps there was something in Roger Maris that made him think of his old Boston and New York opponent, Babe Ruth. He would keep an eye glued on the doings of young Maris for the next three seasons.

Stengel was at his peak as a manager in those days, winning every year since 1949 (except for 1954), talking about his team endlessly, selling baseball everywhere he went, entertaining the press, driving his players on to greater heights, constantly alert to the needs of the Yankees. He made it clear as he approached his late sixties that he had no idea of retirement. The press might hint that sixty-six or sixty-seven or sixty-eight was too old to manage, but Casey never acted as though such a thing were a real possibility. To hear him tell it, he would be managing for many, many more years. Why not? That was what he did, and he did it better than anybody else in baseball. He had brought along a youngster named Mickey Mantle to true stardom, and now in his ever-alert mind he must have been planning the merger of that developed talent with the raw talent of Maris. As early as 1957, Maris's first season in the majors, Stengel clearly envisioned the day when he could write out the names of both players, the M and M Boys, on his lineup card.

The front page of the New York *Times* was filled with the usual signs of world crisis. One story described how King Hussein was tightening his hold in Jordan. Another described the complaints of Egypt over an Israeli raid. In this country the United States House of Representatives approved budget cuts in the operation of the United States Information Agency. President Eisenhower was criticized by his own brother, Edgar, for his large budget requests. Edgar suggested that the Ike he knew wouldn't advocate such a thing. "He must be getting bad advice," he said.

On April 16, 1957, none of this mattered much to the millions of people across the country who had waited since October 10, 1956, the last day of the World Series, for another big league baseball game. For so many people there was only one season, the baseball season. All time was measured by it. The last year ended in Brooklyn with Johnny Kucks shutting out the Dodgers for still another Yankee triumph. It was a happy new year for baseball fans in Chicago with the White Sox playing the Cleveland Indians. Left-hander Billy Pierce, a 20-game winner for the White Sox, opposed left-hander Herb Score, a 20-game winner for the Indians. Al Lopez, manager of the White Sox, for the first time brought out a lineup with the names Aparicio, Fox, Minoso, Lollar, Doby, Landis, Hatfield, Phillips and Pierce on his card. Kerby Farrell listed Smith, Avila, Wertz, Colavito (right field), Maris (left field), Carrasquel, Hegan and Score. It would be the first time the name of Roger Maris would appear in a big league box score.

Maris had a fine opening day, had three singles in five at bats, scored a run, made a nice running catch of a fly ball and faced one of the toughest left-handers in the game in Pierce. The White Sox beat the Indians 3-2.

The club took the train the next morning from Chicago to Detroit. The Indians enjoyed an off day with a short workout. The Tigers' Jim Bunning, another fine American League star pitcher, awaited the Indians. At least he was a right-hander. Maris could read in that morning's Detroit papers about Whitey Ford's 2-1 victory over Washington, with Mayor Wagner throwing out the first ball at Yankee Stadium and Edna Stengel, wife of the manager, wearing a new fur coat for the occasion. Stan Musial hit two doubles as the Cardinals beat the Reds 13-4, and Gino Cimoli's home run gave the Dodgers a 7-6 victory over the Phillies.

The next day, April 18, the Indians finally rallied and pushed across a run in the top of the eleventh when Bobby Avila hit a sacrifice fly to score George Strickland. A walk reloaded the bases and Maris was up. Bunning was long gone and a thirty-one-year-old right-hander named Jack Crimian faced Maris. He was 0-for-four until that point. The count went to 3-2 and Maris unloaded on Crimian's fastball. The ball landed deep in the right field bleachers for a grand slam home run, four Cleveland runs, and the first of Roger Maris' 275 big league round-trippers.

**JOHN MELVIN CRIMIAN** is sixty years old, father of four, grandfather of four, who watches baseball on television, roots for his hometown Philadelphia Phillies and works as an auto body repairman outside Philadelphia in Claymont, Delaware.

**CRIMIAN:** "I really didn't know anything about the home run being the first of Maris's career until some local sportswriter called me one day about three years ago. I remember I gave him one, though. The bases were drunk and I threw this high outside fastball. I had faced him the inning before and struck him out on the same pitch. He was a kid and nobody knew much about him. He had had a good year at Indianapolis, but there were a lot tougher hitters on that Cleveland club.

"I had a pretty good slider in those days. I had learned it from Bill Sarni, my catcher on the Cardinals in 1951 and 1952. I bounced around the minors and then I came back and used that slider to pitch another couple of years in the bigs and then three or four more years in the Mexican League. I had good control of it, but I didn't want to use it with a 3-2 count and walk a runner in. I was a pretty good relief pitcher and that was the worst thing you could do. I threw what I thought was a good pitch, maybe a little high, around the shoulders and just off the plate. The last thing I saw, that ball was going out of town.

"Years later Maris hit all those home runs for the Yankees. I was retired then, but I felt good about it. I knew he must have been a pretty good hitter because there were a lot better pitchers on that home run list than me. I've stayed interested in baseball all these years. I grew up in Philadelphia and went to Olney High with Del Ennis. He is a good friend of mine and we still talk on the phone about the old days. I really can't think back to my emotions at the time Maris hit that one off me. I guess I was just mad about it. You never look good giving up a home run, and you certainly don't look good when the bases are drunk. I probably would have been better off if I had walked him for one run and got the next guy.

"Maybe not. With Maris hitting 61 home runs, more than anybody, all of his home runs become significant, so I guess I sort of started him on his way. Anyway, it's a good way for my grandchildren to know that I played in the big leagues, like I said, and faced some of the real famous hitters of the day. I remember Maris as a strong young man. You knew he wasn't going to be a Punch and Judy hitter. I'm not walking around bragging that I gave up a home run to Roger Maris. But when somebody asks me about it, like you did, I don't deny it, either."

Maris suffered several serious injuries that summer. He pulled a hamstring, he hurt his wrist running into a wall and he severely pulled a rib muscle. Maris was out a couple of weeks, and manager Kerby Farrell wanted him back in the lineup. Maris said he wasn't ready. Farrell said he thought Maris was ready. A few days later Maris saw his name back in the lineup. When he went to Farrell, the manager said, "You're in there." Maris could not swing normally. He saw his average plunge from .280 to the low .240s. He was angry when the Cleveland sportswriters began pointing out that the rookie may be in over his head. Maris knew he could hit big league pitching if he were healthy.

He struggled through the rest of the season and ended with a .235 average, 14 home runs and 51 runs batted in. He was asked in the final weeks of the season if he wanted to play winter ball in the Dominican League for $1000 a month. Maris said it wasn't enough. "I told him," new general manager Frank Lane later reported, "that .235 hitters don't hold out, they hold on." Maris went home to Fargo and got a job with a local radio station doing sports reports. Lane called and said he could get the $1500 a month Maris had asked. The rookie told him it was too late now. He had that radio job, he didn't feel like spending the winter in Latin America, and besides all that, he didn't feel as if he needed that extra work.

"I guess you could say we never got along after that," Frank Lane said.

Maris spent a quiet winter in Fargo. He paid little attention to winter baseball news. He would not know that the winter baseball meetings had begun in December in Sarasota, Florida. He would certainly not care that the Yankees had made inquiries about him again with Lane. Casey Stengel still remembered that left-handed swing.

# 5
## kansas city kid

**THE** 1958 season would be a pivotal one in baseball. There were profound changes in the game, many of which would later have significant bearing on the life and times of Roger Maris.

In New York, the Yankees were alone. The Brooklyn Dodgers, led by Walter O'Malley, finally took the long-rumored plunge and moved the franchise to Los Angeles. O'Malley convinced Horace Stoneham, owner of the New York Giants, to move west with him. Stoneham settled in San Francisco. His team would begin play in an old minor league park called Seals Stadium. The Giants would soon have a new stadium called Candlestick Park. Stoneham visited the site of the proposed stadium early one morning. A soft, gentle breeze blew across San Francisco Bay. It was well before noon. What Stoneham didn't know—and the local builder did—was the fact that the San Francisco winds come up howling at the spot shortly after three o'clock every afternoon. It would make Candlestick

Park the most wretched stadium in baseball—cold, raw, windy, miserable for fans and players. The wind would be so strong that a small relief pitcher named Stu Miller would be blown from the mound during the 1961 All Star game. "I hate it here," visiting Dodger center fielder Duke Snider would say, "because the peanut shells blow in your eyes."

Attendance in Yankee Stadium, despite the absence of the Dodgers and Giants for the first time in history, would actually plunge from 1,497,134 in 1957, when there were three teams, to 1,428,438 when the Yankees were alone.

Baseball Commissioner Ford Frick—a man who would have a strange impact on Maris's life later—seemed unconcerned about the absence of a National League franchise in New York. Cherubic Warren Giles, the National League president, was queried about the success of the league without a team in New York. "Who needs New York?" Giles said.

While the National League fans stayed away from Yankee Stadium, New York Mayor Robert Wagner set the wheels in motion for another team, possibly in a new league. He appointed a bright, articulate, politically connected lawyer by the name of Bill Shea to head a committee to study the possibility of bringing another team to town. The plan would center around a new stadium. Shea believed he could get a team if he could get a stadium. City funds would be used. There was talk of a new league, and before long a group of wealthy business men had created teams in Houston, Buffalo, Toronto, Denver, Dallas and New York—on paper, called the Continental League. The league would never come to fruition but it would serve as the trigger for American League expansion in 1961 to Los Angeles and Washington, and National

League expansion to Houston and New York—in a place called Shea Stadium, in 1962.

The Indians had finished sixth in 1957 under Kerby Farrell. GM Frank Lane fired Farrell and hired Bobby Bragan as his 1958 manager. Bragan was a volatile personality, a creative baseball man and a very outspoken Texan. He could rub people the wrong way without half trying. He was soon platooning Maris and downgrading his ability. The Indians had obtained Larry Doby, a former Cleveland star, and Minnie Minoso from the White Sox over the winter. Doby, Minoso and Colavito got most of the playing time in the Cleveland outfield. Maris faced only right-handed pitching. His anger grew.

By mid-June he was hitting only .225, but had 9 homers and 27 runs batted in with 182 at bats. The trade deadline approached. Scouts were everywhere. One of the most active scouts around the Cleveland ball club was Tom Greenwade. He had brought a young Mickey Mantle to the Yankees and now he had been assigned by George Weiss to follow one ballplayer: Roger Maris.

"He was around us for a long time," Lane once said. "We knew he was there only to watch Roger Maris. The Yankees were hot after him because they saw home run potential in that left-handed swing. The Yankees were pretty tricky about it but they couldn't fool me. I would see Greenwade around and I knew he was trailing Maris and we'd get to talking. In that slow Oklahoma drawl of his he would start running Maris down. 'He can't do this and he can't do that.' When a scout from another ball club starts doing that with your player, you know they are after him. They just want to get him for a cheap price."

Lane had this passionate dislike for the Yankees, for

George Weiss and for Casey Stengel. He saw the Yankees as too uppity, stealing players from other clubs, pushing their money around, trying to dominate the league from their position on high.

"One day I got a call from the Kansas City owner, Arnold Johnson, and he inquired about Rocky Colavito. Rocky had hit 25 homers for us the year before. They wanted a right-handed hitter. They figured with their left field fence, Colavito would hit 50 for them. I told Johnson, 'Rocky's too popular here now. They'd run me out of town. You take Maris instead. He's a better all-around ballplayer with more potential. He can run. He's a good outfielder. He's got a good arm and one of these days he'll be a real good hitter.'"

Johnson said he would think about it. He called Lane back at the Shoreham Hotel in Washington. "Johnson was in New York and Bobby Bragan and Mel Harder, our pitching coach, were with me in the room. I told Johnson I would make the deal for Maris on one condition. I didn't want Johnson passing him on to New York right away. I knew he would end up there later in any event, but I wanted to stall it as long as I could. Maybe my team would be strong enough to beat them by then."

On June 15, 1958, the deal was announced. Roger Maris was traded to Kansas City with pitcher Dick Tomanek and infielder Preston Ward for infielder Vic Power and infielder-outfielder Woodie Held.

With Maris hitting only .225 and squabbling with Lane and Bragan, the deal caused little fuss in Cleveland. Held was a fine player and Power was considered the best first baseman in the league, certainly the flashiest with his one-handed snatches of popups and long throws.

For his part, Maris was upset at being traded, especially because he was forced to leave some of his good Cleveland buddies, but he recognized Kansas City as one of the most comfortable places to play in baseball, especially for a low key, soft-spoken, basically shy youngster such as he. The press was mild. The fans were tolerant. The crowds were gentle. Maris would fit in well in Kansas City.

It is not unreasonable to speculate that Maris would have enjoyed playing his full career in Kansas City.

The Philadelphia Athletics, under the ownership and field manager leadership of Connie Mack, had been one of the dominant teams in baseball in the first quarter of the twentieth century. They fell on hard times with the Depression, sold off most of their good players and rattled around the depths of the American League through the 1940s and early 1950s. Mack, who was to die at the age of 93 in 1956, was a well-known baseball figure wearing his old-fashioned stiff collars, managing the club from the bench in street clothes, waving his scorecard to move fielders and riding up and down old Shibe Park (later called Connie Mack Stadium) in a tall, thin elevator, good enough for his angular physique but horribly uncomfortable for short, fat sportswriters who would later pile in it as a press elevator. The Athletics played their last season in Philadelphia in 1954, moved to Kansas City in 1955 and would eventually settle in as a successful franchise in Oakland in 1968.

The Kansas City A's of 1958 were a sad ball club. Their younger players always seemed to last only until the Yankees wanted them. Their veteran players seemed used up. Kansas City had been a famed Yankee minor league franchise, and New York seemed to retain some under-the-table hold on the A's. Arnold Johnson was a businessman with vast real estate holdings. It would later be revealed he actually owned part of the land on which Yankee Stadium was built, clearly a conflict of interest within the

American League. As players shuffled back and forth between the A's and the Yankees, more credibility was added to this notion of an interlocking relationship. Sportswriters began to liken KC-NY deals to the Underground Railroad, the network by which escaping slaves were moved from the South prior to the Civil War.

That A's team would have more than half a dozen players, including Maris, Hector Lopez, Joe DeMaestri, Bob Cerv, Ralph Terry, Duke Maas and Hal Smith, who would later play in the World Series elsewhere, but at the time were tied together in a bond of failure and frustration. The manager was an easygoing professional baseball man named Harry Craft.

**HARRY CRAFT** is seventy-one years old, lives in retirement in Conroe, Texas, outside of Houston, after more than fifty years as a baseball player, coach, manager and scout. He broke into the big leagues with the Cincinnati Reds in 1937 and managed in Kansas City in 1958 and 1959 when Roger Maris played for the team. Craft is a gentle man with good understanding of people, well spoken and well liked by all who know him.

**CRAFT:** "I had good rapport with Roger. We had heard he was tough to get along with because of that deal with Frank Lane over not wanting to play winter ball. I never held that against a player. Some guys use the winter seasons to improve themselves, other players feel it is more important to rest over the winter and get ready for the next season. I was in the press room with the ball club in Comiskey Park in Chicago. Lane was in there and he kept telling me Kansas City better get Maris, because if we didn't he would go to the Yankees and nobody would

ever beat them. I knew he was an up-and-coming young
hitter. I also knew he could pull the ball because he hit
like a maniac in a place like Detroit, which had the short
right-field wall.

"We made the trade for him and I called him into my
office and we talked. I told him I didn't care what had
happened in Cleveland, how he got along with Lane or
didn't get along, none of that mattered in Kansas City. I
just wanted him to hustle for me, play hard, and if he did
that we would never have any trouble. He did play hard
and we never had any trouble. I just put him out there
and he played good baseball.

"Roger learned to hit the ball in the air in Kansas City.
That's what a hitter needs to hit home runs. He had a
good, quick stroke, good actions at the plate and good
concentration. It was easy to see he would be successful.
He didn't hit tape measure jobs the way Mantle was doing
then, but he hit hard line drives and they got in there.
That was all that counted. On defense I likened him to
Joe DiMaggio. He was real smooth in his moves and always made the right play. I may have helped him some
with his positioning of hitters because he was a young
player, but he didn't need a lot of teaching of mechanics.
He just had the sense of the game. I remember in the 1962
Series against the Giants, Willie Mays hit a hard drive to
right with Matty Alou on first. He was a good base runner
and when Willie lined the ball down there, everybody
figured it was a double and Alou would score easily. It
was the ninth inning and the Yankees led 1-0. Maris went
into the corner, caught the ball on the bounce, fired to
Bobby Richardson and Alou had to hold at third. Then
Ralph Terry struck out Willie McCovey to end the Series.
Roger had saved the game.

"I got to really like Roger and we had a lot of visits

together through the years in Gainesville during spring training or at some banquet or playing golf. He never changed. He was still a gentleman, a quiet fellow and not somebody you had to worry about embarrassing you. We didn't have a real good ball club at Kansas City in those days but we had some fine individual players. A lot of them went on to fine careers. Roger was a complete player for me, he could hit, field, run and throw and he never let down in any game I was managing him. I've been around a long time and seen a lot of players. He is certainly a Hall of Fame player in my book. Forget about the home runs. Just look at his overall record. How many years did he play in the big leagues, twelve? How many times he get in the World Series, seven times? That's a pretty good credential for the Hall of Fame, isn't it?"

Maris adjusted quickly to Kansas City. He and Pat would soon buy their first home together in Raytown, Missouri, just outside of Kansas City, some twenty minutes by car from the ballpark. It was a quiet tree-lined suburban street with pleasant surroundings and unobtrusive neighbors. Maris wanted privacy with his family away from the park, and he got it in Raytown. One of his neighbors in Raytown was Kansas City outfielder Bob Cerv.

**BOB CERV** is sixty years old, a native of Weston, Nebraska, who now makes his home in Lincoln. He is the father of ten children and the grandfather of nine. He broke in as an outfielder with the Yankees in 1951, was traded to Kansas City in 1957, came back on the Underground Railroad in 1960, went to Los Angeles in the expansion draft, returned to New York in 1961 and finished out his career in 1962 with Houston. He was a baseball coach at John F. Kennedy College in Liberal, Kansas, for many years, and coached in summer semi-pro leagues helping such future big league stars as Ron Guidry, Steve Rogers and Phil Garner. A husky brute of a man, Cerv now spends a good part of his leisure time walking the fields around Lincoln with a metal detector, seeking gold and silver coins, some dating back to the days when no white men dared invade those Nebraska lands.

**CERV:** "One day Harry Craft called me into his office in Kansas City. He told me we had just traded for this kid Maris. Craft had heard the scuttlebutt that Maris was tough to get along with. I didn't know much about it, but I knew Roger had played with the Indians and for Frank Lane. Lane was one of those guys who liked to tell you to jump and when you did he wanted to hear, 'How high?' Maris couldn't get along with a guy like that. Roger was too independent. Anyway Craft asked me if I would room with him after he joined us, look after him and tell Craft what kind of a kid he was and if I thought he would help our ball club. I had been with those successful Yankee teams in the early 1950s and I knew that if a player didn't fit in he would cause more trouble than he was worth. We went out on the next road trip and I watched over Maris. We went to the park together, we had a beer after the game, we went out to dinner, we rehashed the ball game, we spent a lot of time together. I came back after the trip and went up to Craft. 'There's nothing wrong with him.' That was it. We were real close friends from that day on.

"He moved out near me in Raytown and we spent a lot of time together in the offseason. We used to go quail hunting in the winter and we used to fish in the summer. Roger was a real good fisherman. He had a lot of patience, was a quiet guy and I liked to talk a lot, so that's why we got along. We'd be out in the boat together for a long time and he might not say anything for an hour. I would be doing all the talking and finally we would be quiet, as we thought the fish were biting, and Roger would haul one in and then he would say, 'Now I can do some talking.' He was like that in baseball. He never talked about what he would do or how he could handle this pitcher or that one, but if he got him he would talk about it if you asked him afterward.

"I came back to the Yankees in 1961 and Roger had been there a year by then. I was living in the Emerson Hotel downtown and Roger was living in the Henry Hudson Hotel in Manhattan, and we got to talking one day about sharing an apartment so we could avoid the hassle. Roger was hitting a lot of home runs by then and he was getting bothered everywhere he went.

"We got Mickey to come in with us because he was getting hassled in the hotel he was in, and it worked out well. We made ourselves coffee and juice in the morning, or a sandwich, and ate our meals out in some neighborhood place in Queens after the game. We had these two big bedrooms and a huge living room. That was our putting green. We had contests, me and Roger and Mickey putting for a few bucks on that living room rug. We had a ball living out there, and avoided the hassle."

**JULIE ISAACSON:** "One time Roger told me this great story about living with Mickey. I laughed for an hour. One day Cerv was out and Mickey and Roger decided to stay in that night and cook their own meal. It was an off day or something, and they drive over to the neighborhood grocery store. This was late August or early September, when that home run thing was really hot in 1961. The

whole country was talking about it and all the sportswriters wanted to know was where Mickey and Raj were
living. I got the apartment for them, rented it in my name
but kept it a secret. This one day they drive up to the
grocery store and walk in to buy some steaks and ice cream
and a couple of beers for dinner, the two of them, Mickey
and Raj, the two hottest guys in the country. They are
pushing this grocery cart down the aisle.

"Mickey throws a few things in and Raj throws a few
things in and there is a kid putting away some groceries.
He was standing on this ladder and he looks down at the
two of them and waves his friend over. 'Man, isn't that
Maris and Mantle over there, I mean that's them, right?'
This other kid is down the end of the aisle, he walks by
and shakes his head that it ain't them. Then he walks back
toward where he is working and takes another look. He
knows there is no reason in hell that Mickey Mantle and
Roger Maris would be in that grocery store. Then he stops
and takes a real good, slow look. His face freezes and he
walks back to the other kid and says, 'That's them, dam-
mit, that's them, Mantle and Maris, in here, in this store,
now. What the hell are they doing here?' This other kid
on the ladder wants a better look since he has been convinced he's right. So he leans closer and closer and closer
and pulls the ladder and all of a sudden, whack, the ladder
falls, the kid falls, the cans are flying down those shelves
in every direction. I bet that happened a lot of times in a
lot of places that year. When people saw Mickey and Raj
they would just stare. It was wild."

CERV: "It never let up around the hotels on the road or
coming into the ballpark or any public place the ball club
had to go. But in a private place like our apartment it was
all quiet. That's the way they wanted it. The neighbors in

the building saw us after a while and knew who we were, but they would just say hello and keep walking. Heck, they didn't want a hassle in their neighborhood any more than we did. That really worked out well all season. We stayed there until maybe the middle of September. Then I had to have that knee operation, Mickey was getting sick and would be in the hospital soon, and both Roger and Mickey had their wives coming up for the last week or so. And then the Series. So we left the apartment. It was a helpful thing. I think Roger got some peace there I know he would never have gotten any place else. It was a great deal for all of us.

"I made it through that 1961 season, and then got into the 1962 season before I was traded to Houston where I finished up. I got into college coaching after that, and saw Roger through the years around the Kansas City area and at a golf tournament or a banquet after that when he moved to Florida. We talked on the phone when he got sick and I didn't think that disease would get him. He was a strong guy. You never know who will go first, but I certainly didn't expect anything like that to happen to Roger. He was a good friend and a terrific ballplayer and I was happy he really enjoyed his later years with his family and a good business in Florida. I guess I was watching a game on television when they just said they had a news bulletin that Roger Maris had died. It was a pretty empty feeling. When I heard the funeral was going to be in Fargo, I just got in my car and started driving. I wanted to see him one last time."

That season of 1958 turned out to be a remarkable one for Maris. He was beginning to make an impact on the league with his long ball hitting. He slugged nine homers in 182 at bats for Cleveland before being traded, and hit

19 for Kansas City in 401 at bats. Harry Craft knew he had something special in the blond twenty-three-year-old, and he thought the A's could rebuild their offense around the husky youngster from North Dakota.

"He took a few days to get adjusted, but once he saw that he was going to be in there every day he just let his natural talents take over," Craft says.

Maris finished the season with .240 average, 28 homers and 80 RBIs for the combined season with two teams. The average was the only thing that kept him from being considered a truly outstanding second-year player.

"It was always a funny thing with Roger and his batting average. He was just one of those guys whose eyes lit up when there were men on base," says Cerv. "He was about as tough a hitter as there was with a man on third and less than two out, or a man on second in a close game. If it was a one-sided game, one way or another, he just didn't seem to concentrate. Roger could have been a .300 hitter easy if there was a man on second every time he came up all season. In those spots he really bore down and he really made sure he got his pitch to drive. Good hitters do that. Roger seemed to care about getting hits only when it mattered. 'RBIs, that's what I'm after. That's what they pay off on,' he would say. He felt there wasn't a lot of money to be made hitting singles and having a big average if you had to cut down on your swing to do it. That's why the Triple Crown, like Mickey won, is such a great achievement."

If a ballplayer could ever be described as being the perfect player for the perfect team, it was Roger Maris in KC. Maris, by personality, background and emotion, was made for that club. He could do his job without a fuss. He could live in privacy. He could avoid crowds and noises and the pressures exerted by fans. He told Cerv and other teammates he was anxious to play out his career in Kansas City. There were some good young players coming along, and maybe the A's could even get into a pennant race in a few years. They had the makings of a pitching staff with a solid veteran named Ned Garver, who had broken in a decade earlier with the old St. Louis Browns, and a handsome, hard-throwing right-hander named Ralph Terry. Garver was 12-11 that year and Terry was 11-13, impressive figures with a seventh-place ball club.

**RALPH TERRY** is fifty years old, one of the most handsome men to pitch in the big leagues over the last quarter of a century, with a lanky frame, a dimpled chin and wide open brown eyes. He was born in Big Cabin, Oklahoma, signed with the Yankees as an eighteen-year-old, made the big club in 1956 and went to Kansas City in 1957 as part of a big deal involving tempestuous Billy Martin. Terry came back to the Yankees in 1959 on the Underground Railroad, pitched on five pennant winners, finished up with Cleveland, Kansas City and the New York Mets. Baseball fans remember him for two significant pitches: a home run ball he gave up to Bill Mazeroski of Pittsburgh to end the 1960 World Series, and a fastball Willie McCovey lined violently to Bobby Richardson for the final out in the 1962 World Series victory of the Yankees over the San Francisco Giants. Sportswriters remembered Terry for an even more significant event. In the early 1960s sportswriters began probing deeper and deeper into players' private lives and personalities. This new wave of reporting was described as "Chipmunk journalism," because Jimmy Cannon saw one of the practitioners as a buck-toothed chipmunk-like young man. Cannon was a veteran New York *Journal American* and New York *Post* sports columnist. (Terry was the recipient of the ultimate chipmunk question when he left an interview after the final Series game in 1962 to receive a congratulatory call from his wife. "What was she doing?" asked sportswriter Stan Isaacs of *Newsday*. "Feeding the baby," replied Terry. "Breast or bottle?" asked Isaacs.)

**TERRY:** "I was with Denver of the American Association in 1956 and Roger was playing in the same league at the Cleveland farm club at Indianapolis. He was a pull hitter with a good swing. Every swing looked the same and it was clear he would be the next great hitter to come out of that league. He was also an excellent bunter. He could drag bunt and beat it out. You would think he was about to go for your fastball and try to hammer it and instead he would lay one down, get on base and start a rally. He was just an all-around fine baseball player. We got to be real pals.

"I was real happy to see him come over and join us at Kansas City. We were about the same age and we enjoyed hanging around together. We would go out and have a beer together after a game and we both enjoyed talking it over. His father used to come down and see him play a lot, and we would take him out for a nice dinner and a few laughs. He was a real nice man. I think both of us got along real well with everybody on that Kansas City ball club. The only difference between us was that I laughed everything off. Roger didn't. If he trusted you and you crossed him, you didn't get a second chance. He could be real cold and cut you up if you did something he thought betrayed his trust. I'd laugh about it, kid a guy out of it and forget it. Roger wasn't that way. He was a very serious man.

"I remember when he came over from Cleveland, most of us just thought there was something fishy about it. Roger was too good a young player to be traded away like that. Young guys who can hit home runs don't get dealt like that. I don't care who the Indians had to get in the deal. We always had the idea that the deal was part of something bigger, and since so many players in those days went back and forth to New York we thought sure that would happen. Roger didn't want to hear that. He was interested in playing in Kansas City and staying there.

"Roger could do everything on the ball field. He was an exceptional base runner. He would always slide hard and he could go in and break up a double play as well as anybody I had ever seen in baseball. He had been a football player in high school and we knew that he had been offered a scholarship to Oklahoma, and in those days all the players who went to Oklahoma were blue-chippers. He could have been a great football star, I'm sure. He played very aggressively and he would jump into the wall if he thought he had a chance, and when he came to Yankee Stadium he saved me a lot of home runs by climbing over that low right-field fence. You had to be brave to do that because you could get killed out there when you hit that concrete with your head. Or you could bang yourself up pretty good on those outfield seats when you went there after one. Roger never seemed to worry about it.

"There was nothing like the 1961 season, of course, and when he hit number 61 I remember jumping up and down on that field like a wild man. He was just in a great groove that year and that's all there was to it. It was a thrilling thing to see and everybody on the club felt part of it.

"The trouble around Roger really started in the 1962 season, when a couple of bad articles were written about him by Oscar Fraley and Jimmy Cannon. The players didn't believe any of that stuff for one minute. To us Roger was a great guy, a real hero. I remember thinking in those days I would like one of my kids to be like Roger when he grew up. He was a real hero. I think he was a hero to a lot of people in those early days of the 1960s, the way John Glenn was a hero. He had done something nobody else had ever done and he had conquered incredible odds to do it.

"I'm a golf pro now out here in Larned, Kansas. We are a few hours from Dodge City and Boot Hill and a few of those cowboy towns of the old west. There were a lot of heroic guys in those days, and to me Roger was always the same kind of hero. I play in a few golf tournaments around here and I do some teaching, and I think back often to those days with Roger when I'm out on the course. He was a good, tough competitive golfer and he was the kind of guy you enjoyed shooting a round with, because you knew you would have a few laughs on the golf course and you would have a few more after you finished. Roger didn't like to lose at anything and when we'd play golf he would kid around if we were just out for some fresh air, but if we had a few bucks a hole going or we were playing with some other guys he may not have known he could be real serious. Roger liked to win at everything he did. He was a guy with a lot of pride in what he did and he wanted to perform as well as he could in everything he tried.

"Roger could get mad once in a while, sure, but he usually had good reason. I remember once in 1962 he had this pulled hamstring and Ralph Houk told him to take it easy. He wanted his bat in the lineup and he said, 'Roger, if you hit a ground ball and you know you're out, just jog down the baseline.' Jim Bouton was a rookie then, and he was very intense and he was pitching in this tough game. Roger hit a ground ball to second and jogged down the line. The second basemen juggled it and Roger tried to speed up, but it was too late. He was out easy. Bouton got up from his seat on the bench when Roger came in the dugout. Bouton was a rookie that year and Roger had hit 61 homers— and Bouton jumped all over him. 'I'm busting my ass out here and you're not hustling.' He was screaming at him and Roger just sat there and took it. Houk didn't say a word, either. We all knew Roger was hurt, but what could you do? Roger's face got all red and that was about it. I don't think Roger ever talked to Bouton again the rest of the time they were together on the Yankees.

"I was out in California when I heard that Roger had died. I was playing golf in some tournament and I just couldn't leave to go to the funeral. I thought an awful lot about Roger since and I was just glad I had a chance to play with him. He was really a terrific baseball player, a Hall of Famer for sure, and the kind of guy you could really trust. He was a man's man and you enjoyed being around him because you knew there wasn't going to be a lot of double talk. I think he was a great man, really a hero to me—a John Glenn, like I said, and somebody I admired very much. There are a few things I'm real proud of in my career. One was winning 25 games, including those two in the World Series in 1962, the most by any Yankee right-hander, and the other was playing with Roger Maris, the greatest single-season home run hitter of all time. That's quite a lot for a kid from Big Cabin, Oklahoma."

On May 26, 1959, Terry was traded to the Yankees with Hector Lopez for pitcher Johnny Kucks, pitcher Tom Sturdivant and infielder Jerry Lumpe. It was another in the growing list of Underground Railroad deals between Kansas City and the Yankees.

Just a week before, Terry had been with Maris after a game in Kansas City. "Roger had been complaining for a couple of days of not feeling well," Terry remembers.

He was having the finest season of his young career. He was among the batting leaders in the early weeks of the 1959 season with a .328 average. (Harvey Kuenn of Detroit would win the batting title that year with a .353 mark.) He had ten home runs and 26 runs batted in to lead the Kansas City club. Then, as Terry remembers, he became ill.

On May 22, 1959, Maris was rushed to Kansas City General Hospital for an emergency appendectomy. The operation was performed at 2:00 A.M.

Maris missed a week in the hospital, recuperated for another two weeks, and then began playing again less than three weeks after surgery. He was weak and tired. Over the next 25 games he hardly hit at all, going four for 60 in one streak and 11 for 90 in another. His average disappeared. He started coming back in late July and finished strong. He batted .273 for his big league high, had 16 home runs and knocked in 72 runs for the A's in 122 games.

Yankee scout Tom Greenwade, a tall, thin, taciturn man, continued to send weekly reports to the Yankees about Maris. He told George Weiss and Casey Stengel that Maris had been ill; then he told them the youngster had recovered and was hitting the ball hard again.

The Yankees, meanwhile, were struggling. The Chicago White Sox, under Bill Veeck and Hank Greenberg, won the pennant.

New York finished third. The New York press was restless. They began pointing out that manager Casey Stengel had just passed his sixty-ninth birthday. Owner Dan Topping was quoted as saying, "The managerial situation will be examined."

In a few weeks Stengel was given a contract for the 1960 season. Topping gave every indication that it would be Stengel's last as the Yankee manager. He would be retired after the 1960 season, to allow Ralph Houk to succeed him. He would not go gently into that good night.

Stengel met with Weiss before the winter baseball meetings that year and said, "We need a left-handed power hitter." Norm Siebern had hit only 11 homers and Stengel had been sour on him ever since Siebern blew a couple of fly balls against Milwaukee in the Stadium sun during the 1958 Series. Hank Bauer had been a tremendous player for Stengel, but the grizzly ex-Marine was thirty-seven years old and Stengel knew he was just about finished. It was time to exercise their option on Maris. The Yankees had followed the young slugger for nearly two years. No one can confirm today whether or not Maris was sent to Kansas City with an understanding he would eventually move to New York. Frank Lane, Arnold Johnson, George Weiss and Casey Stengel, the men who might know, are all gone now. It is important only because Roger Maris was about to walk into baseball history.

On December 11, 1959, Maris was traded to the Yankees with Kent Hadley and Joe DeMaestri for Don Larsen, Marv Throneberry, Bauer and Siebern. Maris would now be an outfield teammate of Mickey Mantle's. He was projected to play right field in Yankee Stadium, the position vacated twenty-seven years earlier by Babe Ruth. All the elements of this impending drama were coming together.

In Raytown, Missouri, Roger Maris heard the news of the trade on the radio. He was very upset.

"I don't want to go to New York," he told Pat.

He could hardly imagine the wonders he would experience there in the next seven years.

Roger as a member of the Kansas City A's in 1959 before he was traded to the Yankees. *Credit: Wide World.*

Roger attending his first Yankee spring training camp. Also shown: his wife, Pat; his son, Roger, Jr.; and his daughter, Susan. *Credit: NY Yankees.*

Roger collected numerous awards. This one was for fielding, proving he was more than just a home run hitter. *Credit: Bob Olen.*

Roger at the 1961 All-Star game with Willie Mays and Mickey
Mantle. *Credit: Bob Olen.*

Roger was always comfortable with kids, his own and others. *Credit: Bob Olen.*

The M and M Boys in September, 1961. Roger, for a joke, poses in a right-handed batting stance with his switch-hitting teammate. *Credit: Bob Olen.*

# 6

## new york, new york

"**NEVER** bet against Joe Louis, Notre Dame or the New York Yankees," went an old sports cliché. Joe Louis had retired, Notre Dame was still winning, but the Yankees had some questions to answer for their fans in 1960.

There was an air of urgency around their spring training camp as the Yankees gathered in St. Petersburg, Florida. The Chicago White Sox had defeated the Yankees and the Cleveland Indians to win the pennant in 1959. New York had won only 79 games and lost 75, the worst season in ten years since Casey Stengel took over the club. Much of the furor surrounded the gnarled old manager.

Stengel would be seventy years old that summer, give or take a year. His age was always open to question and endless scrutiny by the press. No soul had ever seen his birth certificate, but Yankee public relations director Bob Fishel was a witness in a cab when Stengel and his wife Edna began arguing about his age. "She always insisted he was a year older then he was listed in our press guides.

I don't know if it was true or if she did it just to needle the old man a little," Fishel said.

Yankee owners Dan Topping and Del Webb showed less support. It was clear Topping, especially, wanted to move in coach Ralph Houk as the future Yankee manager and make Roy Hamey the general manager, succeeding George Weiss. The manager was clearly on the spot and was more testy and less funny than usual that spring. He saw his brilliant baseball career ending—saw that he was marked for the scrap heap despite winning nine pennants in eleven years. Stengel's Yankees had blown the 1957 World Series to Milwaukee after leading two games to one, had been forced to rally from three games to one down to win the Series in 1958, and finished a sorry third in the AL race in 1959. Topping sensed that the team was in decline.

Stengel expected to throw Roger Maris into the breach.

"I'm not all that happy coming to New York," Maris told sportswriters on his arrival in camp. "I liked Kansas City. I expected to play out my career there."

Ballplayers could not become free agents then. They were bound to their ball clubs for life unless traded, sold or released under a paragraph in the standard baseball contract called the reserve clause. Maris had only one other choice when he was traded. He could quit. He was twenty-five years old that summer, the father of two children with a third on the way, and a responsible man. He reported to St. Petersburg.

"I got this new man and I expect him to hit some long balls for me," Stengel said of his new outfielder.

Maris had had a fine season for Kansas City in 1959. He had established his credentials as one of the finest young hitters in the game. He also had established his hold on right field in Kansas City. That is where he expected to play for the Yankees. Stengel seemed to have other ideas that spring. Mickey Mantle was the center fielder. Hector Lopez, who had come over to the Yankees with Ralph Terry the previous May, had played an inadequate third base. Stengel had decided to make him into an outfielder. Everybody expected the line drive hitting Lopez, a Panamanian, would be the Yankee left fielder. Everybody figured wrong.

When spring games began, Maris was in left field, Lopez was in right field and Mantle, of course, was in center field. When sportswriters asked Stengel why Maris was playing left instead of his accustomed right, the manager replied, "I want to see if he can do it." It was not as insignificant as it seems. Left field in Yankee Stadium is much more difficult to play because of the contours of the park, sloping deepest in that area, and because of the way the sun falls late in the season. It makes fly balls disappear. Maris, who had been in the league since 1957 and played in Yankee Stadium many times, knew all that. He was testy when reporters queried him.

"I'm new here. I'll play anywhere the manager wants me to play. Of course, I'm more comfortable in right field. That's where I played most of my career," he said.

Stengel drove his players wild with platooning. He used left-handers and right-handers in strange ways. He maneuvered players in and out of the lineup. He shifted positions of several players. He grew more agitated as the spring games ran down. He played Maris in thirty spring games, all of them in left field. The Yankees played poorly, as was their tradition, through most of the spring, winning 13 times and losing 19. Maris hit .315 in the spring with only one home run. There was a great deal of concern about the success of the ball club as the Yankees flew north from Florida to their 1960 opener at Fenway Park in Boston.

The Yankees were shut out five times in spring training and Stengel fooled with his lineup cards before the Boston opener, hoping to add some punch to the lineup and change the pattern of weak hitting he had seen through March from his "shutout lineup." The Red Sox started a tall, skinny right-hander named Tom Brewer. Brewer had a 10-12 record in 1959.

Stengel always wanted right-handed hitters in Fenway Park to attack the short left-field wall, the Green Monster of Fenway fame. He decided to start Hector Lopez in left field and bat him fourth, use right-handed-hitting catcher Elston Howard instead of veteran Yogi Berra, and put switch-hitting Mickey Mantle, batting left-handed, in the fifth spot. Then he filled out the rest of his lineup card. He led off with Roger Maris in right field. Then he had Bobby Richardson at second, Gil McDougald at third, Lopez, Mantle, Bill Skowron at first, Howard, Tony Kubek at shortstop and Jim Coates pitching. Maris was shocked to see his name leading off on Stengel's posted lineup card, but he was pleased to be back in right field.

Maris made it clear at the batting cage before the game that he did not like the idea of leading off. He told sportswriters he was a number 3 or number 4 hitter and was most interested in runs-batted-in. "That's what they pay off on," he said. He was asked how he felt about playing right field after so many games in left. "It's like coming home again," he said.

The man who was to break Babe Ruth's single season home run record played his first game as a Yankee in Boston, the same city Ruth had started his career in some forty-six years earlier. It was a debut worthy of Ruth. Maris hit a double his first time up as a Yankee, then he hit a home run, then he singled, and finally he hit another home run before flying out in his final time at bat. He was four for five with four runs batted in, two runs scored, and a perfect day in right field. It was an auspicious Yankee start. The Yankees won 8-4.

Stengel was enthused after the victory. "It was the funniest thing," the old manager said, as he pulled his baseball socks off his legs. He sat bare-chested in the small Boston clubhouse with only a red, silk pair of undershorts with the NY logo. "We hadn't been doing anything all spring so I changed the lineup. I picked all the right-handed hitters to hit that fence and I put Lopez batting fourth because he hit in some ninety runs [92] for me last year. I was really slick. Then Maris hits the two home runs to right field and Lopez doesn't get a hit."

Fenway Park measured 315 to the wall in left field and only 302 to the wall in right, but unless the ball was pulled sharply in right it sloped off quickly to 380 feet in front of the Red Sox bullpen, a huge shot for most hitters. Ted Williams, playing his final season, slugged a long home run out there for his 494th career homer (he was to finish with 521) that day, and Maris hit two even longer shots. Stengel was duly impressed... "He'll be batting lower in the order where he can do more of that," Stengel promised.

The two-run homer Maris hit in the fifth inning broke open the game, and the Yankee players, usually cool and professional when a teammate homered, erupted with uncommon enthusiasm, greeting Maris warmly as he came to the dugout, slapping him on the back, pumping his hand all down the dugout line and rubbing his head. Maris took it in stride.

"I didn't pay much attention," he said later. "It was a mob scene. All the guys pulling for each other, I guess."

In a scene that would grow all too familiar over the next few years, Maris leaned against his locker and talked to the press. He had taken off his Yankee gray uniform shirt with the large number 9, threw it in a basket that clubhouse man Pete Sheehy had placed in the center of the room, lit up a cigarette, puffed on it in between swallows of beer, and answered all the questions he was asked. He was direct, unemotional and unsmiling. It was clearly a chore he did not relish. He did it because it was required of him as a professional baseball player. He looked the questioner directly in the eye. He spoke in a monotone. He would answer each and every question. He clearly gave the impression he wished he could be someplace else.

The next stop for the Yankees was in Baltimore before coming home. Stengel had always chosen to keep his marvelous left-hander away from the Red Sox in Fenway. Whitey Ford pitched and won, of course, in Baltimore.


**WHITEY FORD** is fifty-seven years old, a gregarious, witty, even-tempered man who was one of the truly great pitchers of baseball in his distinguished Yankee career from 1950 through 1967. He was a Yankee coach for many years and now scouts for the Yankees. He lives in Lake Success, Long Island, during the baseball season, when he is a frequent visitor to Yankee Stadium, and in a condominium in Fort Lauderdale during the winter. He won 236 games and lost only 106 in his brilliant career. His catcher for many of those years, the late Elston Howard, called Ford the Chairman of the Board for his pitching acumen. Ford's locker in the Yankee clubhouse was always an oasis of humor and civility even when tense, high-pressured teammates were exploding in anger at the press. His best friend, Mickey Mantle, has often said, "I wished I could have been more like Whitey."

**FORD:** "We got back from Baltimore early in that 1960 season and we wanted to break Roger in. We decided to show him New York. That meant a long night at Shor's." (Toots Shor was a bombastic New York restaurateur who catered to the sports crowd. He was famous for his friends—Joe DiMaggio, Joe Louis, Charlie Conerly, and other top athletes—as he was for his enormous drinking capacity. He once said the only night of the year he didn't drink was New Year's Eve. "That night is for amateurs," he said.) "We went over there as soon as we got back from Baltimore, in the early evening, and started drinking. It was Mickey, myself, Ken Hunt [a young Yankee outfielder who had grown up with Roger in Grand Forks] and Roger. We started to down the double Scotches pretty good and Roger kept up for a while. He wasn't like me and Mickey. He slowed down about midnight. Toots used to stay open until three or four in the morning and we figured that would be it. Toots wasn't about to quit. He got a cab and we all piled in and we went back to his apartment on Park Avenue, and he told Baby [Shor's wife] to get out the good stuff for his special guests and we kept going until eight o'clock in the morning. We had an off day—we wouldn't have done that if it wasn't an off day—and Casey had scheduled an early workout. There wasn't much sense in going home by this time, so the four of us just got into a cab and went up to the Stadium. We didn't have a great workout but we were set to go by the next day. That's what counted.

"Roger was a good guy to have on the club. He could laugh, he could kid around, he could take a joke. He was quiet around the press but he was loose around the guys. He and Mickey got along well. They wouldn't have lived together if they didn't. It's one thing to be a teammate and get along around the ballpark; it's another thing to share an apartment. You're only going to do that if you are comfortable with a guy.

"Mickey and Roger probably got even closer in the years after they stopped playing. Mickey had a golf tournament each year in Wildwood, Florida, and Roger would play in it. He was a tough competitor. We were both left-handed golfers, and he hooked a lot of balls to the right and I sliced a lot of balls to the left. He was an erratic golfer. He would shoot 75-76 one day and come back the next day and shoot 88. He was always tougher when there was money on the line.

"Roger tried to act loose during that 1961 season but it was impossible. The pressures on him were enormous. I had a pretty big year myself, 25 and 4, but nobody noticed because there was so much attention on Roger. That was great for me but it was really rough on Roger. Sometimes I wondered how he did it, day after day, night after night. The big thing that helped was getting away at home to that apartment with Mickey and Cerv where he could really relax during the day. That couldn't have happened if he had stayed in a hotel. The press would have found out and been all over him.

"There was probably even more pressure on him in 1962 than in 1961. A lot of people thought the home run year was a fluke and he wasn't that good a player. He proved he was with another terrific season. I think Roger was liked by everybody and got along with everybody on the club, except maybe for Jim Bouton. Bouton just rubbed him the wrong way. Jim had some kidding remark in the press one time about Roger, and Roger took it seriously. It upset him. Another time Jim was running for player representative and actually campaigned. He put up a poster in the clubhouse asking guys to vote for him, and he

handed out pamphlets to his teammates with his quali-
fications. Roger thought it was bush. He tore the poster
down and threw away his pamphlets. Then Jim tried to
get his running in before the game. Roger told him, 'Don't
ever try and run in right field.' He really intimidated Jim.
It was funny to watch Jim run from left to center before
the games, and never run with the other pitchers from
right to center.

"When Roger got sick I would call Pat and keep up on
how he was doing. The reports weren't good. I was down
here in Lauderdale in December. Mickey and I and Phil
Rizzuto were making a film for Little Leaguers. I was at
home one afternoon, talking to Joan, and the phone rang.
I was sitting in this very same chair. Some sportswriter
from Fargo, North Dakota, called me on the phone. He
identified himself and then he asked me, 'What do I think
about Roger?' I knew Roger was quite ill by now and I
said, 'I hope he gets better.' The sportswriter said, 'He
died. I thought you knew.' We had known he was very
sick, but that was a shock. I called Mickey at the Yankee
Clipper where he was staying. He just started crying.

"We made arrangements to go to the funeral in Fargo
and traveled there together. Mickey kept talking about
Roger. He said he just couldn't get him out of his mind.
Mickey always used to kid about how Roger had stolen
all his fans in 1961. He meant those boo-birds. They had
always booed Mickey every time he had a day without a
home run, and now they started booing Roger and cheer-
ing Mickey. 'Stop stealing my fans,' Mickey would yell.
Mickey and Roger really did become great friends, and I
think Mickey admired Roger a lot for what he did. Mickey
always said he thought Roger belonged in the Hall of Fame
for doing that, if for nothing else. But Roger was a terrific
all-around player. He was a terrific competitor and he

played the hell out of right field. I think he went into those seats out there and saved me a few home runs. Roger did everything well on the ball field. If there was any one thing I'll always remember about Roger, it's that he was a team man and he really liked to win."

Stengel soon had the Yankees straightened out and playing good baseball. It would remain a tight pennant race with the young Baltimore Orioles under Paul Richards through early September. Richards had built a fine young pitching staff, labeled the Baby Birds, but they couldn't carry the burden of a head-to-head fight with the Yankees. They came into New York in September for a four-game series, only a game out of first. The Yankees swept all four and moved on to the 1960 pennant. The inexperience of the Baby Birds showed in the first game when young shortstop Ron Hansen and young third baseman Brooks Robinson collided under a pop fly. The ball fell safely and the Yankees broke the game open, a typical Yankee performance.

Maris had settled into the fourth spot in the batting order by midseason, batting behind Mantle, and had been slugging away at a rapid pace. He had 25 home runs in a little less than half a season and found himself about to be compared with Babe Ruth for the first time. A sportswriter examined the Ruth record in 1927 and saw that Maris was four games ahead of Ruth's schedule. Many players had been ahead of Ruth's pace of 1927 but all had lost out later in the season, especially when confronted with the reality of the 17 Ruth had hit that September. Described in the press as the "newest, new Babe Ruth," Maris was asked about his chances of making a run at the Ruth record.

"No one is going to beat the Babe's record," Maris said.

"Certainly I won't. Furthermore, hitting home runs does not interest me that much."

Maris was asked what did interest him in that 1960 season.

"I'm not looking for any records," said Maris. "I'm just hoping to have a good season and help the Yankees win. I know much better than to start setting any fantastic goals for myself."

To astute observers it was clear what Maris had in mind. Of course he enjoyed the home runs. Every slugger did. Even Punch-and-Judy hitters did. Even pitchers become most animated over homers. When Dwight Gooden hit his first big league homer for the Mets, the normally shy, soft-spoken young man talked about it excitedly for many weeks. Maris understood the essence of the Yankees. They simply had to win. They did not win in 1959, and another losing season in 1960 would not go down well with the owners. If he was to really have a good year, if he was to get a substantial raise, the Yankees had to win.

To that end, Stengel continued to juggle his lineup. Mantle and Maris, still a season away from being linked as M and M, were playing every day. Others platooned. Then Stengel was forced into a major change. Maris injured himself in a collision with Washington shortstop Billy Gardner. He wrenched his knee and damaged a ligament. He was out of the lineup more than two weeks.

All talk of catching Ruth ended. Maris did return strong, though, and continued to hit well. New stories about Maris filled the newspapers. Now he was being discussed as a candidate for the Most Valuable Player award, the most prestigious honor in baseball. It was heady stuff for a twenty-five-year-old playing only his fourth year in the big leagues. While Maris was out, Yogi Berra, Bob Cerv and Hector Lopez got more playing time in the outfield.

**HECTOR LOPEZ** is fifty-four years old, a native of Colón, Panama, who now works as a recreation department official for the Nassau County, New York, town of Hempstead. He spends much time in his native Panama giving baseball clinics. He was a solid line drive hitter with the Yankees, very tough in the clutch with his ability to spray the ball all around. His fielding, or lack of it, kept him from a more successful career. New York *Post* sportswriter Leonard Shecter captured that weakness in print when he began calling him Hector (What a Pair of Hands) Lopez.

**LOPEZ:** "We had this running pinochle game that went on all the years we were together—Roger, Clete Boyer, Hal Reniff [a portly blond relief pitcher] and myself. I was Roger's partner, and Reniff and Boyer were partners. We'd play for a few bucks and then go out and have a big dinner together. Roger was a very good card player, very smart, and seemed to remember all the cards all the time. His expression never changed. Reniff and Boyer kidded around a lot but Roger and I paid attention to the game. Maybe that's why we won most of the time.

"My locker was near Roger's and when things really got hot in 1961 I just moved into the trainer's room. I would take my shower and come out, and go in there with the other players and Gus Mauch, and just wait out the press. As the season went on those stays in there took longer and longer and longer. There would be fifty reporters waiting for Roger when he came out to talk to them, and then another fifty would be around his locker after he had finished with the first bunch. It was an amazing thing to see how he stood there day after day, every day, just answering all those questions.

"The 1961 season just had to be the most exciting thing I had ever been part of in baseball. Everybody could feel the pressure Roger was under, and everybody else was under some pressure as well. You didn't want to do anything or make a bad play that would cost Roger anything. I felt excited and relieved when he finally hit that sixty-first homer. I knew it would be a big part of Yankee history. I was on the top step when he came back to the dugout, and I think I was the first guy to block him from going in and pushed him back out. I just felt he deserved that applause. Roger was a modest guy and he probably would have just gone into the dugout and sat down. I'm glad he took those cheers. It was an emotional thing to see.

"I saw him a couple of times and he was always very friendly to me. I got along real well with Roger. I was real upset when I heard he died and I thought back to those days with all that pressure and I thought, well, maybe that had something to do with it. Who knows? The man took a lot, you know."

Traditionally, the Yankees had been a strong second half team. Most good baseball teams are. The idea is to stay close through July and August and put on the rush to win in September. The Yankees had some pressure from Chicago and Baltimore most of the summer. The series against the Orioles at the Stadium in September would give them the pennant. It was a series against the White Sox in late July that kept them close when it seemed Chicago had a chance to pull away. Whitey Ford was pitching the first game of a doubleheader against the White Sox. Tony Kubek was at shortstop for the Yankees.

**TONY KUBEK** is fifty years old, one of the brightest, most articulate young men to play for the Yankees during the late 1950s and 1960s. In only nine seasons from 1957 through 1965, Kubek established himself as one of the finest shortstops in the American League. He was a tough, left-handed line drive hitter and a leader among the Yankees. He suffered a serious neck injury when a line drive bounced at him off Bill Virdon's bat in the 1960 World Series against the Pirates. It forced him to retire early. Kubek became a sportscaster and now does the weekly National Broadcasting Company Game of the Week telecast.

**KUBEK:** "We were playing this game against the White Sox and we were struggling a little. If they won, we would be two or three games back and it might have been tough to catch up again. Whitey was on the mound in a 2-2 game about the seventh or eighth inning. The White Sox had the bases loaded. Gene Freese was up. He hit a line drive into right center field and I figured it was easily a double, maybe a triple for three runs, and we were out of the game. I ran out to take the throw and I watched Roger chase after the ball. He could really run. He had a smooth stride and it didn't seem as if he was moving all that fast. He simply overtook that ball, jumped in the air and backhanded it before it hit the wall to end the inning, a tremendous catch. After the game, which we finally won 7-2, Whitey came over to me and said, 'If Roger didn't catch that, I was finished.' There was a lot of feeling in the clubhouse that Roger's catch had not only turned the game around for us but turned the season. You don't want to start falling three games back in July. It is just too hard to catch up. Everybody talks about home runs with Roger but he was as good a right fielder as I ever saw. I think the standard in those days was Roberto Clemente in the National League with Pittsburgh. I didn't see all that much of Clemente except for the World Series against him that year, but Roger was every bit as good.

"Roger got a bad rap from the press because he was a yes-and-no guy. He just didn't feel comfortable talking about his personal life or predicting what he would do or wouldn't do. He was really a shy guy who just went out and did the best job he could every day. His personality had a strong impact on the press and I think he never was appreciated as a complete player because of it. They like the guys who talk easily. I can understand that. It's tough for me to interview guys on television who won't talk.

"I used to locker across from Roger and in 1961 I would watch this parade every day, and it was an amazing thing to see. He was really in a meat grinder. I remember one day we were in a very tough game. Moose Skowron finally hit a home run in the seventh inning and we held on to win 1-0. When the game was over all the sportswriters gathered around Roger. 'Moose won the game. Go talk to him.' The press didn't care about Moose. They were still on Roger. It was during the last part of the streak and they wouldn't go to anybody else until they had some stuff from Roger. He found that tough to deal with. Another time Ellie Howard won a game, and Roger stayed in the trainer's room until he was sure all the press had talked to Ellie. He didn't want anybody to think he was taking any attention from them.

"There was all that talk of Roger and Mickey not getting along. It was nonsense. Mickey was very supportive of Roger. The big Yankee players were Joe DiMaggio and then Mickey Mantle. Nobody else came close. When they both started hitting home runs, we all pulled for both of them. There may have been some feeling early that if anybody was going to do it, it would be nice if it was Mickey. He had succeeded DiMaggio, he was the heart of the Yankees for a long time, and he was just about at his peak as a player. He wouldn't have many more chances. By the middle of the season I think the feeling was maybe both of them could do it. When Mickey got sick at the end and dropped out, we really pulled hard for Roger to make it.

"The pressure was enormous on Roger. He broke out with this terrible rash on his face for a while, and then his hair started falling out. Mickey was out of the race by then, and one day he told Roger to take a couple of the younger players and go to Shor's and ask for his table and sign the check to him and just relax. Roger had trouble relaxing.

"I don't think anybody experienced the pressure Roger did that year. One time in Detroit, some nut threw a folding chair from the top deck that landed a foot away from Roger. The game was stopped and he walked off the field. He was real angry. 'I don't get paid enough to take that.' You could see he was not going out there again unless he was protected. They made an announcement and cops were sent to the stands to police the crowd.

"I guess my biggest thrill that year was batting ahead of him. Late in the game I was always trying to get on somehow to save him an at-bat. Whenever I made out last to end the game, I would get some letters from fans, getting on me for preventing Roger from hitting again. What was amazing was that he hit 61 homers and never got an intentional walk all year. That's how much the batting order, with Mickey hitting behind him, meant to the record.

"Roger was sensitive about his average. People used to get on him about that, and one day when he had 40 or 45 homers he said, 'I'll settle for 50 if I can hit .320.' I don't know if he meant it, but he was bugged by that constant reference to his never hitting .300.

"The amazing thing was how calm he was on the field

during the game. In a way, that's when he really relaxed. I remember one day in Detroit when he had 56 home runs, and all of a sudden he is at bat and looks up and sees these Canadian geese flying over the park, maybe 200 of them, moving south, and he steps out of the box to watch them. Ed Hurley was the umpire and he called time, and the two of them just stood there watching those geese fly overhead. Roger got back into the box after they disappeared, dug in at the plate, and hit the next pitch 385 feet for a home run.

"What hurt Roger the most was his loss of privacy. There was always somebody ready to interview him. The Yankees kept scheduling these interviews for him with magazine writers earlier and earlier in the day—*Time* magazine, *Sports Illustrated*, *Newsweek*, all the big ones. One day he said, 'I just don't have any private time any more. I've been too busy to even call Pat.' He was playing ball, eating, and giving interviews over those last few weeks.

"I can't say enough about what Roger accomplished. Mickey once said he couldn't imagine going to Cooperstown without having Roger there in the Hall of Fame. It was such a remarkable performance.

"I knew Roger was failing and it couldn't be a shock when he finally died. I was in the Dominican Republic watching some winter baseball and I was going on the air to do some interviews. Just as the red light went on, this producer handed me a piece of paper. It was the wire service story saying Roger had just died. I couldn't talk. I broke into tears and stammered a few things about Roger. There wasn't much I could say. I knew he had suffered a lot at the end. He had gone through so much as a player, especially in that 1961 season, and he'd gone through so much pain at the end of his life. In a way, when he died, it was like the end of that 1961 season. I remember him saying how much of a relief it was to have that season behind him. I felt that same way when he died. All that pain was finally over."

The Yankees ground the Orioles down in that September series and were moving into Pittsburgh for the 1960 World Series. The Yankees had last been there in 1927, Ruth's 60-homer season. Now the Yankees were coming back with Roger Maris (39 homers, 112 Runs Batted In, a .283 average), Mickey Mantle (40 homers to win the title, 94 Runs Batted In, and a .274 average) and Moose Skowron (26 homers, 91 Runs Batted In, and a .309 average) as their big three sluggers. It was as awesome a group as the 1927 sluggers, Ruth, Lou Gehrig and Tony Lazzeri.

BILL (MOOSE) SKOWRON is fifty-five years old, a Yankee first baseman from 1956 through 1962. He finished his career as a part-time player with the Dodgers, Senators, White Sox and Angels. He lives in Chicago and is a sales representative for a company manufacturing blank checks for banks. "I got my nickname during World War II as a kid growing up in Chicago. My grandfather started calling me Mussolini because he thought I looked like him. The kids changed it to Moose. I didn't mind it. My brother they called Hitler," he says. Skowron, like Roger Maris, always wore a crewcut.

SKOWRON: "Maybe that's why we got to be friends right away. We both wore crewcuts and we both were bashful guys. He was a great team player and he played every game like we were losing 2-1. We used to go out together a lot. Roger could really eat. It was nothing for him to put away a bushel of those crabs they used to bring into the clubhouse in Baltimore for an appetizer and then go out and have a big steak.

"When he hit that sixty-first homer I don't think he wanted to stand out there and wave to the fans, but he knew we wanted him to do it. He was bashful, like I say, and that wasn't something he enjoyed. But after doing that you have to give the fans something or they won't stop hollering.

"I think he missed being around the guys after he quit, but he was mad at the Yankees for what they did to him after the home run year, with his hand being hurt and not helping him and getting traded like that at the end. Anyway, the regime had changed and I used to call him in Florida all the time and say he should come back. 'Roger, the guys want to see you, they want to see if you got fat, they want to see if you still have your hair.' He would say, 'They'll boo me.' I told him those fans are all dead. He would be cheered. I was really happy when he finally came back for Old Timers Day.

"We saw each other in Florida or at some Old Timers Game or at the Cracker Jack game in Washington and then, later, at his golf tournament in Fargo. That was always fun. In 1985 he was too sick to travel from Florida to Fargo for the tournament, and I talked to him on the phone. 'Moose, when I'm gone, I want you to keep that thing going, you get those guys to come out. You're in charge. It's for a good cause.' I didn't want to hear anything like that, but I told him I would do it, and I will.

"Then in December my son, Gregory, called me from Scottsdale, Arizona, to tell me his wife had given birth to a baby boy, and me and Cookie [Skowron's wife Lorraine] were grandparents again. That was terrific news. I put the phone down, and a minute later it rang again. It was Pat.

'We lost Roger. We want you to be a pallbearer at the funeral. He asked for you.' I just started to cry."

In his first season as a Yankee, Maris was in a World Series. The 1960 Series was one of the most exciting ever played, with the Yankees scoring 55 runs to Pittsburgh's 27 and still losing, four games to three. Bill Mazeroski won it for the Pirates with a ninth-inning leadoff home run over the left-field fence, with left fielder Yogi Berra not even bothering to look up at the long ball in the seventh game. Mazeroski's homer off Ralph Terry set off a wild Pittsburgh celebration.

Maris hit a home run his first time up in a World Series, collected three hits in that first Series game, and finished with a .267 average—eight hits, two homers and a double.

After the final game Casey Stengel was surrounded by members of the press. They wanted to know if that losing Series was his final game as the Yankees manager.

"I didn't make my living here. Why should I tell you anything," he grumbled.

None of the Yankees were concerned at the moment. More important, Tony Kubek, who had been struck by Bill Virdon's hard shot off the Pittsburgh infield dirt, lay on the training table with blood dripping down his neck. Mickey Mantle walked into the trainer's room, took one look at Kubek and burst into tears.

Three weeks later Roger Maris was named the American League's Most Valuable Player.

"It's a great honor," he said. "I'm very proud to receive it. I was just lucky enough to play with some great players. They deserve this as much as I do."

The MVP award was not unexpected. It was also not the most dramatic event of the offseason between 1960

and 1961. Stengel was. He was supposedly being "retired." The Yankees threw a press conference and party
for him in Le Salon Bleu of the swank Savoy Hilton Hotel
in Manhattan. Before the announcement there was some
uncertainty. Then Stengel was ushered to the microphone.

"Were you fired?" a reporter yelled.

"No I wasn't fired," Stengel bellowed. "I was paid up
in full."

"The Associated Press has a bulletin, Casey," another
reporter yelled, "it says you were fired. What about it?"

"What do I care what the A.P. says. Their opinion ain't
going to send me into any fainting spell. Anyway, what
about the U.P.?"

Stengel was gone, George Weiss would soon follow, and
the 1961 Yankees would be run by general manager Roy
Hamey and field manager Ralph Houk.

There was one other significant baseball change that
winter. The American League announced that it would
expand from eight teams, a format that had lasted sixty
years, to ten teams. Franchises were awarded to Los Angeles and to Washington. The existing Washington franchise owned by Calvin Griffith would move to the Twin
Cities of Minneapolis and Saint Paul and be known as
the Minnesota Twins. To accommodate the 10-team league
the schedule would be expanded from 154 games to 162
games.

There was no word from the office of Baseball Commissioner Ford Frick about any proposed changes in baseball's record-keeping.

# 7

## mickey, maris and the babe

ON a bitter cold February morning in 1961, Roger Maris got behind the wheel of his 1960 blue Buick and headed for the Yankee spring training camp in Saint Petersburg, Florida. His wife Pat, two months pregnant, sat alongside him as they pulled out of the driveway of their Raytown, Missouri, home. Three sleepy children, Susan, four, Roger Jr., three, and Kevin, four months old and fast asleep in a porto-crib, shared the back seat. Maris had decided to leave for spring training early for a week of sun after the hectic 1960 season.

He was twenty-six years old, about to start his fifth big league season, the American League's Most Valuable Player and, for the first time in his baseball life, making some serious money. He had been rewarded with a huge raise, from $19,000 to $37,500. He had made the adjustment to New York as well as expected, enjoyed playing in the World Series, felt comfortable with his teammates and looked forward to another successful season.

124

Halfway through the state of Georgia, still some 500 miles from the beach apartment they had rented in Florida, the car mysteriously broke down. Maris pulled off the road.

"I first looked around to see if any snakes were crawling around," Maris wrote of the experience, "and then I lifted the hood. Not to make any repairs, but as a sign of trouble."

A tow truck found the car, but a nervous Pat Maris and three sobbing youngsters could hardly be consoled as they were hauled to a garage more than twenty-five miles away over dusty, bumpy Georgia country roads. The repair was made and the car drove on to Florida without incident. When Maris arrived along St. Pete Beach, he decided to knock on the door of teammate John Blanchard. Pat Maris was obviously quite ill, the children were restless and uncomfortable and there was need of comfort from somebody who understood. John and Nancy Blanchard had become close friends in 1960. Nancy was also pregnant at the time.

**JOHN BLANCHARD** is fifty-three years old, a rugged-looking, hard-living former Yankee catcher and pinch hitter extraordinaire. He was with the Yankees from 1959 through 1964, was traded to Kansas City in 1965 and finished up with the Milwaukee Braves. His lifetime mark was only .239 but he hit 21 home runs in 1961, including four in a pinch-hit role.

**BLANCHARD:** "When Roger was at Reading in 1955, I was catching in that league at Binghamton. We got to talking, became real friendly and used to have a few beers together when we played against each other. Roger was from North Dakota and I was from Minneapolis and we liked to do the same things.

"I remember in December of 1959, when I read in the paper that Roger had been traded to the Yankees. We had lost the pennant that year but we knew we had a good ball club. Casey kept saying if we could land a left-handed slugger we could win again. When I read about Roger joining us I went out and bought a brand new Pontiac Ventura for three or four thousand dollars, a lot of money then. 'We can't afford that,' Nancy said. 'Now we can,' I said. 'We got Roger Maris.' I really looked forward to his coming to the team, and he lockered next to me and we became good buddies.

"It was about 10 o'clock at night that time when I heard a knock on the front door of my beach apartment. I don't even know how he got the address, but I opened the door and there was Roger and the kids. They all looked pretty beat and when I asked Roger what was going on, he said, 'Pat's out in the car having a miscarriage.' Roger wanted to drop off the kids and take his wife to a hospital. Nancy got the kids into our place and Roger took off for the hospital. We kept them for a few days and then Roger's mother came down from North Dakota to take care of them once spring training started. [Quick medical care had saved Pat's baby. Randy was born that summer.] It was a very tough spring for him.

"Roger finally got settled down that spring and went into the season in pretty good shape. He started slowly, but once he started hitting home runs there was no stopping him. There was a lot of attention on Roger and Mickey both, but after Mickey got sick at the end, it was all Roger. The pressure was incredible. I remember when his hair started falling out in patches and I said to him, 'Roger, are you going bald or what?' He said, 'Ah, hell, it's just nerves. The doctor says it will all grow back after this is over.' It was real scary to me.

"The press would be all over him every day and he never had time to breathe. He just stood there and they fired questions at him and he just answered, and that seemed to go on day after day. Once in a while some reporter would ask a real dumb question, Roger would answer as best he could, and then later he would say, 'Do you believe the garbage they want to know?' I remember when some guy asked him if he played around on the road. Here was a clean living guy like Roger with three or four kids and they are asking if he plays around on the road.

"We had a good time together, even under all that pressure. The most fun was going out to eat together. Especially in Baltimore. They'd bring those crabs into the clubhouse and Roger would finish off a bucketful, let out a good burp and then say, 'Let's get a steak.' I'd eat a few crabs and drink a few beers, but nobody could eat like Roger. That's why he didn't drink much. He was too busy bearing down on those crabs."

Blanchard was emotionally tied to the Yankees. Not even one of the most embarrassing incidents a big league catcher could live through could change his feelings toward the team. He sat on the bench once in Chicago when the temperature climbed near 100 degrees. Yogi Berra was catching in the 1959 game and Casey Stengel didn't like the pitch Berra called and they argued about it. Stengel turned to Blanchard and told him to get his catching gear on. Blanchard put on all that heavy catching equipment and sat fully ready on the bench while Berra continued to catch the game. When it finally ended, Blanchard picked up a bucket of ice and dumped it over his own head. When he was finally traded to Kansas City he wept openly for more than an hour.

**BLANCHARD:** "Roger never really talked much about the home runs when we would go out that year. He kept everything inside. That's the kind of guy he was. I think that may have had something to do with his getting sick. You could see his mind was always working but he wasn't talking much about his problems.

"We stayed close through the years. I used to run a liquor store in Minneapolis and he would call me up every so often. Then I got into sales for a heavy equipment company, and I would travel around and catch him here and there. I was really happy when he came back for the first time to an Old Timers Day. He had really mellowed by then, a lot of that anger about the way the Yankees had treated him was gone. He was a little fat the way most of us were, and we kidded him about that and he laughed. 'Hey Roger, you really turned out to be a nice guy.' He laughed like hell at that.

"I don't know if this means anything, but I had a cancerous kidney removed about three weeks before Roger died. I had some pain and I was peeing blood and I went to see a doctor. He examined me and put me right in the hospital. I was operated on the next day. About a week after I got out of there, Roger died. I just got in my car and drove to Fargo. I know Roger would have done that for me."

Maris had a poor spring as was his custom. He hit only one home run. He batted .235. Rookie manager Ralph Houk was under a lot of pressure. He fooled with the lineup and decided to go with Maris in the third spot and Mantle hitting fourth. Camilo Pascual, a Cuban right-hander with a big curve ball, opened for the new Minnesota Twins and shut the Yankees out, 6-0. Maris was hitless.

In 1985 Maris would say, "Camilo Pascual was the toughest pitcher I ever faced. His curve ball was the best in baseball, he had marvelous control of it and he could change speeds. I just never could get a good swing against the guy."

Maris was miserable at bat. His swing was off and his average fell below .200. He did not hit a home run for the first ten days of the season. Finally, on April 26, at Detroit, Maris hit homer number 1 off right-hander Paul Foytack. Mantle hit two homers that day in a wild 13-11 Yankee victory. It gave Mickey seven home runs in 11 games, the finest home run start of his career.

Maris hit number 2 off Pedro Ramos, number 3 off Eli Grba (the 100th of his career) and number 4 off left-hander Pete Burnside of Washington. Number 5 was a rocket off Cleveland's Jim Perry, number 6 a long drive off Cleveland's Gary Bell and number 7 on May 21 off Chuck Estrada. Mantle had slackened his home run hitting pace by then, and had only 10.

Maris's average was still below .240, and when the team returned from Cleveland the right fielder was summoned to the Yankee offices at 745 Fifth Avenue for a chat with owner Dan Topping and GM Roy Hamey. They had been discussing Maris and had decided that they wanted the outfielder to hit home runs. He had hit 39 in his MVP year of 1960 and, with Mantle off to a strong start, they figured 40 or 45 or even 50 homers by both sluggers would make for a bountiful Yankee season. Maris was uncertain of the purpose of his visit. He was always a worrier, and a visit to the boss was an extra worry he didn't need as he battled to get his average up.

The owner and the general manager took Maris around the corner to Reuben's Restaurant, a pleasant place for corned beef sandwiches, cheese cake and beer.

"We want you to stop worrying about your hitting," Topping said. "We're not worried and we don't want you to fret about it. Forget your batting average and go out and swing for home runs. We would rather see you hit a lot of home runs and drive in runs than hit .300."

Maris was relieved. That's the way he had always seen his role. Topping had one more thought. He figured maybe Maris was having trouble with his eyes because he seemed to be swinging a bit late at some balls.

"Just in case there may be something wrong with your eyes, we want you to have them checked," he said.

Maris was sent by car to an eye doctor. He was examined thoroughly. There was nothing wrong with his eyesight but the eye doctor suggested there might be a little strain in the eyes, perhaps from the tension of his slow start. Maris was given a solution to put in his eyes. He put a few drops in his eyes before the game and ran out to his position. Soon his vision was blurry. He stopped the game to get his eyes washed out by trainer Gus Mauch. It didn't help. His vision remained blurred and, when the half inning ended, manager Ralph Houk had to replace Maris with a pinch hitter. Houk was livid. The Yankees won but remained five and a half games behind first place Detroit.

Maris hit number 8 off Gene Conley on May 24, number 9 off Cal McLish, and number 10 on May 30, again off Conley. Mantle hit two homers that day and had 13. On May 30, 1927, Babe Ruth had 14 homers.

Maris hit number 11 off Mick Fornieles on that same day and hit another, number 12, off Billy Muffett the next day. Then he got number 13 off Cal McLish, number 14 off Bob Shaw and number 15 off Russ Kemmerer. Maris had now passed Mantle, who had 14 home runs. It was Yankee game 45. Ruth had 16 homers in 1927 after 45 games.

The press began noticing the growing total. Comparisons were being made between Maris and Mantle, and between both of them and Babe Ruth.

George Herman (Babe) Ruth was born in Baltimore on February 6, 1895. He came from a poor background and soon wound up in St. Mary's orphanage, despite the fact that both parents were still alive. He was a troublesome kid but found status and salvation in baseball, a left-handed pitcher, a left-handed catcher, an outfielder and, above all, a tremendous hitter. He was signed by the Boston Red Sox and made it to the team as a pitcher in 1914. He pitched and played the outfield for Boston until sold to the Yankees on January 3, 1920.

Babe Ruth won ten home run titles in the next dozen years as a Yankee, rescued baseball from the doldrums of the 1919 Black Sox scandal, revolutionized the game with his slugging, lived the high life with women, booze and garishness, and clearly was the most famous person in America—and probably the most loved—as he set the home run record of 60 in the season of 1927. Growing fat in his later years, he was an almost comical figure with his huge chest and spindly legs, his bulbous nose (causing opposing players to needle him by suggesting he was half Negro), his careless habits (he called most people "Kid" because he could not remember names) and his enormous capacity for food and drink. He was quoted constantly and probably was the most photographed man of his time. When his salary reached $80,000 he was allegedly criticized for making more money than Herbert Hoover, the President of the United States. According to legend, the Babe retorted: "Why not? I had a better year than he did." He epitomized the rousing lifestyle of the Roaring Twenties. Every kid in America wanted to grow up to be Babe

Ruth. He played with the Yankees through 1934, but never was offered the managerial job he so intently desired because general manager Ed Barrow said, "How can he manage other men when he can't manage himself?" He coached for the Brooklyn Dodgers for a spell, then lived out his life as a Manhattan celebrity, attending fights and first nights, traveling abroad, showing up at various public events and finally dying of throat cancer on August 16, 1948. He was fifty-three.

In addition to all the pitchers in the American League, Roger Maris would have to battle the heroic legend of Babe Ruth—a legend that, in the summer of 1961, was firmly planted in the American consciousness.

To many of Maris's 1961 teammates, Babe Ruth became a comic, if annoying, figure throughout that summer. More than once, as a young sportswriter patrolling the Yankee clubhouse during those days, I would hear some player scream out with venom. It was often an obscenity ending with Ruth's name. They had become tired of hearing it, angered that a man dead thirteen years whose feat of 60 homers had been accomplished thirty-four years earlier, could have such overwhelming importance in a 1961 season.

**BOB TURLEY** is fifty-six years old, a bright, handsome man from Troy, Illinois, who pitched for the Browns and Orioles before being obtained by the Yankees. He was the best pitcher in baseball in 1958 with a 21-7 season. He won the Cy Young award. Turley retired after the 1963 season and is a successful insurance executive in Atlanta.

**TURLEY:** "There were so many pressures on Roger that year. Anything you could do for a laugh would be important. I was having breakfast one morning on the road in Chicago or Detroit or Cleveland, I can't remember, and Roger and Bob Cerv came into the coffee shop and we sat down together. We were reading the sports pages and having coffee. Some little kid came over.

"He was about ten or twelve and maybe he had been sent over by his parents, I don't really know. Anyway, he wanted all our autographs. I don't even know if he knew who each of us was except that he knew we were Yankee ballplayers. Cerv wrote his name on a piece of paper and then he passed it to Roger. Roger scribbled 'Babe Ruth' and laughed as the kid walked away. I don't know now why he did it—just for fun, I guess, just because he was getting all that Babe Ruth talk and once in a while it really got to be too much. Somehow or other the kid went back to his table and the parents looked over and said something, and I didn't think anything of it until the next day when I read these big headlines in the paper. Roger was getting ripped for signing Babe Ruth's name on a kid's autograph book, and how could he do such a horrible thing and what a bad man he was and all that. It was just a joke, really, and it had been blown up into huge headlines. It was something Roger had to deal with all year.

"I go back a long way with Roger, all the way back to 1949, when he was about fourteen or fifteen years old and I was pitching professionally in Aberdeen, South Dakota. Somebody hit a ball against a fence in batting practice and I went to retrieve it and this kid came rushing over the fence trying to race me to the ball. I was standing just about where it stopped rolling and when I picked it up he asked for it and I wouldn't give it to him. I couldn't give away baseballs. Anyway, I remembered the incident years later, and when Roger joined us he reminded me of it and told me he was that kid. I picked a ball out of the ball bag and flipped it to him. We both laughed a lot.

"Nobody had a tougher time in baseball than Roger did that summer. No matter what he said, he seemed to get in trouble. If he said he wasn't going for the record, they didn't believe him. If he said he was, it came out as if he was attacking Babe Ruth. People portrayed him in the press as public enemy number one because he wasn't Mickey Mantle. I remember one time he hit a home run in Detroit toward the end of the year, and the ball landed back on the field and Al Kaline [the Tiger right fielder] picked it up and threw it into the Yankee dugout for Roger. After the game somebody asked Roger if that wasn't a nice thing that Kaline did. Wasn't that something special? 'No, not really. I'd do the same for him. Anybody would do it.' That was just Roger. He couldn't say the political thing. He only said the honest thing. He was right. Probably anybody would have done it. But it didn't sound right, and it came out like a rip at Kaline.

"We played golf a couple of times in Gainesville when I would travel on business through there. Roger's personality had mellowed. He wasn't angry any more. He had found peace. Roger was a man. He said what he believed. And don't forget his skills. He was the finest right fielder I ever saw."

Maris hit number 16 off Ed Palmquist and number 17 off Pedro Ramos. Then he hit number 18 off Ray Herbert. That day Mantle also got one off Herbert. He had 16. The date was June 9. Ruth had 18 homers after 48 games on that date in 1927. Maris got Grba again on June 11 for number 19, and ex-Yankee Johnny James in the same game for number 20. He went to 21 against Jim Perry, 22 against Bell again, and 23 against Don Mossi, the jug-eared Detroit reliever. Number 24 was off Jerry Casale and number 25, on June 19, was off Jim Archer.

It was about this time, with Maris at 25 homers and Mantle at 20, that the criticism surfaced. Casale, Archer, James, and several others were clearly expansion pitchers. They probably would not have been in the majors, except that twenty more pitchers made big league rosters that season. No one bothered to point out that Ruth hit a home run, number 59, off Paul Hopkins, a right-hander who was pitching his only big league start that season and would get into only ten more big league games, all in relief, or that number 43, number 45 and number 46 were off Tony Welzer, a German immigrant who pitched two ineffective seasons for Boston in 1927 and 1928. Not all of Ruth's pitching victims in 1927 were Hall of Famers.

Number 26 came off Joe Nuxhall, the youngest man to ever pitch in a big league game with Cincinnati back in 1944, number 27 off Norm Bass, number 28 off Dave Sisler, number 29 off Burnside again, and number 30 off John Klippstein. It was July 2. Mantle had 28.

Maris hit number 31 off Frank Lary, number 32 off Frank Funk, and number 33 off Bill Monbouquette. On July 13 the Yankees beat Early Wynn and the White Sox, 6-2, and moved back into first place in the seesaw battle with Detroit. Maris hit number 34 off Wynn. On July 17 Mantle hit number 33.

The press was picking up steam. Both Maris and Mantle, now paired in the press daily as the M and M Boys, were several games ahead of Ruth's pace. This was no longer a kidding matter for baseball fans. It has been traditional that when a batter has five or ten home runs early, he is compared to the Babe Ruth total of 60 in 1927 and projected to be able to hit 65, 70 or 75 homers if he keeps up the current pace. The hitter and the press know it is all in fun. No one is ever taken seriously until he can get about half the season behind him and still stay ahead of Ruth's pace, as Jimmy Foxx (1932) and Hank Greenberg (1938) once did in relative tranquility.

But Maris was being interviewed daily, additional home run or not. He would stand before his locker and answer all the questions. He would show little emotion and no enthusiasm for the interview. He would simply do it. Mantle, with the experience of ten Yankee seasons, more mature at almost thirty and naturally more witty, was more fun for the sportswriters, especially after home runs. He wasn't much fun after losing games, when he often sulked, but his boorishness was excused by a fawning press. Maris was awarded no such dispensation.

Mantle was good at small talk. He could tell hilarious stories about his drinking bouts with Whitey Ford or Billy Martin, or bring a sportswriter into his orbit with a raunchy story about some young lady who simply couldn't prevent herself from offering her body to Mantle. Many of the sportswriters, especially the young ones, were in awe of Mantle's drinking, womanizing and huge home run hitting. It was always possible he could hit a Herculean homer out of Yankee Stadium—a feat never achieved even by Babe Ruth—even after a long night at Shor's.

Maris shared none of his inner secrets. He barely even talked of his family. Sportswriters seemed intimidated by him. Few, outside of Jim Ogle, were close enough to even know how many children he had or what his wife's first name was. Maris's answers to questions were filled with clichés. Sure, he liked hitting homers, sure he wanted to get a big contract next year, certainly he enjoyed knocking in runs—but the winning games were all that counted.

Sportswriters tended to disparage his remarks because he was bland. He never told colorful drinking stories. He never bragged about womanizing. He never seemed to be anybody's hero. He was, in the vernacular of the time, a working stiff, a guy who simply happened to be good— great that summer—at knocking baseballs over fences. For most of the press, that wasn't enough.

The fan mail reflected the press. Mantle got more. Some of Maris's mail was nasty. He might not tip his cap after a homer or show public appreciation of applause. He was a private man in a public business. It was a burden he would be forced to carry.

From early June on, when both sluggers had 15 or 16 homers, the press began examining the Babe Ruth record. There was constant discussion of the expanded schedule, the decrease in quality pitching and the most often heard bromide, the lively ball. Not only Maris and Mantle, but Rocky Colavito, Harmon Killebrew, Jim Gentile and Norm Cash were all having incredible seasons. It had to be the lively ball.

More and more fans, old-time players, press and baseball executives seemed determined to protect the Ruth record. Babe's widow, Claire, who had spent the years from his death in 1948 until 1961 living off her late husband's name and fame, was even asked to comment on a possible challenge. "I hope he doesn't do it," she replied. "Babe loved that record above all."

Ford Frick had been a journalist for many years before becoming the president of the National League. He had been close to Babe Ruth in the 1920s and 1930s, ghosted articles and books about him, dined with him often, told endless stories about him and enjoyed being in the glow of the light the great baseball eminence radiated in his lifetime and beyond. He could hardly be described as an impartial man when it came to protecting the glory of the Babe. In his brilliant biography of the Sultan of Swat, entitled *Babe: The Legend Comes to Life*, author Robert Creamer writes of Ruth's final hours. He describes the visit of Frick to the Babe's bedside at New York's Memorial Hospital. "Paul Carey [a close friend of the Babe] phoned Ford Frick one day and told him Babe would like to see him. Frick said the hospital was like a three-ring circus, with reporters and photographers waiting and the death watch across the hall. He spoke to Claire for a moment and then went into the room.

"It was a terrible moment," Creamer quotes Frick as saying. "Ruth was so thin it was unbelievable. He had been such a big man and his arms were just skinny little bones and his face was so haggard. When I came in he lifted his eyes toward me and raised his right arm a little, only about three or four inches off the bed, and then it fell back again. I went over to the bed and I said, 'Babe, Paul Carey said you wanted to see me.' And Ruth said, in that terrible voice, 'Ford, I always wanted to see you.' It was just a polite thing to say. I stayed a few minutes and left and I spoke to Claire again across the hall and then I went home and the next day he was dead."

This was the final anecdote in Creamer's book, Frick and the Babe together, ending the biography of Babe Ruth with that vivid description. Could that possibly be a man who could fairly rule on the significance of what Roger and Mickey Mantle were doing in the summer of 1961?

With the pressures building, with comment everywhere from sportswriters and non-sportswriters alike in the press, with the public aroused enough to inundate Pete Sheehy in the Yankee clubhouse with fan mail for both Yankee stars, Frick announced he would hold a press conference and address the subject of the home run record in 154

games, as Ruth had done it, or 162 games if either of the
Yankee stars did it.

Frick quickly stated that no batter would be credited
with breaking the home run record of 60 unless he did it
in 154 games. The Yankees had played 88 games. Under
the 1927 Ruth formula Mantle, with 33, was ahead of the
Babe's pace by eight games and Maris, with 34 homers,
was up by 19 games. A player, Frick said, would get "a
distinctive mark" in the record book to note he had compiled it in a 162-game season.

"Any player who may hit more than 60 home runs during his club's first 154 games would be recognized as
having established a new record," Frick said. "However,
if the player does not hit more than 60 homers until after
his club has played 154 games, there would have to be a
distinctive mark in the record books to show that Babe
Ruth's record was set under a 154-game schedule and the
total of more than 60 was compiled while a 162-game
schedule was in effect."

Dick Young, the sports columnist of the New York *Daily
News*, then said, "Maybe you should use an asterisk on
the new record. Everybody does that when there's a difference of opinion."

It was the first use of the word "asterisk" in that connection. It would be a word that would follow and haunt
Roger Maris to his grave in Fargo. On that winter afternoon, when the wind howled and the frost nipped at every
nose, Roger's older brother Rudy Maris asked me, "Could
you see that the Commissioner [Peter Ueberroth] issues a
statement that the asterisk is gone from Roger's record
forever?"

In fact, it was never there. The 1962 baseball record
books simply listed the Ruth record in 154 games and the
Maris record in 162 games on separate pages. There never

was then and there is not now any "distinctive mark" or asterisk in the baseball records about that home run total.

In 1973 Frick wrote his autobiography, *Games, Asterisks and People*, and showed that, as far as he was concerned, Maris was a second-class home run citizen. "A lot of my newspaper friends have enjoyed kidding me about the Asterisk incident," he wrote. (Frick had newspaper friends only among the veteran reporters. The younger reporters made fun of his fuddy-duddy, conservative ways in this matter and in others. In any controversial question he would often say, "It's a league matter." It became a standing joke for an excuse not to make a decision. "It's a league matter," one might say when asked to decide between a free beer or a free soda in the press box.) Frick continued, "As a matter of fact no asterisk has appeared in the official record in connection with the Maris feat. Roger hit 61 home runs that season to set an all-time record and he is given full recognition for that accomplishment. But his record was set in a 162-game season. The Ruth record of 60 home runs was set in 1927 in a 154-game season."

It was clearly a biased decision and any legal test would describe it as a post facto law and clearly unfair in that context. Baseball records are always subject to some interpretation; but in a game which has succeeded because the records are so significant, where past and present can always be measured because 20 wins in 1905 meant the same excellence in 1985, where a .300 average in 1910 meant the same skillful hitting in 1985, where the most home runs in a regular season should clearly have been the all-time standard, Frick's decision was outrageous. Neither Pete Rose, who broke Ty Cobb's hit record of 4191, or Hank Aaron, who broke Ruth's career mark of 714 homers, ever had to contend with the length of their season.

Baseball clearly recognizes Rose as the career hit leader, Aaron as the career home run leader—and should, by all tests of fairness, recognize Maris as the single season home run leader.

The ruling would create an awful barrier for Maris and Mantle. They were now faced with a countdown each day that separated them from all other attempts at a baseball record. Mantle would kid about it from that day on. When he hit his 48th homer on August 31, he yelled to Roger, "I got my guy, Raj, you get yours." He was referring to the fact that Lou Gehrig had 47 homers in 1927 as Babe hit 60. Maris had 51 that last day in August.

After the Frick ruling, reporters gathered around Maris's locker. He was concerned about a negative fan reaction and watched his words carefully. He suggested he didn't make the rules, he didn't have anything to do with it, he wasn't really concerned because the possibility of 60 or 61 seemed difficult and remote and he was really only interested in helping the Yankees, still in a bitter pennant race with Detroit, win the pennant. He turned away from the press after the game, put his glove on his locker shelf, pulled off his undershirt and turned back one last time to a few waiting reporters.

"A season's a season," he said.

The muscles in his face were taut. His eyes stared fixedly. His expression could only be described as a sneer. Roger Maris would not have a quiet day the rest of that season.

# 8

## the countdown

THE Frick decision exploded on the public. Editorial comment was everywhere. In bars and ball fields, fans argued the decision. Old timers were being interviewed. Roger Hornsby, who had hit over .400 three times, including a .424 mark, was quoted as calling Maris a "bush league" hitter because his batting average never exceeded .283.

Maris and Mantle continued hitting home runs. Maris hit number 35 off Ray Herbert. He hit what he thought was number 36 in Baltimore. Clete Boyer hit a homer in the same game. Then, with two out in the top of the fifth inning, the rains came hard. Mantle had hit what he thought was his 34th homer of the season. The umpires waited for more than an hour but finally called the game. The homers were stricken from the records since the game had not gone five full innings with the home team, behind in the game, batting in the fifth. History would little note that Maris had actually hit 60 homers in 154 games (one not counting), or 62 homers for the season.

"What about me?" says Boyer. "If it hadn't rained I would have had 12."

The official number 36 came in Boston against Bill Monbouquette. Maris exploded for four home runs on July 25, in a doubleheader, to reach 40, with number 37 coming against Frank Baumann, number 38 against Don Larsen, who had pitched a perfect game for the Yankees in the 1956 World Series, number 39 against Russ Kemmerer, and number 40 against Warren Hacker.

On the night of July 25 Maris had 40 homers, Mantle had 38, and the Yankees had played 96 games. Ruth had only 33 homers after 96 games. The country was in a dither. Teammates of the Babe, Joe Dugan, Bill Dickey, Waite Hoyt, Mark Koenig and Earle Combs were being interviewed constantly. Nobody, not even the Babe, had ever hit 40 home runs before the end of July.

Maris escaped at home to the apartment with Bob Cerv and Mantle. On the road he hid in his room or in a teammate's room. The phone never stopped ringing. The lobbies of the hotels were being inundated with fans. People were constantly knocking at Maris's hotel door at all hours. Young fans seemed to have a knack for discovery, always finding Maris's room. Once, a pretty girl with a tight-fitting sweater made a mistake. She knocked at the door of my room at 2:15 in the morning after a long game.

"Mr. Maris?"

"No."

"Aren't you Roger Maris?"

"I'm not that lucky."

"I was told he was in room 679."

"Might be. This is 697."

She set off hurriedly to find the missing room.

**BILL STAFFORD** is forty-seven years old, a Yankee pitcher from 1960 through 1965. He pitched two years for Kansas City before retiring to private business in Canton, Michigan.

**STAFFORD:** "We were very close. We used to have adjoining rooms on the road. What was tough was how much Roger loved baseball and loved talking about it. He couldn't do it that year because he couldn't walk into the hotel lobby to look for other guys. We used to play the game, come back to the hotel on the team bus, order room service and spend the hours talking with one or two other guys.

"That was the thing that hurt Roger the most about that season. He couldn't sit around the lobby and share it all with the other guys on the team."

After each game, as it got into late July, there were anywhere from twenty to forty members of the press, radio and television around Maris or Mantle or both. Magazine writers began collecting. More and more newspapers were sending two, three or four sportswriters to cover the Yankees, one to watch the game and two or three to write about Roger. They approached him immediately as he entered the clubhouse, dogged his steps, hounded him for reaction to quotes and interviews about him appearing around the country, followed him to the batting cage, studied his hitting style, watched the game, and repeated the cycle after the game. He found no rest until he entered his car at home and drove off with Cerv or Mantle or Julie Isaacson or some other friend. On the road he was never safe until he was in his hotel room. Sometimes not even then. Babe Ruth never saw press after a game because sportswriters only started visiting baseball clubhouses for postgame quotes after World War II. When Ruth chased the home run record in 1927, it was his own mark of 59 in 1921 he was chasing. Maris and Mantle were chasing history.

More important, as the days passed, Maris needed protection from the press. He got none.

"Maybe," says Bob Fishel, the American League vice president and the public relations director of the Yankees then, "we didn't do as good a job of protecting Roger as we could have. We should have done something like the Reds did with Rose. An organized postgame press conference each day as he chased the Cobb record. That was it. But who knew? The record chase got too big too fast."

Maris hit number 41 off nemesis Camilo Pascual on August 4. It was one of the most satisfying homers of the season because the Cuban right-hander was such a tough pitcher for him. The press expected rousing enthusiasm. They got nonchalance, blandness and boredom.

"I'm not thinking about the record," he told the writers. "I'm just trying to do the best I can. I'm trying to help the ball club win."

The Yankees were only a game and a half ahead of second place Detroit in a bitter pennant race, but few of the sportswriters bothered with that. By that time they had all received instructions from their editors: write Maris and Mantle every day. That meant: regardless of what happened in the game, regardless of heroics by any other Yankee, the story was the enthralling home run chase— Maris, Mantle, and the Babe.

By now baseball fans had chosen sides. They wanted Mantle to break the record, or Roger, or both—or neither. The "neither" group, the loyalists to Ruth, seemed to get the most attention. A fan wrote baseball's bible, *The Sporting News*, "I'd hate to see a bum like Maris break Babe's great record."

"I admire Ruth and all he stands for," Maris told the press. "He was the greatest and there will never be another hitter like him regardless of how many anyone ever hits."

Instead of cooling passions, Maris's comments stoked more fury. One fan wrote a letter to the New York *Post*. "Who the hell does Maris think he is comparing himself to the Babe. What an insult to baseball he is." The tone of Maris's own fan mail was becoming more vicious. Why? Psychological explanations abound. In retrospect, one explanation seems reasonable. The fans were divided mostly by age. Young fans supported Maris or Mantle, or both. Older fans defended Ruth. This was the summer of 1961, the beginning of the youth revolution that would reach its peak in the latter half of the decade. The kids who were in the forefront of that revolution may have started emotions churning as outspoken baseball fans during 1961 by issuing the first of what would be many challenges to the past. Maris was perhaps, in some sense, a victim of his time.

Two days after Maris hit number 41, Mantle hit his 41st. As Maris cooled off, swinging on top of many pitches instead of slightly under them to lift the ball, Mantle got hot. He hit three homers to get to 43 by August 11, and one that day to get to 44. Maris broke a week-long drought and hit his 42nd off Pete Burnside. Maris hit one on August 12 off Dick Donovan for number 43, another on August 13, and still another in the second game that day, with Bennie Daniels and Marty Kutyna the latest victims. Mantle had also smacked one against Daniels for his 45th. The race was breathtaking. The Yankees had played 117 games. Ruth had not hit his 45th until game 132 in 1927.

"At that point," Mantle says, "I really starting thinking about Ruth's 17 in September. How the hell could he do that?"

Maris hit number 46 off left-hander Juan Pizarro (he would wind up with 12 homers against left-handers and 49 against right-handers); number 47 and number 48 against another fine left-hander, Billy Pierce; and number 50 against Ken McBride. It was August 22, the depths of a baseball summer when the heat wears most players down. Mantle had 46. Maris became the first player to hit 50 homers before the end of August. He was only the ninth man in the history of baseball to hit 50.

The Yankees were flying to Kansas City for an off day and a three game series against the Kansas City A's. Before leaving the hotel Maris received a wire telling him that Pat had given birth to a healthy son, his third boy and fourth child. The cares of the spring were forgotten. When he returned home to Raytown, he was shocked the next morning to find cars driving by his home and kids parked on his doorstep for autographs. A local paper had printed his address. It enraged Maris. He called the paper and berated the editor. "I would put anyone who does a thing like that in the idiot class," he said. Any public figure could understand his rage. Unlisted phone numbers and hidden apartments are a standard for people in the public eye. One wonders if John Lennon would still be alive if it were not so publicly known that he owned an apartment on Manhattan's Central Park West in a building called the Dakota. He was shot dead there in 1980.

Maris hit number 51 off Jerry Walker on August 26. The pressures by now were brutal. The crowds booed when he failed to hit a home run. They booed the pitchers when they walked him. Every word Maris uttered seemed to make the newspapers. His actions, from blowing his nose to taking his uniform off, made news. His nerves were shattered. His hair began falling out. A rash developed on his face. His temperament seemed always a hair trigger away from exploding. One day he went to a barber for a haircut. The barber suggested the last man to cut his hair had done a terrible job.

"What do you mean? I always use the same barber. He knows how to cut my hair," Maris said.

"Well, take a look," the barber said. He held a mirror up behind Maris's head. "Look at all those uneven spots."

A visit to a doctor several days later revealed that the nervousness was manifesting itself in his scalp, with patches of hair falling out almost daily. The spaces could be seen even with the disguise of the tight, blond crewcut. It was a page one story.

On the morning of September 1, 1961, Maris had 51 homers, Mantle had 48. Ruth had only 43 on that date in 1927, and the countdown to game 154, scheduled in Baltimore for September 20, was occupying everyone's mind.

A young, handsome outfielder joined the Yankees that morning from the farm club at Richmond. It was Tom Tresh.


**TOM TRESH** is forty-nine years old, the baseball coach at Central Michigan University in Mount Pleasant. He had several fine seasons as a Yankee until a knee injury terminated his career. He was close to Maris from 1961 through 1966. The son of a former big league catcher, Mike Tresh, Tom Tresh is the father of four and grandfather of one.

**TRESH:** "I was the only minor leaguer called up by the Yankees that September. What a thrill that was just to watch what was going on. It was such a tremendous race when I got there, and even though Roger was ahead I still had the feeling people were pulling for Mickey. People just wanted Mickey to do it if anybody did. You could see the strain on Roger's face each day. He was the first guy in the clubhouse and last to leave. It was as if he didn't want to leave. He felt safe inside there.

"I lockered next to Mickey and across from Roger. I could see everything going on with the press and Roger. It was brutal. They never let up on him. Roger did have a little bit of a Dr. Jekyll and Mr. Hyde personality. He tended to shut people off. During that period he had to do that. It was his protection. If not, they would swallow him up."

On September 2 he hit number 52 off Frank Lary and number 53 off Hank Aguirre. He hit number 54 off Tom Cheney and number 55 off Dick Stigman. It was September 7. Mantle, who had picked up a slight cold, had 51 home runs. Mantle hit his 52nd on September 8, in game 142. Maris hit number 56 on September 9 off Mudcat Grant. It was game 143. On September 10 Mantle hit his 53rd homer. Maris still had 56. The games dwindled down to a precious few. The interviews continued relentlessly.

"I'm finished," Mantle said. "I can't do it. I hope Roger can."

Mantle's cold had worsened. He felt weak.

The Yankees had blown open the pennant race by now and every bit of attention was on Maris. When he failed to hit a home run he was booed. One night he attacked the fans for booing him.

"The fans are a bunch of front-runners. Hit a home run and they love you. But make an out and they start booing. Give me the fans in Kansas City any time," he said.

The press attacked Maris again. They pointed out that fans pay their way into a ballpark and pay the salaries of the players. "I didn't ask them to come," Maris said.

The Yankees flew to Detroit for their final road series of the season against the Tigers, then the Orioles and the Red Sox. Yankee game 154 (actually game 155 because of an earlier tie)—the one the Babe's fans would be watching carefully—was scheduled for September 20.

The Yankees had won 13 games in a row to blow open the American League pennant race; they could clinch it in Detroit, where they played two games on September 15. They won the first and lost the second. Maris went one for nine in the doubleheader without a home run. He walked into the clubhouse, threw his glove in his locker and continued into the trainer's room, an off-limits-to-the-press sanctuary. Maris's brother, Bud, was in town for a visit and he was invited in to kid with Roger, Mickey, Boyer, Tresh and the rest of the Yankees. The trainer's room had no door and Maris sat on a table with his back to the waiting press. They waited and waited and waited. He did not come out as writers began worrying about missing editions. They approached Bob Fishel and asked him to ask Maris to come out and meet with them. He told Fishel he had nothing to say and Fishel, one of the brightest, hardest working, most dedicated executives in baseball, was chagrined. He could do nothing. The press asked Houk to ask Maris to come out, especially since Roger's brother was allowed in where they were not. Houk screamed at the press, knocked a notebook out of one sportswriter's hand and stormed off with a zinging obscenity. The tension in that room could be cut with a knife.

All through that season—from June on, when it really started, through July, August and September, through 56 home runs—Maris had been decent, patient and considerate with the press. He was not always revealing or terribly communicative, but he was civil, more so than

Mantle, who could unleash an obscenity or be cruel, especially with younger sportswriters. Mantle was a tougher interview on a bad night, but a more charming, witty, emotional one on a good night. Maris was almost always the same: calm, bland and direct.

The Detroit night was Maris's worst performance. He finally came out to dress, was approached cautiously and was sarcastic in his answers. "What record? Am I close to it? I don't want to talk about it. Do you want me to concede defeat? If you do, I'll concede. All right?"

This was red-assed Roger at his best. This was the essence of so much of the bad publicity that Maris would have to deal with throughout his career. He had been approachable through 149 games of that season. That one game in Detroit, with the press held at bay, did severe damage to his image. It was simply, for some strange reason, that the press chose to accentuate the negatives regarding Maris and accentuate the positives regarding Mantle.

Maris hit number 57 the next night against Frank Lary. It was game 151, including the tie. He had four games to hit three homers to tie Ruth's 1927 record, and needed four home runs in the four games to break it, a near impossible feat.

The next night he hit number 58 against Terry Fox. The Yankees flew to Baltimore for an off day and a twinight doubleheader. That afternoon Maris received a call from Baltimore outfielder Whitey Herzog, a good friend from Raytown. Herzog had been asked if he could get Maris to visit a boy in a local hospital who was dying of leukemia. Legend had Babe Ruth visiting many kids and always hitting home runs for them. Maris would visit on one condition.

"No publicity," he told Herzog.

Maris visited the child, signed some baseballs, hugged him and soon left. Because of the visit he was late to the ballpark. He had forgotten an appointment he had made several days earlier with a magazine writer. The writer was livid at being stood up. He was so outraged that he told the Yankee executives he would "destroy" Maris. When that got back to Maris, he was so angry that he called his pal Julie Isaacson in New York. Isaacson immediately flew down to Baltimore to be with Roger.

The Yankees split a doubleheader, but Roger failed to hit a home run. He was at 58. Mantle still had 53 and now was out of the lineup.

It came down to the night of September 20. Maris needed two home runs to tie Ruth within 154 games, as Frick had decreed, or forever be attached to that hated, if artificial, asterisk. In more than twenty-five years as a sportswriter, it was the most dramatic, exciting, tension-filled game I have ever witnessed, even more than the Yankee pennant playoff in Boston in 1978, than any championship series game, than any World Series game. It was one man against history.

"At the ballpark," Maris would write, "the situation was unbelievable. People all looked at me in a funny way. It was as if they were studying me to see how I was reacting, to see if I was cracking up."

Throughout the last five or six weeks of the home run chase, Maris had dealt bravely with the pressures. Now he would surpass himself. He had often described himself during the case as a "freak show," and now he was clearly king of the jungle.

"I had only one thing in my mind," Maris wrote. "Whatever happened, I was determined to give it my best shot. I was going down, if I went down, trying my best. I knew I was going out on that field and I was going to be swinging. If it was humanly possible I was going to try for three homers, but three ... two ... one ... or none, I was ready to give it everything I had."

Pat Maris watched the game from a Kansas City television studio. Claire Ruth watched the game from her Riverside Drive apartment. The rest of the country waited.

In the first inning, with Tony Kubek on first, Maris faced right-hander Milt Pappas. He was a fastball pitcher with a hard curve. The fans were silent as they awaited the swing. Maris got on top of Pappas's fastball and lined it toward the right-field wall. There was a roar from the crowd, but the ball was only shoulder high and Whitey Herzog, Roger's Raytown pal, caught it three feet in front of the fence. One swing gone.

Now Maris had three, possibly four more chances, to hit three home runs to break it, two to tie it and one to fall short with a courageous effort. Frick watched the game from his Bronxville home. He did not comment on his feelings publicly after the game and did not describe his emotions in his book. One can only guess where his heart was that night.

In the third inning Maris faced Pappas again. The count went to 1-1. Pappas threw a fastball. Maris ripped at the pitch and sent another high line drive toward right. He had gotten under this one. The ball continued to rise as it neared the wall. It crashed into the concrete seats above the 14-foot wall. It was number 59 off Milt Pappas.

The Yankees knocked Pappas out in the third inning and right-hander Dick "Turkey" Hall was the Baltimore pitcher when Maris batted again in the top of the fourth. The lanky, side-arming right-hander threw an inside pitch and Maris rocketed the ball deep, but foul, down the right field line. The count went to 2-2. Hall came back at Maris with a high, outside fastball. Maris swung hard and missed for strike three. Another chance lost. He had one homer, one long fly out, one long foul—and now the strikeout.

In the seventh inning he faced Hall again. He hit a long, deep foul. The crowd was on its feet now. Who could know what Claire Ruth or Ford Frick or millions of people who had loved the Babe were thinking now? This quiet, small-town, blond-headed crewcut twenty-six-year-old baseball player from North Dakota had caused more excitement in this country that summer than most people had witnessed in their lifetime.

The next pitch jumped off Maris's bat. It was high enough. The crowd followed the flight and screamed.The ball seemed to stay in the air for an eternity. Now it started settling. Again Herzog, in right field, moved for it. This time he was farther towards center, his back resting against the wall, his eyes staring at the baseball. He leaned forward a bit, patted the pocket of his glove, caught the ball and seemed to hold it still for an instant. It seemed over.

The Yankees, who wanted to win to lock up the pennant, got a couple of hits in the eighth. Maris would have a turn at bat in the ninth. There was a new Baltimore pitcher. It was Hoyt Wilhelm, the famed knuckleballer. There were two out when Maris faced him in the ninth.

Wilhelm not only had this weird pitch, he had a strange way of throwing it. He seemed to tilt his head sideways and jerk forward as he released the ball. He threw the knuckler. It ticked foul off Maris's bat. He threw it again. Another foul ball. The count was 0-2. There was one swing left in this long march. Maris never got it. The next Wilhelm knuckler caught the handle of Maris's bat, dribbled slowly back to the mound and was picked up. Maris stood at the plate. Then he leaned forward and began jogging towards first. He carried his bat with him. Wilhelm tagged him. The race was over.

Roger Maris had hit 59 home runs in 154 games. Babe Ruth had hit 60 within that schedule in 1927. The past had stayed inviolate.

Maris jogged to the outfield in the ninth inning. As he passed second base, cheers still ringing in his ears for his heroic effort, umpire Charlie Berry crossed his path and said, "You gave it a good try, son."

The Yankees had won the game, had clinched the pennant with that victory, and champagne was flowing in the clubhouse in that childish rite of summer. Maris, pinned by the press against the clubhouse wall, was tired and proud.

"I tried hard all night," he said. "Now that it is over, I'm happy with what I got."

He was asked about chasing the Ruth record in 162 games.

"Commissioner Frick makes the rules," he said. "If all I will be entitled to will be an asterisk, it will be all right with me."

The tensions began again the next night as the goal of 60 home runs still lay ahead. Maris faced young Baltimore right-hander Jack Fisher. He went hitless. The Yankees went to Boston and Maris again failed to hit a homer.

Mantle, meanwhile, told Ralph Houk he felt better and wanted a chance to play. On September 23 he hit number 54 off Don Schwall. Maris still had 59.

There were only five games to play in the regular season schedule. It seemed impossible for Mantle to suddenly start hitting two a game to catch Maris. Some people thought he could do it. Mantle knew better. He was finished.

**MANTLE:** "I was really feeling bad by then. I was tired and weak and achey all over. I was thinking I might be able to hang in there and get two or three more, maybe 58, to tie Jimmy Foxx and Hank Greenberg. I knew I couldn't catch the Babe or Roger any more. Anyway, on the plane home I mentioned to Mel Allen [the Yankee broadcaster] how lousy I was feeling. He said, 'I have a doctor. He'll give you a shot that will fix you right up.' He gave me the name of this guy, Dr. Max Jacobson, and made an appointment for me right that night. Mel told me he had famous actors like Elizabeth Taylor and Eddie Fisher as patients and would really take care of me. He took care of me, all right."

Dr. Max Jacobson was later known in some quarters as Dr. Feelgood, a New York physician who was said to have pioneered a new form of vitamin therapy medicine together with the use of certain drugs. Many well-known people were rumored to be his patients, including President Kennedy.

"He stuck this huge needle in me and it hurt like hell. I feel like I'm paralyzed. He slaps me on the back and tells me to walk back to the St. Moritz Hotel, where I was staying by then, to get in bed and forget about it. I'd be fine in the morning. In the morning I almost died. Merlyn [Mantle's wife] was coming in from Dallas for the last few games and the World Series, and when I woke up she was next to my bed. I'm dizzy as hell, I'm burning up with fever and I'm sick as a dog."

Mantle was taken to Lenox Hill Hospital. The area around Dr. Feelgood's shot had become infected and had to be surgically repaired. The scar remains to this day.

There would be no more distractions from Mantle. It now was Maris and Maris alone. He had missed the Ruth record in 154 games and now needed two more homers. It was Tuesday, September 26, the Yankees at home in

Yankee Stadium against Baltimore. Jack Fisher was the Baltimore starter.

**JACK FISHER** is forty-six years old, a burly right-hander known as Fat Jack in his playing days. He was one of Baltimore's Baby Birds, a regular starter in 1960 at the age of twenty. He gave up the last home run ever hit by Ted Williams in the Red Sox star's final home game in Fenway Park.

**FISHER:** "A gale was blowing out there that day when Ted Williams came up. It was coming from right field toward home, and I didn't think there was a chance in hell that anybody could hit a homer off me that way on that day. I pitched Williams inside because I wanted him to pull into that wind and fly out. He hit it out there and I just watched it and that thing just kept going and going and going. Then it cut through that wind, Williams ran around the bases, and that was it. He was the greatest hitter I ever faced.

"Roger was different. He was a mistake hitter, very strong, but if you got the pitch up and in on him he couldn't do much with it. I wanted to throw him hard stuff inside. I definitely didn't want to make a mistake. He was a hot hitter and I knew he could drive it over the wall without much trouble.

"Gus Triandos [the catcher] called for a curve ball, and I thought it was a good pitch in that spot since I knew he'd be looking for the fastball. As I delivered it a thought flashed in my mind that I should take something off the pitch, throw it with less speed and get Roger's timing off. I didn't snap it real good and it hung up there about belt high and he drove it."

Maris drove the ball deep into the right-field stands for number 60 off Jack Fisher. No man had more home runs in one season, and only Babe Ruth had as many.

"As I trotted around the bases I was in a fog," Maris said later. "I was in a complete daze. I couldn't believe what happened. Had I really hit 60 home runs? Had I tied Babe Ruth for the highest total ever hit in a season?"

As the game ended a television camera was set up on the field. A young producer escorted a small, elderly woman wearing a brown beret to the Yankee dugout. It was Mrs. Babe Ruth. She shook Maris's hand, and he bent over to kiss her as cameras recorded the historic moment.

"You had a great year. I want to congratulate you, and I mean that, Roger, sincerely. I know that if Babe were here he would have wanted to congratulate you, too," she said.

She was now saying all the right and kind things she had not said as Maris challenged the record in 154 games. It was easier now and she was magnanimous. She had enjoyed her place in the sun that summer and could return to being a professional widow and enjoy her box seat at the Stadium, each opening day until her death, alongside Eleanor Gehrig. (No baseball historian would have expected Mr. Babe Ruth and Mr. Lou Gehrig to share a Yankee box seat had they remained alive into their sixties and seventies.)

Maris later said that the affection shown by Claire Ruth had sincerely touched him. On television and before the listening press he said, "I'm glad I didn't break the Babe's record in 154 games. This record is good enough for me."

Pat Maris was in town now, and Roger asked the press if they could be quick. They said they would and he answered all of the questions, described his hazy feeling, admitted he was warmed by the presence of Mrs. Ruth, stood pressed against his locker as he had been almost every day for two months, and finally ended the session.

Mrs. Ruth talked to the press and she repeated what she had told Roger on the air.

The next day, Wednesday, the Yankees were scheduled for a day game against Baltimore. It was another day of Maris furor. He had 60 home runs, and Thursday was an off day. Counting Wednesday, he had four games to pass the Babe, to ride alone into history as the man with the most home runs in any baseball season in history. He chose to sit this one out.

When he arrived at the park Wednesday afternoon he went in to see Houk. They talked behind closed doors for several minutes and Maris came out. Reporters rushed in.

"I'm going to give Roger a rest," Houk said. "He's bushed."

It seemed incredible. He had this chance at immortality and he was taking a day off. The press questioned him before the game and all he would say was, "I'm tired. That's it. I'm too tired to play."

Houk looks back on that decision now and has the same feeling he had then.

"He was exhausted. Nobody but Roger could know how exhausted he was. When he came in that day we talked about it for a while, and I realized he simply needed a day off. I wanted him to take it off but I wouldn't do it unless he wanted it. I wanted to give him every chance. He made it clear he thought he would have a better chance at hitting another home run if he rested. So I didn't play him."

Yankee owner Dan Topping asked to see Maris after the game started with the home run hero on the bench. He said to Maris, "Since you aren't playing, why not ask Ralph to let you leave and really take a day off?"

Houk, who always knew who was the boss, agreed quickly. A clubhouse boy was sent into the stands where Pat Maris was sitting with Julie Isaacson, and Roger and Pat took off. They spent the afternoon shopping, had dinner out together that night, slept late the next day, enjoyed a quiet hotel breakfast, shopped some more that afternoon, had another fine dinner and relaxed in the midst of this emotional storm.

"It's the most relaxed I had been all year," Maris said.

On Friday he would try again to become the single-season champion. He knew a home run could mean big bucks, not only in salary but in commercial endorsements, that would pay for lots of clothes and toys for his growing brood. Maris had made it clear all season that he was more interested in financial security than he was in the honors he would soon collect.

This would all be made so clear in the spring of 1985 when we talked in his Gainesville office. He simply volunteered this information.

"You know what I got from Topping for hitting those 61 homers that year? Nothing. Not a cent. Not a gift. Nothing. I don't know what the Yankees drew that year (1,747,736, the largest attendance at the Stadium in ten years), but they gave me nothing."

The Yankees lost to Baltimore, 3-2, on Wednesday. On Friday night Bill Monbouquette, a proud guy who didn't want to be the 61st home run victim, pitched away from Maris. He got him out three times on bad pitches and walked him in the ninth. Maris stole second. He scored on John Blanchard's single. The game was over. Two games to go. One homer to go.

Don Schwall was the Boston starter on Saturday afternoon. All of the Yankees were ready in the bullpen for the magic home run. One of the pitchers out there was Al Downing.

**AL DOWNING** is forty-five years old, a handsome, hard-throwing left-handed pitcher. He was a Yankee from 1961 through 1969. He also pitched for Oakland, Milwaukee and the Dodgers. He is famous for allowing Hank Aaron's 715th homer, the one that broke Babe Ruth's career mark. He is the only man to witness both historic home runs. Downing is now a sportscaster for KABC in Los Angeles.

**DOWNING:** "Roger was all business around the ballpark. Once in a while he would kid me about sleeping a lot, the way all the players did, and I remember him playing cards in the clubhouse but we didn't have a special relationship.

"I sat in the bullpen the last few weeks of that season and it was a unique spot to watch baseball history. I was just a kid then and I was thrilled to be part of it. I don't think I ever sat down out there any time Roger came up. We would all jump up, wave at him from out there and hold our gloves up for a target. I was ready to catch that baseball."

Don Schwall was the Boston pitcher on Saturday. He worked Maris tough and allowed him only a weak single to center. There was nothing resembling a home run. It would all be over the next day, the last regular scheduled game of the season.

The drama of 1961 was coming to a close. Roger Maris, with 60 home runs, was at peace with himself. As he went to sleep that night in his hotel room he had to be proud of what he had achieved. No man in baseball history had ever performed as nobly for so long under such pressure.

Mickey Mantle was still in pain as he rested in Lenox Hill Hospital. He had contributed his 54 home runs and his charisma to that incredible season. He would not be there in person for the closing act, but he could be proud of his own marvelous season and prouder still that in some ways he was most responsible for the record challenge, pushing Maris onward and taking some of the heat off him. Tracy Stallard, uncertain he would start the final game of the season, enjoyed a night out with his buddy Gene Conley. No matter what happened on Sunday, they would be on their way home soon.

At 2:43 Sunday afternoon, October 1, 1961, in Yankee Stadium, New York, the House that Ruth Built, Roger Maris hit number 61 off Tracy Stallard.

Pat and Roger during the 1961 season. The pressure can be seen in the tired eyes of the slugger. *Credit: NY Yankees.*

The end of the chase. Roger Maris hits home run number 61 off Tracey Stallard at 2:43 p.m. October 1, 1961. The fans are crowded into the right field area for a chance to catch the home run ball. *Credit: Bob Olen.*

The fans fight for the home run ball as it bounces off someone's jacket into Sal Durante's hands. *Credit: NY Yankees.*

A standing ovation leads to a tip of the cap from baseball's new single-season home run king. *Credit: Bob Olen.*

In a post-game interview Maris and nineteen-year-old Sal Durante answer questions from the press about what it was like to hit and catch the record-setting home run. Roger looks completely spent after the ordeal, the tension showing most around his drawn mouth. *Credit: Bob Olen.*

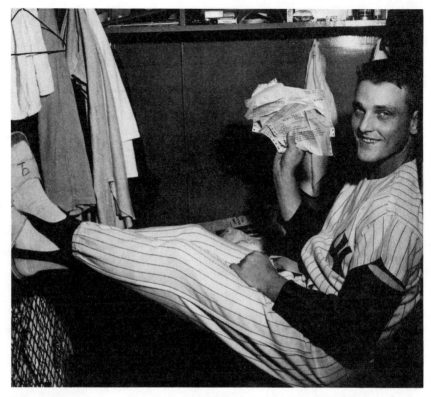

Roger reads the stack of telegrams he received after hitting the historic home run. *Credit: Bob Olen.*

# 9

## the man who...

ON the Monday after that Sunday, Roger Maris casually walked into the Yankee clubhouse. The World Series was a day away and Maris, wearing a tan windbreaker, a light shirt, dark slacks and brown shoes, settled comfortably in front of his locker. Ralph Houk had told him he need not work out, so Maris sat in front of his locker, read his mail, talked easily with the press, kidded with his teammates and enjoyed a day free of tension. One wire caught his eye. MY HEARTIEST CONGRATULATIONS TO YOU ON HITTING YOUR 61ST HOME RUN. THE AMERICAN PEOPLE WILL ALWAYS ADMIRE A MAN WHO OVERCOMES GREAT PRESSURE TO ACHIEVE AN OUTSTANDING GOAL. JOHN F. KENNEDY. Maris kept the wire in a prominent spot on his wall at home and always displayed a photograph of himself and the President, taken at a later White House visit, on his office wall.

As always around the Yankees, there seemed to be more focus on Mickey Mantle than on Maris. Mantle had been released from Lenox Hill Hospital that morning and walked gingerly into the clubhouse. He appeared pale and weak. He revealed a huge gauze bandage over his right hip. Mantle would play only one full game in the Series, the third game, and leave the fourth game after blood seeped from the wound onto the Yankee bench.

Maris played in all five games of the World Series, going hitless in the first two and hitting a game-winning ninth-inning home run in the third with the Series tied at 1-1. The shot came off Cincinnati Reds right-hander Bob Purkey. Cincinnati manager Fred Hutchinson, who would be dead of cancer a little more than three years later, called the Maris homer "the most damaging blow of the Series. After that we couldn't seem to bounce back."

Whitey Ford had shut the Reds out in the first game and came back in the fourth game to pitch five more shutout innings before being forced out with a foot injury. The 14 shutout innings gave Ford 32 consecutive scoreless World Series innings, breaking a mark held by a pitcher named Babe Ruth, set with the Red Sox in the World Series of 1916 and 1918 at 29 2/3 innings. There was no discussion of Ford's record breaking the Babe's in a Series played after 162 games, no asterisk jokes, no suggestion of separate record entries.

"It's just been a bad year for the Babe," kidded Ford.

With both Yogi Berra and Mantle out, the Yankees bombed the Reds in the final Series game, with substitutes John Blanchard and Hector Lopez leading the way to a 13-5 triumph. The grueling 1961 baseball season was history.

There were still many days before Maris could settle back into a new house he was building in Independence, Missouri, just down the road from former President Harry Truman's home, and rest for the winter.

One of the earliest chores was a barnstorming home run

exhibition Maris agreed to after the season through North Carolina and Georgia. The trip was to play in ten towns over ten days, with a home run exhibition featuring Maris against sluggers Jim Gentile, Rocky Colavito and Harmon Killebrew. Maris was to receive $15,000 for his contribution to the show, with each of the others collecting $5,000. The pitcher on the tour was Clyde King.

**CLYDE KING** is sixty-one years old, a drawling North Carolinian who pitched seven years in the big leagues for Brooklyn and Cincinnati. He was in the Brooklyn bullpen in the Polo Grounds on October 3, 1951, when Bobby Thomson hit his famous Home Run Heard Round the World, the shot that won the 1951 pennant for the New York Giants over Brooklyn, considered the most famous baseball home run ever hit. After a long career as a coach, scout and manager, King became the general manager of the New York Yankees.

**KING:** "I was managing Rochester that year, and when the season ended I got a call asking me if I would be willing to pitch batting practice for Maris and the others in a tour through the south. I live in Goldsboro, and most of the cities were in North Carolina, so I quickly agreed. They were going to pay me a hundred dollars a day, and when you are making as little as I was in those days, that is big money. I was glad to do it.

"We started out in Wilson and drew 3,700 people the first day. Then we went on to Raleigh, Durham, Charlotte, Greensboro, and one or two other places before the tour sort of petered out. After the first day there weren't many people coming out, and the promoters sort of gave up the idea after the first three or four days that they could make any money out of it. It was a lot of fun while it lasted.

"I had been picked because I was a real good batting practice pitcher. I could get the ball over and I could usually spot it any place the hitter liked. Roger wanted the ball down and on the inside part of the plate. I threw at about three quarters speed and he had that grooved swing and he could really drive the ball. The format was for each batter to take ten swings in turn for three separate turns. We had a local kid catching and a few other local kids chasing down the balls in the infield and outfield. There would be thirty swings in all by each of the guys, and the whole thing took less than an hour. I remember Roger got 11 out the first day, and I was hoping he could hit 62 on the trip and we would claim he broke his own record in North Carolina. Since we didn't play the whole tour I think he ended up with 40 or 45 before the thing fell through. He was pretty tired by then.

"We used to travel together in a new station wagon with the promoter driving us from city to city. We carried all the equipment in it. I wore my old Brooklyn Dodger uniform and Roger wore his Yankee uniform, of course, and since those teams had a great rivalry that was always fun. Gentile was with Baltimore, Colavito was with Detroit, and Killebrew with the Twins, and they wore their regular uniforms. I was wearing those thick glasses then, same as now, and Roger used to call me 'Professor,' and I was always the one that had to settle all the baseball arguments.

"Everybody was having a good time with this, and then one day Roger hit a couple of dribblers, maybe two or three in a row, and he yelled, 'Hey, you trying to get me out or something?' I told him I was throwing the same as always but he kept kidding that I was bearing down. Just for fun I curved the next one, and he missed it by a foot and we all stood out there and laughed a lot at that. I got back in the groove on the next one and got it where he wanted it, and he hit it straight over the center field fence.

"We used to run into each other here and there through the years and Roger was always friendly. We would kid about those days and he would call me 'Professor,' and we would remember some incident in one of those small towns. He was a fine fellow, and when he got sick it was a very sad thing. Norma and I used to pray for him every night."

The man who arranged all of this was **FRANK SCOTT**, one of baseball's first agents. Scott, a small dynamic man, had been the traveling secretary of the Yankees from 1946 through 1951. He then went into his own business, representing players on contracts with outside firms, getting them lucrative endorsements, handling them for public appearances, raising the level of pay for speaking engagements from the common $100-and-a-chicken-dinner to $500, $1,000 and $5,000 for special events and important players.

**FRANK SCOTT:** "During the middle of that 1961 season Mantle came to me one day. I had been close to Mickey for a long time, I knew him as a kid player and he trusted me. 'Frank, we're getting a lot of guys calling us, Roger and me, and they want to sign us up. We want you to help us.' I told them I would, and Roger and Mickey and I sat down and wrote up a contract. We formed a corporation called the M and M Corporation, and all deals made by either of them or both together would be funneled through that corporation. If you hired Mickey or if you hired Roger, it went into the M and M Corporation. By the time that season was over, Roger had made more than $150,000 and Mickey made about $100,000. I'll tell you why the difference.

"We started the corporation early in July, just about when they started hitting a lot of home runs and there was all that talk about breaking Ruth's record. We signed a few things up but I recommended they wait until after the season. I knew the price would really jump if either or both of them hit 60 or 61 homers. They had about 30 or 35 homers when we made the deal, maybe got three or four deals, and we just sat back and waited. In September Mickey got sick. He knew he was out of it and he wouldn't hit 60. 'Frank, I'm finished. I'm not taking any more. It's Roger's.' I told him the contract was set up in such a way that they shared together what each of them earned in deals. It didn't matter who hit how many home runs. Mickey insisted. 'It's Roger's. That's the way it's got to be.' Mickey was always that way. He wasn't going to take a dime if he didn't pull his own weight. So we broke up the corporation, and I handled each of them as separate players.

"After Roger hit 61, everybody wanted him. He could have made three or four times what he did. He put a limit on it. We did the Perry Como show for $10,000, we had a line of clothing, we did some personal appearances and we endorsed a couple of food products. Roger really didn't want anything that would take him away from home too long. He did the home run hitting tour right after the season, and he didn't want anything else that would keep him away.

"There were a few other things, mostly small things, but Roger just wasn't interested. Oh yeah, we did that movie *Safe At Home* with Bill Frawley, the guy from the Lucy show, and that was fun. It was done in Fort Lauderdale that next spring in 1962. Roger and Mickey each got $5000 for that one. [Whitey Ford also played himself with one speaking line, 'Ralph wants to see you,' and remembered years later that he got a $100 residual check in 1984 when it played on television.] In a few months the furor died down.

"Roger was never comfortable doing these things. It just wasn't him. He hated a fuss. By then a few bad things about him had been in the press and sentiment seemed to turn against him, from being a hero to being a bad guy. The press has an awful lot of power that way. Roger didn't care when the endorsements dried up. He always said he just wanted to play baseball. We had a few other things through the years but not very much. People think he made a million dollars hitting those home runs. Like I said, he made $150,000 and that was it. Today he'd make a million or two million playing and he wouldn't even have to bother with endorsements. If he did, he might make five or ten million from what he did at today's prices.

"I really liked Roger a lot and he was an easy guy to work with. If he wanted to do it, fine, he did it. If not, that was it and you couldn't change his mind. I think his personality became more of an issue later on than his playing. I really can't understand why he isn't in the Hall of Fame. For three or four years there he was one of the best players in the game. Then he got hurt. But when he was healthy, he was some player. And he did what nobody else did. That should count for something."

There were a couple of banquets to attend and Maris would be asked the same questions about the pressures. "I'm proud of the record," he would say, "but I wouldn't want to go through it again." When asked if he thought any player could break his record, he pointed toward

Mantle. "If he stays healthy and things break right, Mickey could do it."

At each of these banquets he would squirm through the dinner, usually uncomfortably seated next to some local businessman who bored him, or some local politician, or even a player from another team he did not know and was uncomfortable being around. He felt ridiculous at formal dinners, wearing a tuxedo when he preferred sports shirts and slacks. He never enjoyed the meals of the so-called rubber chicken circuit. He would stare off into space while others talked, even when it was about him, and he constantly looked at his watch, measuring the time he could finally leave without a fuss.

Each of these banquets was accompanied by a press conference. In many of the smaller cities, the local reporters came to him with a negative approach: Would it have been different if Mickey didn't get sick? What about Mrs. Ruth saying she was happy you didn't do it in 154 games? What about the expanded schedule, the lively ball, the Yankee powerhouse supporting him? What about this and what about that, and why don't you show more grace in signing autographs?

On and on it went, eating away at his character, perverting the tone of the home run chase. He was attacked for his inability to be amusing, charged him with crimes he didn't commit: being anti-Ruth, anti-Mantle, anti-baseball. The winter pressures, in their own way, were even harder than the summer pressures. "I always found the game a relief," he once said of the season. "There was no relief from the outside things."

One night he attended a banquet in Milwaukee. He was scheduled the next day in Rochester, New York, to receive the famed Hickok Belt, awarded annually to the country's best professional athlete. The bejeweled, studded gold belt was worth $10,000. He sat through the Milwaukee banquet and was given an award. He then sat down, looked at his watch, got up and left.

"The only way he could make the plane to get to Rochester in time was to leave that banquet," said friend Julie Isaacson. "There were some kids waiting for autographs. When he left without signing, they crucified him."

Maris was always comfortable around kids—his own, those of his teammates, or those of friends. He was not comfortable around strange kids in droves. When he left that banquet, he pushed his way past some waiting youngsters. There were some heated words. The next day's papers reported that Maris had stormed out of the banquet, pushed his way past these kids and offered no explanations. There was no mention of a plane to catch for another award.

All the anger, all the frustration, all the pressures of going against Ruth and Mantle in 1961 welled up in him over that winter. He felt used and abused. He was a private man caught in a public act he neither was emotionally nor intellectually suited for. Stardom is not an easy burden to carry. In most cases, regardless of the business, it is a gradual climb to the top. The classic overnight success in show business is usually a person who has worked at his trade for years. Maris had worked at his trade for years, but had been just another ballplayer until he came to the Yankees in 1960. Even then, the personality of Casey Stengel overwhelmed the team. The stars were Mantle, Ford, Berra, and Elston Howard, the first Yankee black player. Had Maris hit 35 or 40 homers in 1961, he would have been regarded as simply another good player on another great Yankee team.

By January the Maris family had settled comfortably into their new Independence home. Roger would sleep late most mornings, play with the children, visit with friends, shoot a game of pool, watch television with his feet up on a leg of a chair, sip a beer, eat some potato chips, make a few phone calls and wait for the next spring training season. But first there was the 1962 contract. Pat and Roger, with a growing family, were certainly anxious about the numbers on his new pact. Maris had been quoted in the press as saying he expected "a hefty raise" for his record-shattering year. The definition of a "hefty raise" would be a matter of some difference through January and February. Maris had made $37,500 for the 1961 season. He expected to more than double his salary for 1962. The first Yankee contract called for $50,000. The man described in the press so often as "the man who broke Babe Ruth's record" was now the man who was truly angry. He considered this offer a demeaning insult. It would leave a bitter taste in his mouth for years.

There were negotiations back and forth for several weeks; letters and phone calls from GM Roy Hamey; a couple of talks with owner Dan Topping, an icy cold playboy millionaire who leaked figures to the press as well as statements expressing his outrage that Maris had the nerve to think his salary should be the equal of Mantle's. In those days salary figures were closely guarded secrets—unlike today, when numbers are revealed by the Players Association or by the players themselves in arbitration hearings if the club does not choose to reveal them. "Salary figures leaked to the press were always higher than what they really were," says Tony Kubek. "It was a way of getting the public on the side of the club in a holdout."

Maris threatened a holdout, something the Yankees were concerned about. They raised their offer to $60,000, then to $65,000. Maris held firm. "Roger wants to double his salary and we will not do that," Hamey told the press.

Mickey Mantle had signed his contract a month earlier for $82,000. Maris had won the home run title, of course, plus the RBI title and his second straight MVP award in his second Yankee season.

As spring training reporting dates grew closer, Maris decided to drive south. He was a few thousand dollars away from the figure he sought, and he figured he could get it in a face-to-face meeting with Hamey in spring training. He met with the general manager as soon as he arrived and a deal was struck. Maris signed a contract for $72,500, a little less than the 100 percent raise he was after.

"I got almost what I asked for," Maris told the press. "There was a compromise. The main thing is, I'm happy and satisfied and want to go to work."

"We're very happy he's signed," said Hamey. "We're most appreciative of what Roger meant to the ball club last year."

Maris, the last Yankee to sign his contract for the 1962 season, walked into the clubhouse after the press conference, put on his uniform and walked out on the field at Fort Lauderdale, Florida. It was a new spring location for all of the Yankees.

After more than forty years in St. Petersburg, dating back to Babe Ruth's earliest days with the club, the Yankees had moved their camp across Florida to the East Coast, to booming Fort Lauderdale. Their old spring camp had been turned over to a brand-new baseball team from New York. While the Yankees and Roger Maris had been preparing for the 1961 World Series, a familiar old man stepped off a plane from Los Angeles to a waiting press contingent. It was Casey Stengel, who had resurfaced in baseball as manager of the newly created New York Mets after a year as a bank president in his adopted hometown of Glendale, California.

When the press asked Stengel if he could manage a team at the age of seventy-one, he replied, "My health is good enough above the shoulders and I didn't say I'd stay fifty years or five."

With Stengel in tow, with a new team in New York, with attention again focusing on the National League, the Yankees were hard pressed to cause any excitement that spring. They had Maris, of course, and Mantle and Ford and Howard and Berra and Kubek and Richardson. But they were all old, familiar names. The Mets had Stengel and new names. The old man kept hollering, "They're gonna be amazin'," and it was The Amazing Mets who dominated the New York newspapers that spring.

After a winter of what he considered unfair press coverage, Maris was testy most of the spring. He did his work, answered questions cautiously from the press, stayed away from the comments about the Mets and prepared for another season. On March 22, 1962, the Mets played the Yankees for the first time in St. Petersburg. It would be a major event even before one ball was thrown in that spring game.

One of the Mets coaches was Rogers Hornsby, one of the greatest hitters in National League history, but one of the grouchiest of men. He once managed the St. Louis Browns for Bill Veeck and when he was fired, his team partied all night long. He was a fanatic about his eyes, claiming he had never seen a movie during his playing career because "movies ruin your eyes." He was a heavy drinker and would berate almost everybody he saw when he was in his cups. He used to stand by the batting cage, as a Mets coach that spring, and criticize every hitter's batting style. He never smiled. He almost always ate meals alone. He was already ailing and would be dead less than ten months later. On that March day he sat in the Mets dugout while the Yankees came on the field for batting practice.

A photographer got the terrific idea that a photo of all-time home run king Roger Maris and all-time National League average king Rogers Hornsby (his .358 was second only to Ty Cobb's .367) would make for a usable shot. The lensman approached Hornsby, not aware of the fact that the Rajah, on any occasion he was asked about it the previous summer, had downgraded Maris's home run feat. "Yeah, I'll pose with him," Hornsby said. "Bring him over."

The photographer walked towards the Yankee bench as Hornsby sauntered out near the batting cage.

"Roger, would you pose for a picture with Hornsby? He asked if you would come over near the batting cage," the photographer said.

Maris was not in a posing mood that spring, especially with an old timer who had bad-mouthed him all through his challenge. He simply turned his back and walked away. Hornsby witnessed the entire scene. He quickly turned on his heels and went back into the Mets dugout. Reporters saw the commotion and moved quickly to the old player. "He's a busher," Hornsby said of Maris. "He couldn't carry my bat. He is a little punk ballplayer."

Maris was in the middle of another fuss, not entirely of his own doing. Soon Oscar Fraley, a columnist for the United Press, asked Maris for his version of the incident. Maris wasn't talking. Fraley, who would gain fame as the script writer for the hugely successful television series, "The Untouchables," sat down and wrote one of the most scathing articles written about Maris. He called him an "ingrate" for what old players like Hornsby had done for him, described him as a callous, uncouth, loudmouthed ballplayer who had one lucky year with 61 home runs in an expansion season, who could never reach that height

again (who would?), and who didn't deserve to be mentioned in the same breath with greats like Rogers Hornsby
and Babe Ruth. As a wire service columnist, Fraley's story
appeared in hundreds of papers across the country and
did as much to damage Maris's image as any single article
ever written about him.

Maris expressed no regrets for what he had done and,
in tense conversations with those few New York writers
he still trusted, Roger saw nothing wrong in refusing to
pose with a man who had attacked him. He was angry
over what Fraley had written about him and he indicated
that he would be doing even less talking as the season
went on. He simply didn't need the aggravation an interview always seemed to give him. He didn't even need the
aggravation a non-interview gave him.

Jimmy Cannon, the highly respected columnist then of
the New York *Journal American* (he had established his
credentials earlier with the *Post*), set up an appointment
for an interview with Yankee publicity director Bob Fishel.
Maris was supposed to appear early at the ballpark to be
profiled by Cannon, whose columns "Nobody Asked Me
But..." and "You're..." were considered sports journalist
classics. Maris failed to show.

Angered by the slugger's apparent act of thoughtless-
ness, Cannon sat down and typed out a column belittling
not only Maris's home runs but the man himself. Cannon's
columns were displayed even more prominently than
Fraley's in newspapers across America. He was well read
and could make or break an athlete with a stroke of his
pen. Probably one of his most memorable lines was written in his "Nobody Asked Me But..." column about famed
sportscaster Howard Cosell. "If Howard Cosell were a
sport," Cannon wrote years later, "he would be the roller

derby." It was a line Cosell would have trouble escaping.

Now it was Maris who had been cut by Cannon's scythe. He would be left so battered and bruised that, for the rest of his life, Roger Maris never fully trusted any reporter. Before 1961 and throughout most of that year, except for a few rare occasions, he had cooperated with the press. From the spring of 1962 throughout his remaining Yankee years, ending in 1966, he would never again be free of the fear that, somewhere in the crowd of New York reporters he might be addressing after a big home run or a great catch, there was at least one reporter with a desire to cut him up and embarrass him, leaving him without any recourse but to retreat further into himself.

His image had been locked into the public psyche. "Red-assed Roger" would be the description heard most often in the ensuing years. He was generally described as an angry young man. Few could penetrate the wall that rose up between Maris and the press as a result of the two scathing assaults by Fraley and Cannon.

Ralph Houk was unconcerned, though, about those problems. The Yankees tended to disregard off-the-field events and concentrate on the field performance of their players. Maris was healthy, hitting the ball hard all spring and showing no signs of a serious letdown on the field from his spectacular 1961 season. Houk had other problems to solve with the ball club. The Yankees were aging. Yogi Berra would soon have to be replaced. Elston Howard, a Yankee since 1955, would emerge as the first-string catcher. Young Tom Tresh would show much promise and soon move Tony Kubek out of the shortstop position. Three young players seemed set to make the club: Jim Bouton, a smallish right-handed pitcher; first baseman Joe Pepitone, a fast-talking, lovable wise-guy type from Brooklyn;

and Phil Linz, a bespectacled infielder from Baltimore. Bouton would beat out veteran Robin Roberts for the last pitching spot on the staff, Pepitone would soon move Moose Skowron off first, and Linz would emerge as a solid backup infielder, known as much for his wit as his skills. ("Play me or keep me," he once told Houk, after sitting on the bench for several weeks.) The Yankees tended to give young players a hard time until they proved their worth. A young pitcher from Connecticut named Rollie Sheldon remembered what it was like.

**ROLLIE SHELDON** is fifty years old, a tall, lean right-hander who was 11-5 as a Yankee rookie in 1961. He was 7-8 in 1962, and would be out of baseball by 1966. He is in the insurance business in Overland Park, Kansas.

**SHELDON:** "Joining the Yankees was like joining a college fraternity. There was a lot of hazing for a young player. You would come in the clubhouse and there would be a message on your footstool to call a certain Mr. Wolf at such and such a number. You would dial the number, not knowing if it was a chance at a banquet for $100 or what it was. Then the phone would answer and somebody would say, 'Bronx Zoo.' You would be real embarrassed at falling for such a gag. Pete Sheehy was the one who would put those phone messages there, but all of the players would be watching you making a fool of yourself.

"Roger was always one of the guys laughing the heartiest. He was part of the carrying on that went on in the clubhouse. I used to pal around with Ralph Terry and Spud Murray, the batting practice pitcher, and we had fun together. Maris was in a different group. He hung out with

Boyer and Stafford. Ball clubs are that way. You can't go out to dinner with fifteen guys, so it usually comes down to two or three, and those are the guys you get close to.

"Most young players went along with those old tricks. It was part of the ritual. Whitey Ford would yell at me after a game to get him a Coke, and I always did. He had been around a long time and was a great pitcher. It was all in fun. I was a conformist, anyway. I think the three young players who joined us in 1962, Linz, Pepi and Bouton, were different. They were nonconformists. They hung together and went their own ways. They probably weren't close to Roger."

Pepitone, in trouble with the law at this writing on a drug and concealed weapons charge, was a favorite foil for Mickey Mantle. Pepitone wanted so much to belong, to be a Yankee, to run with the stars.

"He was always around Mickey, sort of begging him to go out with him at night," says Clete Boyer. "One night Mickey was getting cleaned up in the clubhouse after a game and he asked Pepitone if he had a date. Joe said he didn't. 'Okay, here's a restaurant I'll be at tonight about nine. Meet me there for dinner.' Pepi was thrilled. He got all dressed up. Then he got in this cab and gave the guy a note with the address. 'You sure you want to go there?' the cab driver asked. Pepi assured him that's where he was going, so he could have dinner with Mickey. The driver took off and he just drove and drove and drove. Maybe for an hour. The cab fare might have been fifty bucks. Then he opens the door and lets Pepi out. It was in front of the darkest, dirtiest, dingiest place you could imagine in the black section of town. Pepi was scared as hell, but Mickey said this was the place. He went in to that joint, asked for Mickey, got a strange look and realized he had been had. Mickey made Pepi tell that story the next day to me and Roger and a lot of the other guys, too. Roger just laughed like hell."

Still comfortable with his teammates if not the press, Maris was anxious for the 1962 season to begin. He knew there would be no chance of hitting 61 home runs because he alone knew how hard a feat that really was. He wanted to hit 40, if possible, lift his average a bit and help the Yankees to their third straight pennant in the three seasons he was there.

Except for those isolated cases when Maris would be involved in a furor that spring with the press, most of the attention in New York centered on the Mets. The new team was putting its first lineup together and Casey Stengel, a folk hero to the retired folks who populated St. Petersburg, was cheered every time he showed his face. The Mets had some former Brooklyn Dodger stars (Gil Hodges, Don Zimmer, Clem Labine, Charlie Neal, and Roger Craig) on that team, plus a few ex-Giants, some over-the-hill players from other teams who had played well against New York (such as Richie Ashburn of the Phillies, Frank Thomas of the Pirates, and Gus Bell of the Reds) and an enormous amount of good will. Even before spring training ended the Mets seemed to be more popular as an expansion team—without playing a single game— than the Yankees were as world champions.

One of Stengel's favorite players was Rod Kanehl. He had been a Yankee farmhand. Stengel remembered him because Kanehl had jumped over a low fence in a Florida spring camp to wrestle a baseball away from a fan. Stengel, always careful with a buck, admired that. Now he was using Kanehl to needle the Yankees.

"We can play him at seven positions," said Stengel of the versitile youngster. "He couldn't do that with the Yankees."

It was clear that 1962 would be remembered in New York not for any home runs hit at Yankee Stadium but for the arrival in town of the ever-popular Amazing Mets. It would help Roger Maris have a peaceful summer.

Roger signs a ball for President Kennedy late in 1961. This picture rested in an honored spot on Roger's office wall. *Credit: NY Yankees.*

Batting champ Norm Cash of the Detroit Tigers, home run king Roger Maris and major league pitcher of the year Whitey Ford at January, 1962 banquet. *Credit: NY Yankees.*

Roger and Mrs. Babe Ruth at a banquet in 1962 after all the furor had settled down. *Credit: NY Yankees.*

# 10

## sour summers in the stadium

**THE** fans had expected so much. Roger Maris had spoiled them with 61 home runs and now, when he didn't hit one, they booed. Not always, not noisily, but enough to be noticed. There would be some fan on most days who felt cheated that he had paid $3.50 to see the greatest single-season home run hitter in history and he hadn't hit a home run that day.

Maris hit 33 runs in 1962. It was only good enough for a tie for fifth with Jim Gentile. Harmon Killebrew hit 48—nothing like 60 or 61—and Norm Cash hit 39, Rocky Colavito hit 37, Leon (Daddy Wags) Wagner hit 37, and Maris and Gentile had 33. Mantle hit 30, knocked in 89 runs and batted .321. Maris batted .256. Mantle won his third MVP award.

After an early challenge from the exciting Los Angeles Angels and a late challenge from the Minnesota Twins, the Yankees won the pennant by five games. Ralph Terry had a brilliant year with a 23-12 mark, Whitey Ford was 17-8, Bill Stafford was 14-9 and relief pitcher Marshall

Bridges (who would later make news by being shot in a night club by his girl friend) was 8-4. Four other pitchers—Rollie Sheldon, Jim Coates, Bud Daley and rookie Jim Bouton—would each contribute seven wins.

The Yankee team personality seemed to change in 1962. Bouton, Phil Linz and Joe Pepitone added some humor. Mickey Mantle seemed more relaxed and secure. Ford was always funny. Yogi Berra, in his last years as a player, was a figure of fun and warmth even though most of Berra's humorous lines ("Thank you for making this day necessary," and his famous Met line as manager, "It ain't over till it's over") were accidents and malaprops. The Major, manager Ralph Houk, was as tough and stolid as always but seemed more at ease generally after his 1961 win. Without any home run chase to fuss over, reporters left Maris alone a good part of the time. It was the way he liked it. Ironically, as a team the Yankees seemed to take their temperamental cue from Bouton. A Seattle teammate, Steve Hovely, once said of Bouton, "He was the first fan to make the big leagues."

**JIM BOUTON** is forty-seven years old, a former Yankee pitching star who also pitched for Seattle, Houston, and eight years after retirement, Atlanta. He was quick, clever, extremely witty as a clubhouse interview in his playing days, a ferocious competitor on the mound (I nicknamed him Bulldog Jim for his pitching intensity as he let fly with his over-achieving fastball and lost his cap) but a guy who could enjoy the status and success of a big leaguer off the mound. He was a sportscaster for many years and a civil rights, anti-war activist. He now lives in Teaneck, New Jersey, and owns and operates Big League Cards, a company manufacturing personalized bubble gum cards similar to those showing off big league stars. In 1970, while still pitching in the big leagues, he published *Ball Four*, an iconoclastic look at baseball, that was humorous, biting and revealing. It shattered many illusions about the game, the people, and the business of baseball. One remark about Mickey Mantle's drinking habits got more attention from the Yankees than all the other 400 pages put together. Mantle swore he would never attend another old timers' game if Bouton was invited. Bouton has never been invited back.

**JIM BOUTON:** "I had one kidding remark about Mickey drinking and he wrote a whole book in which he talks often about his drinking. People said my book offended baseball and baseball players. That's not why the establishment got mad. It was for economic reasons. I challenged their thinking about the game. When Marvin Miller [former executive director of the Players Association] was looking for evidence in the Messersmith case [the landmark baseball decision that led to free agency], he used my book. It became a legal document in that case. Only one player was called to testify against the reserve clause as it stood: me.

"I enjoyed playing baseball but I never saw it as a life career. I knew I would do other things. I certainly enjoyed pitching for the Yankees. As far as Roger Maris and I were concerned, we were from two different planets. I was always different, and the two of us were simply a contrast in personalities. We didn't see the game the same way.

"When I joined the club in 1962 I went out to pitch with the same ratty old glove I had always used in the minor leagues. After the game he came up to congratulate me and he gave me this brand new glove of his. 'Here, use this.' I did, and I always appreciated that gesture.

"We had some problems, of course. There were times I thought Roger dogged it and I would say something about it. I think anybody who was around the club then knew there were days he didn't feel like playing and days he jogged to first base. I spoke up about it. I wanted to be the player rep and I did campaign but it wasn't all that serious. I was interested in those things and not many other guys were. Maybe Roger took all that too seriously, I don't know.

"I felt sorry when some tough things happened to him, like hurting his hand, but I never could have a real discussion with him about it. We just didn't communicate. I palled around with Fritz Peterson and Phil Linz and Roger had his own group.

"I felt sad when he became ill, and I went to his funeral service at St. Patrick's Cathedral. I was a teammate. I wanted to be there. He was a very fine player. It's difficult to discuss things that seemed so important then and are so petty now. I don't want to say anything about him that isn't complimentary. He's gone now and can't defend himself. Just say that he gave me that glove and I thought that was a very kind gesture. I'll remember that when I think of Roger."

As Maris went around the league in 1962 the pitchers worked him more carefully than ever. They knew the man who ... was a very tough out. They had to be careful. **JIM KAAT** was a second-year pitcher with Minnesota. He is now a Yankee broadcaster after twenty-five years of successful pitching.

**KAAT:** "Roger was a low fastball hitter and I kept the ball up and in on him. As a left-handed pitcher I had good success with him. But you couldn't make a mistake on him. He could turn those wrists and explode on you. I think he got one home run off me while I faced him. It was a line shot that hit the foul pole. There was a big argument about fair or foul, but the umpire was waving his fingers over his head so I knew he had called it fair. We would talk about that homer a lot when we would meet someplace at a dinner or at a baseball gathering years later. He was always friendly, an easy guy to talk to. He never talked much about the '61 season, I always noticed that."

Maris completed another fine season in 1962. He knocked in 100 runs besides hitting 33 home runs, his third straight season with 100 or more RBIs. The Yankees won the pennant by five games—the third pennant in a row for Maris—and played the San Francisco Giants in the World Series. It was a stirring seven-game Series, not settled until the final swing of Willie McCovey's bat produced a line drive that was caught shoulder high by Bobby Richardson to end it. Maris had saved the game by scooping up a double by Willie Mays and holding speedy Matty Alou on third. It would be the last Yankee World Series triumph for fifteen years.

Maris had only four hits against the Giants, including one home run, for a .174 average. Mantle had only three hits without a homer for a .120 average. Terry won two games, Stafford won one, and Ford won one as the Yankees captured their 20th Series in 27 appearances.

Maris did not attend a single banquet after the season. He stayed home in Independence, relaxed, enjoyed his family and visited with his baseball friends living in the area, including Bob Cerv, Norm Siebern, Whitey Herzog and Bob Allison.

**BOB ALLISON** is fifty-one years old, a handsome, broad-shouldered former outfielder with the Washington Senators and Minnesota Twins from 1958 to 1970. He works for the Coca-Cola Company and lives in Medina, Minnesota.

**ALLISON:** "I was born in Raytown and my father still lived there when Roger moved to the area. I would visit my father, Louie, who had a construction business in the area and I would often go over to see Roger, play some golf, drink a few beers, enjoy relaxing with him.

"I don't know how Roger was in New York or what his personality was like there, but around Raytown he was a people person. He really enjoyed sitting around with the guys, telling stories, laughing, having a good time. He didn't like to talk about himself and he never seemed to talk of anything that happened in 1961, but he told funny stories about Mantle and Ford and lots of the Yankees.

"We got to be pretty good buddies and I always visited him in Gainesville when I would go through Florida, and he would take me out for a round of golf and we really enjoyed the day. We went to a golf tournament in Sun Valley, Idaho, in 1984. All of a sudden he began complaining about these terrible headaches, and a day or two after we got there he had to leave and go home. It was sad to see the way he was feeling after that. Once it caught hold of him it was very tough. Every time I called and wanted to visit he just said he wasn't up to it. Then he was gone. I went out to Fargo and we were all together, the guys who were really close to Roger, and we talked about him and then we all went home."

The Yankees gave Maris a small raise to $75,000 in 1963. It would be the highest salary he would ever make in baseball. He arrived at spring training in 1963 without his family. Pat Maris was pregnant again and their fourth son, Richard, and their fifth child would be born that year.

Joe Pepitone had replaced Moose Skowron at first base, with Skowron being traded away to Los Angeles for a strong right-handed pitcher named Stan Williams. The rest of the Yankee team was about the same save for Yogi Berra. He had been named a player-coach after eighteen years as a Yankee star. He coached at first base. Years later Whitey Ford would become a Yankee first base coach, and he would ask Berra how the job was handled.

"Just pat the runners on the ass as they cross first base," Berra said, "and point them toward second." Berra always had a simple explanation for things. When asked once by the press after a game-winning home run what he was thinking about as he swung, he replied, "You can't hit and think at the same time."

"There was a plan that had been in the works for a long time," says Ralph Houk. "Roy Hamey [the GM] was retiring, and I would move up from the manager's job to general manager. Yogi would become the manager in 1964. We told him about it in the early days of spring training in 1963 and surprisingly it remained a secret all through that year."

The 1963 season would be the first of Roger's four injury-filled Yankee seasons. He suffered a back injury, several muscle pulls and a problem with his elbow. He played in only 90 games, batted .269, hit 23 home runs (he had 200 homers in six seasons), and managed to knock in 53 runs.

The leg pulls were often severe, and Maris played many games without really being able to run. He didn't run out a lot of ground balls and fans, both at the Stadium and on the road, would boo him. He began to retreat more and more into his private world around the ballpark, communicating less and less with the press.

Early in May of 1963, the Yankees were playing the Twins in Minnesota. There were some fans who had driven over from North Dakota to see the game, not all of them on Maris's side. Many might have remembered Roger's shift from Fargo High to Shanley just a decade earlier. In the first inning Maris hit a routine grounder to Minnesota second baseman Bernie Allen. Maris jogged toward first base and quickly turned toward the dugout. Suddenly the ball skipped off Allen's glove and bounced far to his right. Maris had already turned away from the play. Allen hustled over, picked up the ball and threw Maris out.

When Maris walked toward the Yankee dugout, the fans behind the fence began booing. It got louder and louder with several players turning from the dugout to see the commotion. Many of the fans were yelling things from the stands. As he stepped down into the Yankee dugout, Maris raised his right hand with the middle finger extended in a familiar obscene gesture. Television cameras had followed Maris all the way to the dugout and caught the derisive move. Switchboards at television stations immediately lit up with calls from fans who were outraged at the public display of obscenity.

Maris was questioned later by reporters and screamed at them. It was a bad scene.

Two weeks later Commissioner Ford Frick seemed to come to Roger's defense. He issued an edict that television cameras must not follow a player into the sanctity of the dugout. "Of course I do not condone what Maris did, but I have communicated to the clubs that I don't want to see a recurrence on television. It's all right to follow a player in after a home run, but they move around in there, change shirts and such, and it isn't for the cameras."

By now Maris was chagrined. "It's not that I wanted to do it," Maris said. "I just did it. A loudmouthed guy behind our dugout kept heckling me and I finally got mad. It happened just like that."

"I didn't see what Maris did," claimed Houk, who missed very little of importance. "I'm not trying to excuse it. It isn't right and I'm sure he won't do it again. However, that heckler was way out of bounds. Some of the things he shouted at Maris made the air around us purple."

When the Yankees returned from that road trip there was a gift for Maris waiting on his footstool. It was a wooden carving of a hand with the middle finger extended in that famous obscene gesture. Nobody claimed ownership but it was always expected the donation came from Mantle. Maris would often place the extended finger carving on his footstool when he was unwilling to talk to the press.

**CLETE BOYER** is forty-nine years old, one of the famous baseball-playing Boyer brothers. Brother Ken died of cancer in 1982. Clete was a stylish third baseman who loved to hit home runs. He played for Kansas City, the Yankees (from 1959 through 1966) and Atlanta. He has coached and scouted in the big leagues, and in 1986 was awaiting a new baseball job. He lives in Clearwater, Florida.

**BOYER:** "I was probably closer to Roger than I was to my own brother. We spent more time together. My brother was always playing some place else. You had to get to know Roger. Sometimes he wouldn't let you. But if he liked you he would really open up. He was pictured as a quiet, introverted, reclusive guy. He wasn't that way at all. He loved to laugh. That story with the wooden finger was just one example.

"We would go out and have a few drinks, I would have ten double Scotches, and he would quit at five, and really have a blast. There wasn't anything mean about Roger. He wanted the fans to just leave him alone. He liked to be alone with his friends. That's what caused so much trouble, people butting in where they shouldn't. It's like Billy [Martin]. He never starts any of those things. It's just some guy in a bar who wants to be a big shot and say he knows Billy Martin. So he comes up, makes some remark, and before you know it they're rolling around on the floor again.

"Roger was a tremendous baseball player. There were a lot of things he did people didn't know about. He was the best guy I ever saw in going from first to third, the best on breaking up a double play, the best in getting a run in from third with less than two out. I saw Roger many times, with a guy on third, hit the weakest grounder in the world to the right side, I mean weak, but the guy from third can score. That's a lot better than hitting a bullet that the first baseman catches.

"Roger could also bunt. There were quite a few times with the third baseman back, Roger bunted for a hit. He wasn't just a home run hitter. He was a complete player and deserves to be recognized for it. Roger should be in the Hall of Fame. My brother, too. I don't know what these writers are thinking about some times.

"We were in touch all the time when he got sick, and I knew how bad it really was. I knew he wasn't going to make it. I saw the same thing happen with my brother. You get that special cancer treatment and for a few days you think it has helped, but it never does. Once it starts going, that's all there is to it. I knew Roger was going but

I was still stunned when Pat called me. I just sat there in my house and cried. Not a day has gone by since Roger died that I haven't thought about him."

With Whitey Ford having another magnificent year with a 24-7 season, Ralph Terry winning 17 games, and youngsters Jim Bouton (21-7) and Al Downing (13-5) showing pitching skills beyond expectations, the Yankees won the 1963 pennant by ten games. Mantle broke a bone in his foot and only played 65 games with a .314 mark, but catcher Elston Howard had a tremendous year (.287, 28 homers and 85 RBIs), the defense was very strong and the Yankees were in the World Series again, this time against the Los Angeles Dodgers.

Led by future Hall of Famers Sandy Koufax and Don Drysdale, the Dodger pitchers allowed the Yankees only four runs in the four games, and swept the Series. Mantle had only two singles and Maris, who suffered a leg pull in the second game, was 0-for-five in his turns against Koufax and left-hander Johnny Podres. The best game was the third game when Drysdale beat Bouton, 1-0. Koufax closed out the Series with a 2-1 win over Ford in the final game.

In some way the 1964 season would be remembered by Yankee fans as the finest in Roger's New York career. He almost single-handedly led them to the pennant. Maris was twenty-nine that year (and often ailing), Mantle was thirty-two, and Ford was thirty-five. Houk was the general manager and Yogi Berra, no longer an active player, had been named manager.

Berra was a sweet man but was unable to discipline his old buddies—Mantle, Ford, Maris—and some of the younger, wilder ones such as Pepitone. A familiar clubhouse sight that year was a player or two stretched out on the training tables before a game, not being treated for injuries but sleeping off the results of a long night. By early August the Yankees were slipping back in the race. Two players, Tony Kubek and Bobby Richardson, malted milk drinkers, went to Houk. They complained that players were taking advantage of Berra and something had to be done. They did not suggest that Berra be fired. They simply were concerned about a lack of discipline.

In an intriguing parallel, Johnny Keane, the manager of the St. Louis Cardinals, was in trouble with his team. The Cardinals had talked to Leo Durocher to find out if he was available to manage their club and learned he was. Owner Gussie Busch hesitated, though, about making a move during the season.

Late in August, Houk met secretly with owner Dan Topping. He relayed the feelings of Kubek and Richardson and agreed Berra was simply not doing the job. The decision was made. Berra would be fired after the season ended, no matter how the Yankees finished. Houk also instructed Bill Bergesch, now the general manager at Cincinnati but then a Yankee scout, to sound out Keane about his interest in the Yankee job if it became available. Keane and Houk had been friendly when they managed against each other in the minor leagues. Bergesch flew to St. Louis in a clandestine move. Strictly speaking, it was illegal to discuss a managerial job with a man under contract to another club. Both Houk and Bergesch have always denied that there was ever such a meeting, or that an offer to manage the Yankees was made in August. Keane, who also denied the 1964 contact, died in 1967. In 1965, after Keane was named the manager of the Yankees, columnist Milton Gross of the *Post* quoted Keane's daughter and his wife saying that such contacts were made.

Suffice it to say, Berra was in trouble in August. On August 20 the Yankees lost a 5-0 game in blistering hot Chicago to fall four and a half games behind the league-leading White Sox. The team boarded an old, unair-conditioned bus for the ride to the airport and became ensnarled in late afternoon traffic. Phil Linz, who had purchased a harmonica early the previous afternoon, began playing a few chords. It was horrible, and the players in the back of the team bus, led by Mantle, Maris, Ford and Pepitone, all laughed. Berra, sitting in a front seat near a group of reporters, turned around and told Linz to "cut it out." A few seconds later Linz began again, playing a poor version of Mary Had a Little Lamb. This time Berra jumped up from his seat. He walked towards Linz and screamed, "I told you to shove that harmonica up your ass." Linz lobbed the harmonica at the manager. Berra grabbed it and threw it back toward Linz. It hit Pepitone on the right knee. He feigned serious injury, screaming, "Oh, I'm hurt, Oh, I'm hurt," as all his teammates laughed. Coach Frank Crosetti, self-appointed upholder of Yankee tradition, jumped up and screamed, "I've never seen anything this terrible in all the years I've been with the Yankees. You ought to be ashamed of yourself."

Things quieted down and the team flew on to Boston. Linz admitted he was wrong, pleaded forgiveness and expressed sorrow at the incident. He was fined $200 by Houk, who joined the club in Boston. (No matter: Linz made $10,000 in a deal with a harmonica company.)

Despite Berra's loss of control—or perhaps because of it—the Yankees got hot. They won 30 of their last 41 games and moved into first place on September 17, eventually winning the pennant by a game over the White Sox.

The key player in that stretch was Roger Maris. Mantle had been injured and Berra moved Maris to center field, playing John Blanchard and Hector Lopez in right and Tom Tresh in left. Maris knocked in 24 runs, hit six homers and batted .304 in his last forty-one games, ran the bases hard, and played the best center field since Mantle was a youngster.

**YOGI BERRA** is sixty-one years old, a Hall of Fame catcher who became a coach for the Houston Astros in 1986. He spent eighteen seasons with the Yankees and played four games with the Mets in 1965. He was one of the game's truly great clutch hitters, a three time MVP, a pennant-winning manager with the Yankees and Mets, and one of the most lovable characters in the game.

**BERRA:** "I didn't have no trouble with Roger. He always played hard for me. That year Mickey was hurt, and I went to Roger and said we need him in center field. It was no big deal. He just did it. He played great. He could do everything you needed, run, hit, field and throw. He was some thrower and he got a lot of guys out when they didn't expect it because he got rid of the ball so good.

"I was down in Houston when he was real sick, and I wanted to see him but they wouldn't let me. They said he was too bad off. I was really upset about that. We had a lot of great players on the Yankees and Roger was one of them. Give me nine Roger Marises each year and I'll take my chances."

The Yankees met the St. Louis Cardinals in the World Series. Maris, who had hit .281 for his second highest average of his career along with 26 homers and 71 RBIs, had six Series hits, a home run, and batted .200. Bouton won two games for the Yankees but Bob Gibson, pitching on two days of rest, won his second game of the Series in the seventh game for a Cardinal win. Keane was asked why he started Gibson on short rest when he had more rested starters. "I had a commitment to his heart," eloquently replied the manager.

The Yankees flew home that night. Both the Cardinals and the Yankees called press conferences for Friday afternoon, October 16. All hell was about to break loose.

Yogi Berra, certain he was being rewarded with a raise after rallying the Yankees to the pennant despite the seventh-game Series loss, went to the Yankee offices. Topping and Houk awaited him. "We've decided to make a change," they said.

In St. Louis the Cardinals called a press conference to supposedly announce Keane's rehiring for 1965. Instead, the manager announced he was resigning. He said nothing about his future plans. He cited the meetings with Durocher and the lack of support from executives within the Cardinal organization as his reasons for quitting. He was portrayed in the press as a heroic figure for standing up to the beer baron owner of the Cardinals, Gussie Busch.

Four days later, the image was shattered when Keane was named the manager of the Yankees. In the most tension-filled, abrasive press conference I have ever participated in, reporters screamed at Houk, bellowed at Keane, and cornered every Yankee official in a vain attempt to get confirmation on the subject of the managerial succession. They all believed, but could not prove, that Keane had been offered the Yankee job in August when the decision to fire Berra was made. Keane was coming to the Yankees with a heavy burden since Berra was a press favorite and since most reporters believed his succession was a sham.

Spring training is generally a placid time of year for

players and press alike. There were already tensions from
the pitchers when Maris arrived with the regulars. Keane
had decided to change the pitching rotation, moving Ford
back and Mel Stottlemyre, a 1964 rookie who had won
nine games in 13 starts, up. This angered Mickey Mantle.
He didn't want to see his good buddy being phased out.
One day Mantle expressed that resentment in an interview
with a sportswriter from the *World Telegram and Sun*
named Joe King. Mantle, kiddingly, said he would not
chase any fly balls in center field until Ford was restored
to his number 1 status. The story exploded in the New
York papers and embarrassed Mantle, Ford, and especially Keane. It went downhill from there.

Keane had taken over an aging ball club. He was a quiet,
soft-spoken, smallish gentle man. He didn't understand
the Yankee style of hard living, heavy drinking and serious
playing. He saw only the chasing of women and the heavy
drinking. Incapable of attacking the veteran players, he
jumped on the rookies. He berated a rookie named Bobby
Murcer. He criticized Bouton—who had turned up with
a bad arm—Phil Linz and Joe Pepitone endlessly. He saw
the team quickly slipping away from him.

Mantle's skills had eroded as he approached the age of
thirty-four. Maris, still fighting the fans and the front office, had little heart for a losing season.

The 1965 season had started poorly for Maris. In the
spring he had been drinking at a Fort Lauderdale night
spot known as Nick's Cocktail Lounge with Clete Boyer
and Joe DiMaggio, of all people. (DiMaggio, a frequent
visitor to the Yankee spring camps, had grown fond of
Maris. In 1961 he had even introduced his former wife,
Marilyn Monroe, who had just come from a New York
psychiatric clinic, to Maris. "Miss Monroe," DiMaggio said,
"this is Roger Maris." Maris simply said. "It's a pleasure

to meet you, Miss Monroe." The lady he met was wearing no makeup, a flowing, light-colored summer dress, and a kerchief over her blonde hair; she hardly looked like a movie star. Some seventeen months later Miss Monroe would be dead.)

While at the lounge Maris and Boyer were allegedly involved in a fight with a male model named Jerome A. Modzelewski. He filed a complaint with police and Maris was charged with assault. Police investigated. Maris posted a $200 bond and forfeited it as court costs when the charges were eventually dropped. It made a fuss in the press for a few days.

Keane was upset but did not discipline Maris. The American League champions of 1964 broke camp and flew to Minnesota for the 1965 opener. It was a cold, miserable day and when Twins owner Calvin Griffith demanded the game be played, Yankee player rep Tony Kubek called him on the clubhouse phone and complained. Griffith hung up on Kubek.

The anti-Yankee cabal was growing. Other clubs wanted to get even for the years of frustration. They were tired of seeing the Yankees win all the time. They sensed a change as the Yankees struggled early in 1965 under Keane. There was no more significant change than the sale of the team by Dan Topping and Del Webb late in 1964 to the Columbia Broadcasting System. A new man was now running the Yankees—a handsome, bon vivant, former World War II OSS hero, circus operator and esthete named Michael Burke. He was the Yankee operating head in 1965 and the man who would preside over the next eight depressing seasons.

Maris was still an unhappy Yankee. He was occasionally booed but most often ignored. His glory days seemed far behind him. Keane had counted on Maris and Mantle, and they had not delivered. The Yankees dropped quickly into the second division. Then, on June 28, Roger Maris suffered an injury that would destroy his final two Yankee seasons, diminish his strength, and create a lasting bitterness toward the ball club. Maris slid into home plate that day and hurt his right hand. He couldn't play the next day. When reporters queried him, he said he was in great pain. The Yankees issued a statement saying Maris's availability would be evaluated on a "day-to-day basis." The Yankees had long been famous for hiding serious injuries. It was their impression that the less the press knew about an injury, the better. Dr. Sidney Gaynor, a talented if crusty orthopedic surgeon, examined Maris. He said the injury did not seem serious. X-rays were taken. No break was found. Maris continued to feel pain.

Keane asked him to play and Maris continued to insist the hand hurt too much to play. He played an occasional game but mostly he sat. The Yankees allowed him to be examined repeatedly by Dr. Gaynor and, when the club was on the road, by other orthopedic surgeons. None found a break.

"One day Roger called me," said pal Julie Isaacson, "and I could hear him crying. The pain was unbelievable. I went to see him and he could hardly stand up. 'Julie, I can't play. They think I'm faking it.' I decided that was enough. I called some friends of mine and found out who the best man in the city was for injured hands. I went to him and brought Roger. We did it on our own. We didn't tell Houk, we didn't tell Keane, we didn't tell nobody."

A new set of X-rays were taken. These X-rays finally revealed not only a broken bone but a fragment of the bone lodged in the upper right side of Maris's hand. Surgery was scheduled immediately. In a three-hour procedure Dr. William Littler, a noted Manhattan surgeon, removed the fragment from the base of Maris's hand and repaired the damage. The operation was performed September 28, 1965. Maris was still in the hospital when the sixth-place Yankees ended their dreary season on October 3. He left Roosevelt Hospital later that same day and returned home to Independence. Three weeks later he came back to New York to allow Dr. Littler to remove the cast.

Houk was angered that Maris had gone off on his own and had the surgery performed. It would be a familiar bone of contention between them for many years.

In 1985 Maris said, "The Yankees didn't take care of me. They didn't send me to the right doctor. They were only interested in getting me back in the lineup. I was interested in getting my hand well. Ralph knew how bad I was hurting. He should have told the press. Instead they kept on with that day-to-day crap so it looked like I was a malingerer."

Maris's injury brought into clear focus an obvious medical conflict. Team doctors want players playing, hence they may not have as much concern for the long-term health of the player as they should. They remain team doctors only as long as they can keep the athletes on the field. A related problem is improper or excessive prescription of drugs. Cortisone, which can be dangerous, is administered much too freely by team doctors, many outside observers believe. Sandy Koufax quit baseball at the age of thirty rather than risk permanent injury from excessive cortisone.

Maris ended the 1965 season by playing in only 46 games, hitting .239, collecting only eight home runs and knocking in 27 runs. He would play again in 1966 for the Yankees, but it would be without enthusiasm.

\* \* \*

Things started off badly again in 1966. The Yankees quickly dropped to tenth and last place. Keane called a clubhouse meeting and ripped into Bobby Murcer, a nineteen-year-old shortstop. Elston Howard, a good friend of mine, told me about the meeting. Without using his name I printed the details. Keane was outraged that a description had leaked. He called another clubhouse meeting and asked the informant to step forward. No one did. Finally Howard, now a leader on the team, got up and said, "We shouldn't let the press get this information. We should keep our problems confidential." Everybody but Keane knew it was Howard's way of admitting he was the culprit. He felt it was necessary to get Keane off Murcer's back.

It all ended sadly for Keane, the little man who shouldn't have been there, when he was fired May 7 while the team was in Los Angeles. ("Does this mean I can't date his daughter any more?" asked Pepitone, who had his priorities askew.)

Ralph Houk took over as manager again. Maris knew he would never be happy again in a Yankee uniform. The Yankees made a quick run, collapsed immediately afterwards, and settled into the bottom of the American League. They finished in tenth and last place with a record of 70 and 89. Maris played only occasionally, hitting more to left field since his hand no longer had much power. His lack of enthusiasm showed. That year he batted .233, had 13 homers and knocked in 43 runs.

"I think it was about early September when he came to my office one day," Houk says, "and told me he was quitting. He said the hand bothered him too much, he was sick of the booing, sick of playing in New York, and he was going home for good. I told him not to make any hasty decisions. He should think it over during the winter."

Houk told his boss, Michael Burke, what Maris had said and they decided to trade him.

"We knew we couldn't get much for him, but if we got a usable ballplayer it would be better than nothing if he walked away. We had no idea if, once we traded him, he still would quit. That would be the other club's problem," Houk said.

On December 8, 1966, Maris was in the driveway of his home in Independence. He was fooling with his car when a photographer pulled up next to him and told him he had just heard something about him on the radio.

"What was it?"

"You've been traded, I think."

"Where?"

"To St. Louis, I think."

"Who'd they trade me for?"

"I think the name I heard was Charley Smith."

"Who the hell is Charley Smith?"

Smith was a journeyman third baseman who had been with the Dodgers, Phillies, White Sox, Mets and Cardinals. His lifetime big league average over ten seasons was .239. (He had been with the Mets in 1964 and 1965, and Casey Stengel had always called him Charley Davis, mixing him up with some player he knew a half century earlier.)

I called Johnny Murphy, an executive with the Mets, who had traded Smith to the Cardinals. Murphy had been a great Yankee relief pitcher and had a marvelous knowledge of ballplayer talents. He would know the relative merits of the deal.

"Smith is a red-ass," he said, "just like Maris."

# 11

## gashouse gang revisited

**BABE RUTH** and the Yankees dominated baseball in the 1920s. While Ruth was leading the Yankees to six pennants in that decade, the St. Louis Cardinals built their own winning tradition in the National League with pennants in 1926 and 1928. Led by Frankie Frisch, Jim Bottomley, Chick Hafey, Jess Haines and an aging Grover Cleveland Alexander, the Cardinals became the most famous team in the National League.

After Ruth left the Yankees in 1935, they continued to win with Lou Gehrig, young Joe DiMaggio, Bill Dickey, Red Ruffing, Lefty Gomez and Johnny Murphy. The Cardinals were equally successful through the 1930s with a roster of rousing, flamboyant, hard-drinking tough-talking, brawling players led by Pepper Martin, Dizzy Dean, Joe Medwick and Leo Durocher. It was Durocher, the feisty shortstop, who would immortalize the team when his club was once compared to the lordly Yankees. When told by sportswriter Frank Graham that his Cards were good enough to challenge New York in the American League,

Durocher said, "They wouldn't let us play in the American League. They would say we were just a bunch of gashouse players."

Thus was born the famous Gashouse Gang.

The Cardinals were strong again in the 1940s with the addition of Stan Musial, Marty Marion and Enos Slaughter, slowed down in the 1950s, and regained their status with a pennant in 1964 and the seventh-game victory over the Yankees in 1964.

After two second-division finishes in 1965 and 1966, the Cardinals appeared ready for another pennant challenge. They had a marvelous lineup including Lou Brock, Curt Flood, Mike Shannon, Tim McCarver, Dal Maxvill, Orlando Cepeda and Bob Gibson. This was another freewheeling bunch in the Gashouse Gang tradition with loud, blaring rock music being heard in the clubhouse, stars being needled by scrubs, racial remarks used often to diffuse tensions and an aggressive style of play, typical of the team history.

In the spring of 1967, after thinking about it for nearly two months, Roger Maris decided to play one more year in the big leagues for $75,000. He joined the Cardinals at their training camp in St. Petersburg, Florida, and reported to manager Red Schoendienst.


**RED SCHOENDIENST** is sixty-three years old, a former star infielder with the Cards, Giants and Milwaukee Braves. He was a marvelous player, a very successful manager, and is now a coach with the Cardinals.

**SCHOENDIENST:** "At the end of the 1966 season we felt we had a fine ball club. We needed one more hitter, preferably left-handed, and we needed a third baseman to win.

We talked to a lot of ball clubs looking for a third baseman. We thought we might be able to get Eddie Mathews from the Braves. When that deal fell through, we heard the Yankees were offering Maris around. If we got Maris, we still needed a third baseman. We got the idea that maybe we could move Mike Shannon, our right fielder, to third base and play Maris in right. We talked it over with Shannon. He was very agreeable.

"Our season was over by now and the football Cardinals had the field, so we couldn't work Shannon out there. We got Mike out to Forest Park and Joe Schultz, one of our coaches, hit a few hundred balls at him. They bounced off his chest, his shoulders, his arms, all over his body but he stayed with it. He had a strong arm and he was fearless. I was convinced he could play third. When the [Maris] deal was made [December 8, 1966] Mike already knew he would be the third baseman and Roger would be the right fielder. As it turned out, Mike and Roger became the best of friends.

"Bob Howsam [the Cardinal GM] had asked me several times that winter if I thought Maris could help our ball club. 'Get him,' is what I always told Bob. I went back a long way with Roger. I was playing in an exhibition game in Las Vegas in 1957 or 1958. Roger was with Cleveland then, and when I saw him play I knew he would be a terrific player. He had very quick feet and he was powerful. He also had that home run swing like a good golfer, just exploding on the ball at the right time and really driving it into the air. I watched his progress and I wasn't surprised he became the home run hitter he did.

"We had a press conference with our local media just before spring training and he saw that our park wasn't a home run park. He saw the way the wind blew and he saw the high fences, and he knew it would be a lot harder to hit home runs in St. Louis than it had been in New York. He was thirty-two years old and he had that bad hand, and we explained to our media that we were getting him for his all-around ability and experience and they shouldn't expect a lot of home runs from him. We talked before the press conference and he said he didn't want a lot of fuss made about him. I told him we had already explained to the press he wouldn't hit a lot of home runs for us. 'Thanks, Red.' He seemed real pleased that there wouldn't be a lot of pressure.

"He was a very solid player for us, not flashy, just a guy who did his job, played hard, always made the right play and fit in with the guys. I tried not to play him too much, never played him in a day game after a night game, and really got out of him as much as we could. We won two pennants in those two years he was with us. I knew we wouldn't have had a right fielder after we moved Shannon to third base. I'd have to say Roger was the difference in our winning in those two seasons. Roger knew how to win.

"I think Roger loved being with the Cardinals. After he quit he would come around spring training every year in St. Petersburg, horse around with the guys and have a good time. I used to play golf with him in St. Petersburg and he could still whack that ball. Each year we had a tournament in St. Louis for the Christian Brothers to raise funds for their charity and he traveled each year to St. Louis for that one. He was an important member of the Cardinals and got along with everybody here—his teammates, the ball club executives, the fans and the press. There are a lot of wonderful memories about Roger in St. Louis."

* * *

Maris was the final piece in the Cardinal puzzle. Shannon, with his courage, strength and strong throwing arm, solved the third base problem. Maris, who handled right field with ease, combined with Curt Flood, a wonderful center fielder, and Lou Brock, an explosive offensive player and a speedy left fielder, to take care of the outfield defense. Cepeda, Julian Javier, Dal Maxvill and Shannon played well in the infield, the pitching was solid, and the catching was handled well by Tim McCarver, one of the wittiest men to every play the game and now a Mets broadcaster. It was McCarver, later traded to the Phillies, who acted as locker room spokesman for Steve Carlton, the talented but sensitive left-handed pitcher who decided not to talk to the press ever again after he was burned in an interview early in his Philadelphia career. "We're so close," McCarver explained, "that Lefty [Carlton] and I will be buried 60 feet six inches apart when we die."

"We knew Roger had been a great player with the Yankees," says McCarver. "When he joined us it was a thrill. He had played on all those great Yankee teams, won five pennants in his first five years there, and was going to be a Hall of Famer. We knew he would fit in. He was approachable and we got along well after the first few days. There were no airs about Roger. Everybody enjoyed being with him. When the season started he would ask one or two different guys to join him for dinner each night on the road. For a joke, the one guy who wanted to go out with Roger the most, Hal Woodeshick, a relief pitcher, was never asked. He hung around Roger every day after the game, sort of walked back and forth with him there, but never got asked. It really got funny. Roger used to love to eat crabs, and we would go out and eat crabs all night long. Finally, Roger decided it was time to ask Woody to go out with him. They went out together and the next day Woody was in heaven. I asked him if he had been out with Roger yet, and he began telling me about the night. Then another guy asked him, then another and another. By now it was time to take the field, and guys were still asking him, and he was going into this long, detailed explanation about the night. Finally, I think Woody was telling the clubhouse guy about the night and we were all on the field, and Red sees he isn't there and yells at him: 'Get your ass out here.' Then he fined him. It was just funny."

Schoendienst put Maris third in the lineup behind Brock, who would electrify baseball with his base stealing, and Flood, a wonderful hitter who would become most famous off the field—for fighting baseball's reserve clause. Maris kept the rallies going.

"He didn't have the power he had with the Yankees," says Schoendienst, "but he had marvelous bat control. He could make contact and move runners along and keep an inning alive. Then we had Cepeda, McCarver and Shannon to knock in the runs."

The Mets played the Cardinals for the first time in St. Louis in early May. By now, through the good efforts of Julie Isaacson, Roger had become an easy interview. Isaacson had brought Maris along to Grossinger's, a New York Catskill Mountains hotel in the reknowned Borscht Belt, and we had shared a few drinks and a few laughs. I had finally gotten to see the other side of Maris—the loose, less tense, more relaxed part of his character, away from the pressure of the press. We talked easily that May day.

"I really enjoy it here," Roger said. "These are a good bunch of guys. All they want me to do is what I'm capable of doing. I don't have to hit 50 home runs. Nobody boos me in St. Louis."

A couple of weeks later he made his Shea Stadium debut as a member of the Cardinals. His first at-bat was cause for loud cheers and some few boos.

"I guess they let some Yankee fans in here," he said after the game. "I played a couple of Mayor's Trophy games against the Mets here, so I know the park."

I asked him if he expected to go across the river and visit the Stadium.

"What for? I'm with the Cardinals."

Then he turned and walked away. The hurt was still deep.

Bob Gibson beat the Mets that day, and the pitcher heard some of the boos directed at Maris. He was not above needling his new teammate. "I thought you told me you were very popular here," Gibson said.

**BOB GIBSON** is fifty years old, a Hall of Fame right-handed pitcher for the Cardinals, a pitching coach for the Mets and Braves, and now a St. Louis broadcaster.

GIBSON: "Roger was a good guy. Nobody cared what happened with the Yankees. He showed he was a hard-working ballplayer and he was a member of the Cardinals. On the Cardinals everybody was treated equally. We were all stars. He showed us he would play hard and he wanted to win. That was all anybody cared about. I was proud to have Roger Maris as a teammate.

"We needed that extra bat he gave us and we needed that experience. Nobody on those Cardinal teams felt any resentment or jealousy towards Roger Maris. What was there to be jealous about? I think he was a terrific player. I would have liked to have had him earlier with us, when his hand was sound and he could hit a few more home runs."

While each Cardinal victory was celebrated with Orlando Cepeda's music blaring mercilessly in the clubhouse, Maris seemed to settle back into a quiet routine. He lived in a hotel near the ballpark, spent off days at home in Kansas City (he now had six small children), enjoyed all of his teammates and sat quietly at a corner locker while his teammates screamed obscenities at each other. He was never part of that juvenile conduct but he never seemed to be critical of it, either. If his style was to come to work, put in a full day and leave, he was not against others parading naked through the clubhouse, snapping towels at one another or telling off-color stories in both Spanish and English.

Maris had a strong, steady season. He batted .261, hit nine home runs, knocked in 55 runs, scored 64 and had only two errors in the outfield. The Cardinals won the pennant by ten and half games over the San Francisco Giants. Maris was in his sixth World Series in the last eight seasons. He hit well against the Boston Red Sox, batting .385 in seven games with a home run, his sixth in Series play. Gibson beat Jim Lonborg in the final game as the Cardinals won their second World Series in four years.

After the final game in Boston, the Cardinals flew back to St. Louis. Maris sat on the plane with buddy Mike Shannon and told him, "I'm quitting."

Maris had been thinking about it for several weeks. He had enjoyed St. Louis but he just didn't think he had sufficient intensity any more to play up to his abilities. He wasn't sure what he would do in retirement in Kansas

City but he felt he had been away from the family long
enough, had put enough burdens on Pat and the children,
and felt it was time to stay home.

The owner of the Cardinals, Gussie Busch, was in a
light mood at the party that night in the Chase Park Plaza
Hotel. Maris approached him. They began talking and
Maris said he thought that he was going to retire. He told
Busch he had enjoyed playing with the Cardinals but felt
it was time to go home.

"What will you do?" Busch asked.

"I don't know. I'll find something."

Busch had enjoyed winning in 1964, but had enjoyed
the 1967 season even more since his team had come back
from two poor seasons. He had a magnificent new stadium, named in his honor, and wanted to keep it filled
with a winning team for several more years.

"Have you ever thought about the beer business?"

As a matter of fact, Maris had. Several players had gone
into beer sales after their careers ended with the Cardinals
and all had done well. Maris had heard that a beer distributorship, especially in an area near a college or university, could be extremely lucrative. Busch explained a
bit about the beer business. Then he said to Roger, "Play
another year for the Cardinals and I'll take care of you."

Maris agreed to play one more season for the Cardinals
in 1968. He would be a force again, if a little less so, on
another Cardinal pennant winner. He batted .255 in 1968,
hit five home runs, knocked in 45 runs, scored 25 and
helped the Cardinals to their second straight pennant. His
career totals would include 275 homers, 851 RBIs, and a
.260 lifetime average.

There were several stories in the St. Louis papers early
in the summer of 1968 that this would be Roger's final
season in the big leagues. His teammates all knew it by

July. He was extremely close to Shannon but he had warm relations with all of his teammates—Brock, Flood, Gibson, Cepeda and Maxvill.

**DAL MAXVILL** is forty-seven years old, a smallish, quick, sure-handed shortstop with the Cardinals, Oakland A's and Pittsburgh Pirates. He was a big league coach for many seasons and was general manager of the pennant-winning Cardinals in 1985. In 1986 he hoped to repeat as the pennant winning GM.

**MAXVILL:** "I remember when I played against Roger in the 1964 World Series and he bowled me over at second base. I knew he was an aggressive player. That's the way he played with the Cardinals. I first heard talk about Roger coming to St. Louis after that 1966 season, and I read that the Cardinals wanted Mike Shannon to move to third. Mike was one of the best right fielders in the game. I called him up. 'Mike, are you crazy doing that?' Mike was more understanding of the situation than I was. 'It'll give us another big bat. We'll win if I can do it.' I guess I doubted if he could make that move at that stage of his career. He sure proved me wrong. He was great at third, and Roger played terrific right field and added his bat.

"I remember that first spring he joined us. He was real low key, a quiet, decent guy. He didn't force his way into things. He just sat back and waited to be asked. I liked to kid guys who came to the Cardinals about the boss. 'I hope you like to drink Budweiser.' He patted his stomach and showed me that he did. In a few days we went out and he proved that he did. He could handle that Bud. We were having dinner one night down the beach at the Careless Navigator, and he got to talking about how he was having trouble now controlling his weight. He said he had put on a few pounds every year for the last few years, and he just had to start watching it a little more.

"We were having a great time, I think it was Shannon and me and McCarver and Roger, and he started talking about the Yankees, about what a great player Mickey was and all the things he could do, and he started telling some funny stories about Whitey and Mickey and about Clete Boyer and what it was like over there. You know, all ballplayers like to know what it is like playing on other ball clubs. Ever since he joined us, I kept thinking about him as the guy who broke Babe Ruth's record—and here I am, a .220 hitter [.217, Dal] all my life, and I'm talking to a guy who has the greatest home run record in baseball. 'What was it like breaking the Babe's record?' You could see the muscles in his face grow tense, and he just said, 'Now that it's over, it was extremely tough to do.' He just dropped the subject right there, and we started eating real quietly for a couple of minutes and stayed off baseball conversation for a good long while. After that I never asked him about that year, and I don't remember him talking about any personal achievements with the Yankees. "I used to watch him swing in batting practice and it seemed as if he could hit the ball hard everywhere. I couldn't hit it hard *anywhere*. I'd go 0-for-four a lot and be real down, and he would always come over and say, 'We'll get 'em tomorrow.' Those 'oh-fers' were driving me insane, but one of the things I learned playing with Roger was that there was always a tomorrow in baseball. I think it had a lot to do with me lasting as long as I did."

Late in August, Roger Maris and the Cardinals, on their way to the 1968 pennant, came into Shea for the final time in the season. Maris was sitting in front of his locker, reading the sports pages, when I walked over to him. He seemed heavier than he had been the last time we talked. There were more lines in his forehead and his eyes seemed to squint. His hair was still cut in that old fashioned crew-cut but it was thinner now, with more scalp showing under the blond hairs. He would be thirty-four in three weeks. There had been many stories about his retirement in the St. Louis papers. I asked him if it was official.

"I'm just tired of baseball. I won't miss it. I'll have a job that will keep me busy and I'll be able to come home to my family every night," he said.

He described the operation of the beer distributorship he would be running in Gainesville, Florida, near the University of Florida, a solid beer-drinking campus. His company would be responsible for an eight-county area. We kidded about how much he would miss baseball, about how I thought he would be back in spring training in 1969 after he found out what time guys running businesses outside of baseball have to get up. "I get up early anyway," he said.

"At least you won't have to answer any questions about '61."

"I didn't mind '61," he said. "It was '62 I didn't like."

He knew I understood and he continued to talk easily about those seasons, only six and seven years ago, when every move he made made headlines. He didn't want to relive the misunderstandings, the turmoil, the pain, the pressures, the confusion, the bitterness. He had been a man at peace in St. Louis. He would talk hitting.

"It all goes in cycles," he said. "Nobody thought Ruth's record would ever be broken. Home run hitters will come along again. Maybe next year there will be somebody. Maybe in ten years. That's the way the game is."

We talked a little more about hitting, about the delicate art of the home run, about the joy he found in St. Louis. It was almost game time now, and we had to go to our respective jobs. "The one I'll remember was 154 in Baltimore," I said.

"I won't forget that one, either."

"Thanks, Roger," I said.

There was one last thing. I had brought along a photograph I had blown up years before—of Maris hitting his 60th homer at Yankee Stadium that year, the most dramatic shot that summer, the one with his eyes, the catcher's and the umpire's all staring intently at the historic shot. It always seemed unprofessional for a reporter to ask a player to autograph something. Now it seemed appropriate. I asked him if he would, and he held the picture lovingly on his lap for a minute, stared at that much younger face and trimmer body, and held the pen in his hand before he wrote, "To Maury, Good Luck and Best Regards, Your friend, Roger Maris." It sits above my desk as I type these words.

The Cardinals were winning steadily in the final days of the 1968 season. Maris would be leaving the team after the World Series, but it was still a good, solid baseball team that would challenge for the National League pennant for a while. Roger's friend, Mike Shannon, was suffering from injuries and would soon be replaced at third, in a deal, by Joe Torre. After Maris left, Shannon would last only two more years as a Cardinal player.

**MIKE SHANNON** is forty-seven years old, a handsome, dark-haired, broad-shouldered man who was a Cardinal star about six of his nine big league seasons. He was a regular on the 1964, 1967 and 1968 St. Louis champions and, during the time that Roger was with the Cardinals, was Maris's best friend.

**SHANNON:** "When Red first called me up and asked me about moving to third base, I said, 'Why would I wanna do that?' It didn't seem like a very smart move. He explained that we had a shot at getting Roger Maris, and I knew he would help us win. So I just figured I'd put a good strong cup on and go get 'em. They worked me out on that old, dusty field, saw that I could do it and made the deal.

"I had played against Roger in the 1964 World Series and I knew he was a quality player. He could do everything and he seemed to be a very alert player. I was sure he would fit in with the Cardinals but, of course, I had no idea we would become as close friends as we did.

"Guys were a little wary of him when he came over. We had heard all that stuff about his problems with the press in New York, but you learn to judge those things for yourself. I introduced myself to him in spring training that first day, and we just seemed to hit it off right away. They started giving players single rooms by then, but we told Jim Toomey, the traveling secretary, we wanted to have adjoining rooms.

"We enjoyed doing the same things, playing hard and winning, having a beer and eating after the game, spending an off day together fishing down in Florida or doing some duck or geese hunting after the season, sitting around and just talking late into the night.

"After he retired and moved to Gainesville, he would come to spring training and we'd go out and have some laughs, and you could see he really enjoyed his work and enjoyed being away from the pressures of baseball. His business was very successful and he was making good money and had no financial worries. He enjoyed being with Pat and the kids, and he was real proud when the boys started playing golf and winning some of those junior tournaments around home. He really enjoyed being around those kids after he quit baseball, as they grew up.

"In the fall of 1983 he called me up one day and said he had been feeling bad, and a trip I had planned down there had to be postponed. He thought he had mononucleosis and he said he had gone to a doctor who was doing some testing. A week or so later he called me back and said he had good news and bad news. 'The good news is I don't have mono. The bad news is I have cancer.' That was some jolt. But he was pretty matter-of-fact about it, so I was too. 'I got the kind of cancer where 80 per cent of the people who get it live. I'm under the doctor's care now. I think he's doing a good job.'

"He went up to New York in July of 1984, where they retired his number, and when he came back he started losing weight. They put him on some machine because he had shortness of breath, and it turned out he had a collapsed lung. We talked on the phone almost every day after that. The thing was up and down. He'd have good days and bad ones. I would visit him a couple of times that spring of 1985, and most of the time we just sat around at his place on the lake, drank beer and talked. He wasn't up to anything else by then. Then after the season ended in 1985, I wanted to visit him. But he said he just wasn't up to it. He was leaving for some drastic treatment in Tennessee. We talked a couple of times while he was there, and then he went to that hospital in Houston. Pat called and said he had gone into a coma. The next day he was gone.

"We made plans to fly to Fargo, and it was real nice to

see so many guys out there for his funeral, especially some of those old Yankees, like Mickey and Whitey. That was really something. Roger would have appreciated that. I was real lucky to have him as a friend, and I hope people appreciate him now as a player. He could do everything and he was the best at winning ball games. I think he really deserves the Hall of Fame but I don't think it mattered much to him. He may have wanted it for his kids, but Roger wasn't a guy who liked a lot of attention. I think he was just happy playing ball and winning and drinking a few beers and eating some crabs. He didn't need recognition. I never heard him talk much about 1961, but he was proud of that season. Any ballplayer could appreciate what he did. The winters don't seem as much fun now with Roger gone."

The Cardinals roared through the 1968 season. Gibson won 22 games, Nelson Briles won 19, and young Steve Carlton won 13 games. Flood led the team in hitting with a .301 average, Shannon led the club in RBIs with 79, and Brock stole 62 bases. On September 15, with the pennant about clinched, Maris played right field and batted third against a big Houston right-hander named Don Wilson. (In 1975 Wilson would be found dead of asphyxiation while sitting in his car in the locked garage of his Houston home.) Wilson threw very hard. The wall in right center field was 380 feet from home plate and ten feet high. Houston was the toughest home run park in the league because of the strange effect the air conditioning had on the indoor ballpark.

Maris drove a 1-0 fastball in the fourth inning deep into the right-field stands for his fifth home run of the 1968 season. It was his final big league home run, the 275th of his 12-year career, a productive average of 23 home runs a year over those dozen years. Babe Ruth averaged 32 home runs a year over his 22 seasons.

In the World Series, the Cardinals were ahead 3-1 in games and 3-2 in the fifth game when Lou Brock doubled with one out. Julian Javier followed with a line single to left field. Left fielder Willie Horton fielded the ball quickly and fired a strike to home plate. Brock, deciding not to slide, came in standing up and was tagged out. The Tigers rallied to win the game, won again the next day after an off day to tie the Series and, with Lolich pitching his third victory, won the seventh game and the Series 4-1.

With two out and nobody on in that seventh game, the Tigers leading 3-0, Roger Maris faced the crafty Lolich, a veteran left-hander who would win 217 big league games. Lolich threw a soft curve ball in addition to a hard slider and fastball. Maris had gone out twice against him and, with his club behind, wanted to ignite a rally. Lolich quickly got ahead 1-2 on the count and threw a changeup curve. Maris swung, hit the ball off the end of his bat, and popped a lazy, short fly behind shortstop. Detroit shortstop Mickey Stanley caught the ball for the final out of the inning, the final at-bat in the big league playing career of Roger Maris. The Tigers won the game and the Series, and their clubhouse was a wild champagne-swirling scene. In the Cardinal clubhouse it was quiet. Bob Gibson talked grumpily about his losing effort. Curt Flood described a new art gallery he expected to open soon. Mike Shannon bit down hard on a piece of fried chicken. Tim McCarver said it was just a thrill being in three World Series in five years. Lou Brock said he didn't think his no-slide in the fifth game really cost the Cardinals the Series.

On the far right side of the St. Louis clubhouse, Roger Maris sat in his underwear, a can of Budweiser beer in his hand, a soft smile on his lips. A couple of out-of-town sportswriters came over to say goodbye. He nodded his thanks and looked up when I walked over to him.

"Don't go ripping the Yankees again," he said.

"They aren't good enought to rip," I said.

The Yankees had finished their fourth straight season in the second division under Ralph Houk. Maris had kept tabs on them. He always said he didn't concern himself about the Yankees after he went to St. Louis, but in this small way he had.

I wished Roger well, he wished me well, and I circled around the Cardinal clubhouse looking for other St. Louis players to talk to about the losing Series. On the flight back from St. Louis I kept thinking about what I would write the next day in the *Post* about the Cardinals. They would obviously be strong again in 1969 and contenders for the National League pennant. The Cubs and the Giants would be contenders. The Mets had finished ninth in a ten-team league under new manager Gil Hodges, and I figured a move to eighth would be their best in 1969. It was the Cardinals I thought about for the moment. They would be Gibson, Brock, McCarver, Flood, and Shannon again in 1969, all those wonderful players who had helped them win two pennants in a row. Only Maris would be gone. I thought about that fact as I framed the story in my mind. I kept seeing Roger Maris at bat in Baltimore in game 154 in 1961.

Roger accepts 1962 World Series ring from Commissioner Ford Frick, the man who created so much mistaken controversy with his "asterisk" ruling. Yankee owners Del Webb and Dan Topping, who gave Roger nothing for his historic feat, look on. *Credit: Bob Olen.*

Roger recovers from a hand operation at his Independence home in 1965 with Pat, holding their baby daughter, Sandra, and, left to right, Richard, Susan, Roger, Kevin and Randy. *Credit: NY Yankees.*

Roger and Pat enjoy a relaxing weekend at New York's Grossinger Hotel in 1965. *Credit: NY Yankees.*

Finally at peace with his past, Roger returns to Yankee Stadium for 1984 ceremonies honoring him. Also shown: Yankee outfielder Bobby Murcer and author Maury Allen. *Credit: Lou Requena.*

# 12

## so long, roger

**THERE** had been several possibilities, a couple up north, a couple out west, but Roger Maris told Gussie Busch he would like to have the beer distributorship in Gainesville, Florida. Maris converted an old warehouse near the Gainesville airport into his offices. Soon, with his brother Rudy, Roger was running the Maris Distributing Company, an outlet for the sale of Anheuser-Busch beer throughout central Florida. He would drive through central Florida, visit taverns, supermarkets and restaurants, check on their Budweiser stock, talk a little baseball, talk a little golf— and sell a lot of beer. Like all good beer salesmen, Maris also had to use the product. When he showed up for a visit at spring training in March of 1969, he had added some twenty pounds to his already overblown playing weight.

Maris bought a home at the edge of Gainesville, stayed home most of the time when he wasn't in the office or traveling, played a lot of golf with his sons and showed no withdrawal signs from baseball. His health was less than perfect. He had suffered from Bell's Palsy, a nerve ailment, in his final year with the Cardinals, with some lingering affects from the drooping eyelid and facial paralysis he had suffered. His knees bothered him, especially when he accidentally banged them against a chair or a wall; his rib cage was always tender from so much body contact around second base, forcing him to sleep on his back; and his right hand would never be strong again. His ring finger on that hand was still immobile from the 1965 injury.

He appeared at the Cardinal spring camp in St. Petersburg in 1970 and 1971. He was gracious when reporters chatted with him, but he gave no in-depth interviews. He wanted to be ignored by the press and he managed to chat casually with his former teammates out of the range of reporters' hearing.

On October 1, 1971, ten years to the day of his 61st homer, an interview with Maris appeared in the New York Times. He went over familiar ground.

"Look, I never made up any schedule," he said. "Do you know any other records that have been broken since the 162-game schedule that have an asterisk? I don't. Frick should have said that all records made during the new schedule would have an asterisk, and he should have said that before the season—if he should have said it at all."

The asterisk had never been there, but Maris knew that—symbolically, if not in fact—it had tainted his record.

"When they say 154 games, what 154 games are they talking about? The first 154, the middle 154 or the last 154? If it is the first 154, I'd still have tied the Ruth record because I didn't hit my first homer until the eleventh game that year. If it was the middle or the last 154, I'd have broken the record anyway. A lot of people didn't want me to break Ruth's record at all, especially older people.

They tried to make me into the mold of Babe Ruth, and I didn't want to fit anyone's mold. I'm Roger Maris."

Maris had one more significant thing to say as he put some of his feelings about that season on the record.

"The Yankees always favored Mickey to break the record. I was never the fair-haired boy over there. When I got hurt they thought I could still play. When Mickey or Tom Tresh got hurt, they'd let 'em rest."

Roger was asked if there were any ballplayers among his children. Roger Jr. and Kevin had played in the Gainesville Little League.

"I didn't do anything to encourage them and I didn't do anything to stop them. They didn't ask for my help and so I didn't do nothin' with either one. Better they played the way they wanted to," he said.

He was asked if he planned to celebrate his anniversary of that home run. "I'll just go home and have a beer," he said.

In 1973 Hank Aaron was driving on Babe Ruth's career home run record of 714. There was no time limit and no talk of asterisk, but the pressures were heavy on the Braves slugger. I called Maris at his office in Gainesville. We had last talked a few weeks earlier that spring at the Cardinals camp.

"There's some pressure but not very much. If he doesn't get it this year, he'll get it next year," Maris said.

Aaron ended the 1973 season with 713 homers. He hit one in Cincinnati to tie Ruth at 714 on Opening Day of the 1974 season and, after a controversy about sitting out the next game, he returned to hit one more in Atlanta off Al Downing for 715 and a new mark. It was exciting, but it was not quite the same as hitting 61 in 1961, or 59 in 154 games that year.

There had been another major development in baseball that year of 1973 that would have significant bearing on Maris. On January 3, 1973, a limited partnership led by a Cleveland shipping industrialist named George M. Steinbrenner III ("There is nothing so limited as being a limited partner of George Steinbrenner," John McMullen, an original partner and now owner of the Houston Astros, would later say) purchased the New York Yankees. By the end of 1973 Ralph Houk, Lee MacPhail and Bob Fishel had all left the Yankees. Michael Burke, who had put the purchase package together, had been bought out. Maris knew none of the new owners.

Steinbrenner, active politically in Ohio, would soon be entangled in the mushrooming Watergate scandal. President Richard Nixon would be forced to resign his office in August of 1974. Earlier that year, on April 5, Steinbrenner had been indicted on felony charges of illegal campaign contributions to Nixon's reelection campaign. He was fined $15,000 after a guilty plea. On November 27, 1974, after a long investigation, Steinbrenner was suspended from baseball by Commissioner Bowie Kuhn for two years. Kuhn commuted the sentence to eighteen months, and the Yankee owner was reinstated on March 1, 1976, just in time to participate in and enjoy the 1976 season, which brought the Yankees their first pennant since 1964.

Steinbrenner's Company, American Shipbuilding, had always been located in Cleveland. His father and grandfather had been in the shipping business there. Citing a change in shipping habits, but anxious to escape the storm of investigation around Cleveland, Steinbrenner moved his company headquarters in 1976 to Tampa, Florida. He became active in charity work there. He underwrote many college scholarships for needy students. He sent his own children to college in Florida. He participated in fund-raising programs for several Florida universities. He decided to bring his Yankee team to the University of Florida campus in Gainesville in 1977 for an exhibition game. Traveling secretary Bill Kane made the arrangements.

**BILL KANE** has been a Yankee statistician and radio producer and is now the Yankees traveling secretary. He joined the team out of St. Bonaventure University in 1961 after writing letters to all eighteen teams in baseball that year.

**KANE:** "I was working in the broadcast booth all of 1961 with Mel Allen and Phil Rizzuto. I had all the stats on home runs ready every day. I remember sitting in the clubhouse one day late in the season with Roger and Pete Sheehy. I asked Pete, 'What was it like when Ruth hit his 60?' Pete had been there and he said, 'No fuss. Nothing like this. When he hit 60, the guys came over quietly and shook his hand, and the Babe said he would probably hit 70 the next year. I don't remember a reporter in the clubhouse.'

"I always got along good with Roger. After he quit he would show up at Fort Lauderdale where we were training, and he would sit around and have a couple of beers at night. He was calling on beer accounts in the area and he would jump over to see some of the guys. He had never been back to an old timers game and I said, 'Roger, why don't you come back?' I knew they had written him letters inviting him, but he had never answered them. 'They'll boo me if I do.' I told him they wouldn't. He said he would think about it.

"Anyway, in 1977 we're playing that exhibition game in Gainesville and we needed some beer in the clubhouse, and I figured I might as well get it from Roger as from anybody. He sent a few cases over and came inside to say hello. I told him we had a big luncheon that day given by the school and he was certainly invited. I told him George Steinbrenner was going to be there and would be anxious to meet him. George had always talked about Yankee tradition and the great stars like Mickey and Joe D and Whitey and Roger. He had never met Roger, and he said he had hoped Roger would come back. Billy Martin was the manager, and he and Mickey were very close, and I think they had played golf with Roger that spring. Anyway, they knew each other, and Billy asked Roger to come back. He said he would think about it. Finally, at the luncheon, George comes in and Roger, who had decided to stay after Billy asked him, was sitting there. I went up to George and asked him if he would like to meet Roger, and he said he would very much like to meet him. I brought Roger over, they shook hands and George asked him about the beer business. Roger was having trouble with some of the help, and I think George and Roger talked for thirty minutes about employee relations.

"Roger didn't come back that year, but the next season George called him personally on the phone and asked him to come to Old Timers Day and he did. He really enjoyed it, too."

Roger Maris flew unannounced into New York for the first time in ten years on April 12, 1978. The Yankees had won the World Series in 1977 for the first time in fifteen years, and would be raising the Championship flag opening day. Steinbrenner had arranged for the M and M Boys to be there again. Maris came to town the night before the opener and had dinner with Julie Isaacson. He told his friend he was doing it because Steinbrenner had been so nice to him, but he was still concerned about the reaction of the fans.

"You worried they may boo you?" Isaacson asked.

"They might, but what the hell, if they do, they do," he said.

There were 44,667 people in the stands that next chilly April afternoon. Mel Allen was handling the ceremonies. A grainy film on the Stadium video screen in center field showed Tracy Stallard throwing a pitch and Roger Maris hitting it, running around the bases, halting at the dugout steps, waving, smiling, laughing on that October 1, 1961. Maris, walking slowly as if to enjoy each instant again on that field, moved toward home plate. He was dressed in a light tan suit, a white shirt, a dark tie, and polished black shoes. He was heavier than he had been as a player, of course, but the crewcut gave him away. The fans around home plate spotted him coming towards them, recognized that burr cut and began howling his name, "Roger, Roger," and the applause quickly swept across the Stadium, louder, louder and louder still, as rousing a sound as ever had been directed at Maris. It had been sporadic after home run number 60 and intense after number 61, but that had seemed more like a show by the fans for their own part in history. This day it was warm. He waved to the crowd and seemed happy and at ease, a deep smile creasing his face, his eyes moving from side to side around the park as he rotated his body to wave at all the noisemakers. In some few minutes the Championship flag had been raised by the M and M Boys, and now Maris, more of an attraction to the press than the ever-present Mantle, sat in the publicity director's office behind the press box and talked with a handful of reporters. He was asked if he was surprised at the warmth and depth of the greeting.

"No, I expected it," he said. "It's like obituaries. When you die they always give you good reviews."

Linked again in a public moment, as they had been so many times as players, Mantle and Maris sat in the press room later sharing some reverie. They seemed friendly and completely at ease with each other.

"I asked Roger if he got goose pimples," Mantle told me in a conspiratorial tone, "and he finally admitted he did. I didn't feel the same. I've been here before."

"I didn't get the goose pimples for nothing," Maris said. "I've never been in a situation where people cheered for me like that. It was nice."

Some seventeen years after that summer of '61, the slate seemed wiped clean. The fans—even if they were not the same ones as in 1961—had forgiven Maris for not being Mantle, for driving Ruth from his lofty heights, for not showing more public joy, for surliness under stress, for an obscene finger, for fighting back when he felt he had been abused. On this day, as it should have been in 1961, they cared only that this man had electrified baseball, performed a heroic feat, slugged more homers in one season than any man who ever lived, did it with determination, grace and pride. He had talked that summer, openly and honestly, and some of his words stung. Now the years had softened all the jagged edges on his side and theirs.

Ten years after each of them had last played, with salaries being made in one season almost equal to what they had made in their entire careers, Mantle was asked to compare the present with the past in that respect.

"I felt tension at times. I was making $100,000," Mantle said, "and some guy let me feel he wasn't being treated fairly because he was only making $30,000. There's always pressure, then and now."

"I played on five pennant winners after 1961," Maris said. "I never got another raise after that year."

The years following were easier for Maris. He would appear at a Cardinals old timers day as well as one in Atlanta with Hank Aaron, to celebrate the two men who topped the Babe. He actually played an inning or so a couple of times in the Cracker Jack Old Timers Game in Washington. He gave phone interviews easily when somebody would have 25, 30 or 35 home runs in mid-season. He continued showing up at spring training every so often, had a beer with old buddies, talked easily with teammates, and even awed young reporters by being so approachable for interviews. He was not the ogre they had heard about.

By the early 1980s, he had even let his hair grow out one year and talked kiddingly about why he did it. "I'm trying to look like one of those long-haired kids," he said. He soon found out it wasn't him, and he reverted to a crewcut soon again. He even visited Fargo a couple of times for banquets honoring him, especially on the twentieth anniversary of his 1961 feat, and was inducted into a club of crewcut men as well as North Dakota American Legion baseball honorees.

The business was very successful, and by 1983 Roger no longer needed to call on customers. He had salesmen fanning out across the county and he stayed in Gainesville to handle the business end of the company. He would work hard three or four days a week, take one weekday off in addition to weekends, have lunch with local golfing friends, play a round with Roger Jr. and Kevin, who had now developed into wonderful golfers and good friends, enjoy the birth of his first grandson, relax with visits from old baseball friends, talk often on the phone with Mike

Shannon, Mickey Mantle, Whitey Herzog, Bob Cerv, Julie Isaacson and others. It was a pleasant time.

Late that fall, around Thanksgiving, Maris began experiencing severe headaches. He treated the headaches casually, deciding that he may have been working too hard or that his eyes were giving him trouble as he approached the age of fifty. The headaches persisted. He had been bothered with asthma for some time and now found he had trouble breathing on too many occasions. He took more medicine. Then he noticed the small lumps in the back of his neck. He thought they were from nerves. Soon they grew larger. More lumps showed under his armpits and in his groin area. He visited a local doctor. Tests were made. He waited for the results patiently, went to work each day—and finally got the news. Cancer. Doctors had diagnosed his ailment as lymphoma, cancer of the lymph glands. The lymphatic system is an alternate channel for movement of bodily fluids. These fluids flow into glands throughout the body. The cells in these glands swell when antigens (foreign substances) attack them, and the body attempts to respond to this invasion with naturally manufactured antibodies. If unchecked and uncontrolled, these antigens multiply, cause infection and, eventually, death. Lymphoma is not considered one of the most virulent of cancers and, if checked early, has a high rate of survival. Maris was told his survival chances were quite good. After Maris discussed it with his family, Mike Shannon was the first person to be told. "My doctor told me I have been walking around with it for about five years," Maris told his friend.

Chemotherapy was begun immediately. Maris had good days and bad days. He never complained. He continued working. At times he was too nauseous to talk on the phone. He spent a good deal of time at his home on the lake. Mantle, Shannon, Billy Martin, Steinbrenner, Moose Skowron all called. Steinbrenner, who had learned of Roger's ailment early in 1984, told his friend Howard Cosell about it.

Cosell called Maris and persuaded him to go on the air, make his ailment public, and possibly help others who had hesitated about seeking early medical help. Maris agreed. Steinbrenner told Cosell he had a surprise for Maris. When Cosell did a touching ABC interview with Maris on "Sports Beat," he revealed to the ailing star that his uniform number 9 would be retired in splendid Stadium ceremonies. Maris responded with a choked voice. The man who had never shown much public sensitivity was now tearfully disbelieving of such a high baseball honor.

On July 21, 1984, with many of his old Yankee teammates on hand, Maris was honored at the Stadium. The man who had never received a special day as a Yankee was now being immortalized in the Yankee Memorial Park behind the center-field fence at the Stadium, along with his late teammate Elston Howard. His plaque would join those for Miller Huggins, Lou Gehrig, Babe Ruth, Jake Ruppert, Ed Barrow, Joe DiMaggio, Mickey Mantle, Joe McCarthy, Casey Stengel, ill-fated Thurman Munson (victim of a private plane air crash at the age of 32), and teammate Howard.

Friends from as far away as Fargo had journeyed to the Stadium that day to be with him. Many of them were brought to tears when Maris thanked them for their presence on this important day. The plaque read: ROGER EUGENE MARIS AGAINST ALL ODDS IN 1961 HE BECAME THE ONLY PLAYER TO HIT MORE THAN 60 HOME RUNS IN A SINGLE SEASON IN BELATED RECOGNI-

TION OF ONE OF BASEBALL'S GREATEST ACHIEVE-
MENTS EVER HIS 61 IN '61 THE YANKEES SALUTE HIM
AS A GREAT PLAYER AND AUTHOR OF ONE OF THE
MOST REMARKABLE CHAPTERS IN THE HISTORY OF
MAJOR LEAGUE BASEBALL ERECTED BY NEW YORK
YANKEES JULY 21, 1984.

His entire family attended and most were teary when
the plaque was being read aloud to the jammed Stadium
crowd. His old teammates stood around him and applauded, and the opposing players looked out from the
dugout in wonderment at a man who had actually hit 61
home runs in a single season.

Treatment continued through the summer of 1984. The
cancer showed signs of remission, but when I called Julie
Isaacson late in 1984 to ask how Maris was doing, he
replied, "Not so good."

Spring training approached. I would soon be leaving
for Florida and I called Isaacson again. I asked how Maris
was. He said he was about the same. I told him I'd like
to talk to Roger while I was in Florida. There had been
small items in the press about him after his interview
with Cosell and his Stadium appearance the previous
summer. Isaacson called Maris and Roger agreed to see
me in his office in Gainesville.

The Maris Distributing Company building in Gainesville, just a good outfield peg from the Gainesville airport,
is an unpretentious, functional office building and beer
storage facility. Trucks were loading at the side of the
building as a cab dropped me off. I told the receptionist
I was here to see Roger Maris and I waited for a couple
of minutes before she ushered me in, past a couple of
busy-looking people and into a back office. Maris stood

at the door. He looked well, about much the same as he had when I had last seen him that previous July. He wore a sports shirt open at the collar, dark trousers and cowboy boots. We shook hands, he ushered me to a large, comfortable leather chair, and he walked behind his enormous desk and sat down.

"I just got off the phone with Shannon," he said. "He told me the only reason you want to see me now is to talk about the twenty-fifth anniversary of the home run year in case I died before next year."

I smiled weakly and shook my head. "It's the twenty-fifth anniversary of your 1960 arrival in New York as a Yankee," I said. Maris smiled. He didn't believe that, either.

The wall behind his desk was filled with marvelous old photos of Roger with Mantle, Ted Williams, Rocky Colavito, Harmon Killebrew and with Presidents Truman, Kennedy, Ford and Reagan. There was a blownup listing of his 1961 home run hit parade and some scrolls, some crossed bats and a few certificates of baseball honors, a picturesque diary of the career of the old ballplayer.

We talked first of his health. "I'm prepared for whatever happens," he said.

He described his treatment in detail, the pills that made him nauseous, the four shots he was taking every three weeks, the diet and the blood tests. "I'm tired a good part of the time," he said.

We had talked a half hour when the phone rang. It was Mantle calling from Dallas. The M and M Boys exchanged a few obscenities, and Mickey told Roger he was going to be in Florida soon and expected to play golf with him. He then talked about a cruise he was going on later that summer, saying that he expected Roger and Pat to join him and Merlyn for some good times. "I'd like that," Roger said. Then Mickey asked to talk to me by identifying me with his favorite two-word obscenity and that loud, contagious laugh of his. "Don't you go ripping him," Mantle laughed. "I'll come up there and kick your ass." I told him only young reporters do that to young players now, and none of us were young any more. Then he told me an obscene joke, promised he would see me at the Yankee spring camp at Fort Lauderdale and hung up.

"He's been calling almost every day," Maris said.

We talked a bit about Mickey, and Roger said one of his 1961 motivations was beating out Mantle for home run honors. "In 1960 I hit 39 homers and was MVP. Mickey beat me out for the home run title with 40, by getting two off Chuck Stobbs the final week. I didn't want that to happen again." He then made the statement about Mantle being the New York Yankees, no matter what he, Maris, did. It was said with no anger. It was simply a fact. It was vintage Maris, brutally honest, without any softening of the truth. It had caused him problems all his career. At the age of fifty, fighting terminal cancer, he could still react no other way.

We talked for another two hours and he finally said, "If I had to do it all over again I wouldn't change a thing. There were some problems, but I'm proud of my baseball career."

It was nearly two o'clock, and I asked Roger if I could buy him lunch. We walked out of his office into an adjoining office. He introduced me to his brother Rudy—I had last seen him in Detroit in 1961—and to his oldest daughter, Susan, working as an executive in the company. We chatted for a couple of minutes about the current Yankees and walked outside in the warm Florida afternoon. Roger opened the doors of his red Mercedes and drove me through the college town, pointing out the sights, talking easily, telling me about the beer business, reminiscing a bit about old baseball friends who had gone on to executive jobs. We stopped at a small neighborhood delicatessen across from one of the University buildings. The place was filled with college kids. They made no signs of recognition of the crewcut businessman and the white-haired reporter. There was a picture of Maris hitting his 60th homer on the wall of the delicatessen, and the owner greeted him with a quick hello by name. "The sandwiches are real good here," he said. We each ordered a sandwich and a soda and Maris wouldn't allow me to pay.

We talked about the current Yankees, about Yogi's chances of lasting out the season, about whether I thought Billy would ever manage again, about young Don Mattingly, about Ron Guidry, about the chances of another New York pennant. Then we left, and Maris drove me back to the airport so I could catch my flight to Fort Lauderdale. His handshake was strong, and we parted as friends.

George Steinbrenner, who had so much to do with allowing Maris to smell the roses at last, had invited him back to the Stadium again. Maris was to recieve the Lou Gehrig Pride of the Yankees award at the team's welcome home dinner, and would stay over the next day to participate in opening day ceremonies.

Maris and Mantle were paired again that April day, and each received the expected standing ovation. Then Maris returned home to Gainesville.

"About a week after he got home from New York," Shannon says, "he really started feeling badly. I knew he was going downhill steadily after that."

In late May, he returned to New York privately to be

examined by a cancer expert, Dr. Ezra Greenson, at Mount Sinai Hospital in Manhattan. There was no marked improvement.

By late summer he had grown progressively weaker, stopped going to the office and spent most of his time at home or at the lake. He even began limiting his phone calls.

In early fall, growing weaker, spending more time resting, he no longer could deny the inevitable.

"He just started looking real sick around then," says his father. "One day I came over the house and he was cleaning up the leaves and sweating badly. 'Roger, you shouldn't be doing that.' He said. 'The doctor told me to exercise.' I couldn't argue with him. Around that time he started getting that swollen stomach. I told him he looked like Tony Galento. Every few days they were removing fluid from his body. One day they had to remove three liters. He was still taking treatment and he was sick most of the time. Roger never complained. He was feeling badly all the time the last few months, but let me tell you this: Roger never wanted to die."

In November he was referred to Dr. Robert Oldham, a noted oncologist who ran a clinic in Franklin, Tennessee, a 20,000-population suburb of Nashville, which specialized in biological therapy. Oldham had graduated from the University of Missouri in 1968 and had been involved in medical immunology and oncology since 1972. He had done notable work at the National Cancer Institute in Bethesda, Maryland.

"It was hard not to be aware of who he was when Mr. Maris was referred to us," says Dr. Oldham. "He was a fine gentleman with no façade. We have treated many prominent persons and have a high success rate when patients come to us early. We might have been more successful if we had been able to start the treatment earlier."

Observing the confidentiality of a patient-doctor relationship, the oncologist could not be specific about the treatment Maris received but did describe the general procedures followed in his clinic.

"In cases of lymphoma, some patients respond well to radiation and drugs. Some do not. In these types of cases we treat them more aggressively. We remove pieces of the tumor and inject that into laboratory mice. We create antibodies and then remove these antibodies from the mice and place them back into the patient by injection. Most of this treatment, to be successful, takes anywhere from nine months to a year," says Dr. Oldham.

"I knew that was pretty desperate treatment, getting injected with fluid from mice and rats," said his father, "but Roger was a pretty sick boy by then. They were trying everything. They would inject Roger with these fluids and then remove the lymph nodes to study them. It was pretty awful, but they hoped to put him in remission again."

When apprised that the normal length of the treatment was anywhere from nine months to a year, Maris asked, "If I'm gone before then, what happens?"

"Well," one of the clinic's doctors told him, "we would use it to try and help someone else."

"Do it," Maris said.

Dr. Oldham continued the treatment over a period of four weeks.

"I was told about the treatment later with the rats and mice," says Tony Kubek. "It was typical of Roger to do something that would help others."

This biological treatment, based on the creation of artificial antibodies, was combined with the more commonly used introduction of interferon, a natural substance produced by the body's immune system. There have been some notable successes.

"In Mr. Maris's case," says Dr. Oldham, "there just wasn't enough time for the full exploration of treatment."

When Dr. Oldham explained to the family that time was working against Maris, Roger was transferred to the M. D. Anderson Hospital and Tumor Institute in Houston. The facility, part of the University of Texas system, was opened in 1941 and turned its attention fully in 1954 to cancer treatment.

"They saved my son Billy's life," says Mantle. "He was really in bad shape with Hodgkin's disease [a cancerous lymph and blood disease similar to lymphoma] and he went there a couple of years ago. They gave him some experimental treatment, and it worked. He's fine now. I told Roger about it a long time back, and I wanted him to go there. He said he was under the care of a good doctor."

The entire family traveled with Roger to Houston. They knew the end was near. In San Diego, major league baseball people were completing their annual winter meetings. Maris was to undergo massive blood transfusions in Houston. Three of his four sons donated blood for their father. A fourth wept when told his blood was not compatible. In San Diego, blood donors were solicited. There were 28 pints of blood collected and sent immediately by air to Houston.

Yogi Berra, recently named a Houston coach, was in Houston. He drove to the hospital. He was denied admission to Roger's room. He left the hospital in tears.

"It tore me up not to be able to see him that one last time," says Berra. "I wanted to see him badly. They told me he was too sick."

By Friday, December 13, Maris was barely able to talk.

His family knew it would not be much longer.

"About the last thing he was able to say," says his father, "was that he wanted a radio in his room. They brought him a radio and they put on one of those country music stations. Roger wiggled his toes under that bedsheet to the music."

By nightfall he had lapsed into a coma. His family was at his bedside. At 1:45 P.M. on Saturday, December 14, 1985, the greatest single season home run hitter of all time died quietly.

# 13

## the last farewell

**ROGER MARIS** brought the Yankees together again. Whitey Ford heard the news from a newspaper reporter and called Mickey Mantle. He wept. Later Mantle would be interviewed on television and would say, "You always knew he was your friend. He was the kind of guy who would tell you so, just to make you feel better. Not enough people got to know him that way, that's all. What a great guy." Pat Maris called John Blanchard and Bill Skowron and Bobby Richardson. Tony Kubek was notified in the Dominican Republic, Bob Allsion heard the news on television, and Whitey Herzog was notified by the Cardinals while skiing in Colorado.

Shakespeare wrote in Julius Caesar, "The evil that men do lives after them, the good is oft interred with their bones." All of Roger Maris's obituaries were not good reviews. There were some vitriolic comments about the tensions of those Yankee days. The New York *Times* remembered an interview Maris gave after the 61st home run. "I was born surly," he said that day. "I'm going to stay that way. Everything in life is tough. Even the Yankee clubhouse attendants think I'm tough to live with. I guess they're right. I'm miffed most of the time regardless of how I'm doing. But regardless of my faults, I'll never take abuse from anybody—big or small, important or unimportant—if I think it is undeserved."

There was this in the *Times* obituary from Casey Stengel in 1960: "You ask Maris a question, and he stares at you for a week before he answers."

There were some good reviews. Especially from former teammates. "He tried to do something for the rest of the world and got involved in some experimental research," said Tony Kubek. "Perhaps they will save some other lives with the research they did on Roger." Pat Maris, strong in her husband's death as she had been through their life together, said, "Roger died the way he lived. Strong, private and doing what he thought was right. He was at peace with himself and his God."

Funeral services were set for Fargo. Maris had purchased a cemetery plot during a 1984 visit on a soft, gentle site overlooking a hill in Holy Cross Cemetery. "There was never any question about Fargo," said Pat Maris. "This is our home and these are our people. We moved away in 1957, but our hearts were always here."

By Tuesday night, December 17, the old ballplayers and the old friends and the handsome family of Roger Maris had gathered at the Holiday Inn in Fargo. Pat Maris greeted each of them warmly when she ran into them in the lobby or in the coffee shop, surrounded always by her children and grandchildren and friends. The sons, all handsome young men, played blackjack in the hotel lounge as their sisters and girl friends watched. They asked me things about their father's youth, things they never could have seen—a home run off Jack Fisher and Tracy Stallard, a throw I remembered, a catch I could still describe against the right-field wall. Kevin Maris asked, "Will my father get in the Hall of Fame?" I could only say I had always voted for him and maybe now enough others also would, too.

Wednesday afternoon, with more players arriving in town, the family collected in the hotel lobby. Julie Isaacson, a good soldier always, accompanied them as they went off to Saint Mary's Cathedral to view Roger's casket alone and to see that all was in readiness for the public visitation that night.

Don Gooselaw, handling almost everything with skill and poise, offered me a ride to the airport in his van to welcome Mantle and Ford into town. They had flown to Fargo from Fort Lauderdale. Gooselaw had taken off work all this week to devote himself completely to the Maris funeral. He remembered driving his van to the airport the previous summer to pick up Ford and Mantle for the Maris golf tournament. "I just love to listen to those guys. I remember when Roger was playing and I visited him in Minnesota, and we went out to dinner with Mickey and Whitey. I was one of them. What a thrill that was," he said.

The small airport was crowded as we awaited the plane carrying the two Hall of Fame teammates of Roger Maris. Television cameras were set up in the lobby. Several reporters were on hand. The plane landed and the passengers came through the gate. Finally, there was Mantle, wearing a black leather jacket, a cowboy shirt, a string tie, and cowboy boots. He asked me how cold it was. I told him it was seventeen degrees below zero the night before. He let out a long obscenity. "You got a drink in your van?" he asked Gooselaw.

Mantle, Ford, and Moose Skowron, who was on the same plane from Chicago, were together again now in the van, telling old stories, laughing about summers past, forgetting the real reason they had gathered in this frozen country in December. It was a happy ride to the hotel.

At seven o'clock cars were gathered outside the hotel entrance to take the old players to Saint Mary's. A public visitation had been scheduled. Friends, classmates, townfolk, strangers gathered at the red brick church in the central part of Fargo as a light snow continued to fall. Mantle, Ford, Skowron, Clete Boyer, John Blanchard and the rest hustled into the church and sat quietly. To their right, on a small wooden platform, the casket containing the body of Roger Maris lay opened. "I can't look," said Boyer. "That isn't Roger." Bishop James S. Sullivan conducted the service. He delivered a prayer, intoned some words to his God, and soon was calling on friends to reminisce informally about Maris. Classmates, his high school football coach, local friends, casual acquaintances—all addressed the assemblage in the crowded church. No ballplayer moved forward. There was silence between some touching reminiscences. Mantle sat with his head down. The crowd had expected a teammate. Boyer was rising, finally, from his seat. His voice was choked as he said, "My name is Clete Boyer. I was a teammate of Roger's." He spoke warmly, eloquently about his friend, making the audience smile and even giggle once as he talked of Roger's large appetite. Then he sat down. "That was the most nervous I had ever been in my life," he said later. "I knew one of us had to talk."

It was over for now, and the old players moved down the aisle toward waiting cabs. Bob Cerv greeted Ford and Blanchard kidded with Skowron and Ryne Duren said hello to Julie Isaacson. "It was nice, wasn't it?" Isaacson

said. "Raj would have liked it, especially the singing."
The lilting refrain of "On Eagles Wings"—"and He will
raise you up on eagle's wings, bear you on the breath of
dawn, make you shine like the sun, and hold you in the
palm of His hand"—had touched the congregation.

Now the old players had collected, as they so often do,
in the private hotel lounge. They bought drinks and
laughed and told old stories.

"I didn't finish the year in 1961 with the Yankees because I got in trouble," Duren was reminding his old mates.
"I was a drunk then [he is a recovering alcoholic who runs
a Wisconsin rehabilitation clinic] and we were on this
flight to Los Angeles. The stewardess bent over to hand
me a drink and I pinched her right breast, I remember it
was the right one, and she screamed. Two weeks later I
was gone."

The old players laughed, and Blanchard started telling
a story right away that seemed to fit in perfectly.

"That was the year I started using two falsies," laughed
the old catcher, a John Wayne lookalike with the macho
scar on his cheek. "Jim Hegan, our bullpen coach, used
to have his wife go out and buy falsies for the catchers—
two for me, two for Elston and two for Yogi. They were
great as sponges for a guy's fastball. Rhino [Duren], here,
was the only pitcher I ever caught that made me wear my
two falsies at the same time."

It went that way for a couple of hours as the drinks
continued. They talked and they laughed and they drank
together. There was no sadness.

They were lined up now, at noon on Thursday, on the
steps of Saint Mary's Cathedral, standing as they often did
at stadiums across America. Their faces seemed drawn
and the lines so much deeper. There were twelve of them—

seven old ballplayers, Mantle, Ford, Shannon, Skowron, Boyer, Herzog and Allison, and five old friends, George Surprise, Julie Isaacson, Dick Savageau, Robert Wood and Don Gooselaw, escorting Roger Maris to his last hurrah as honored pallbearers.

The church was filled to its 500-seat capacity and more people stood along the side walls, under the glistening stained-glass windows. Still more stood shoulder to shoulder in the church basement listening to the service on closed-circuit television.

"It is one thing to come here for a golf tournament in the summertime when everything is lush and green," said the Rev. John E. Moore. "It is another to come at this time of year and brave the elements. It shows how much you cared for Roger."

The old Yankees, all of them having shared that summer of '61, sat with heads bowed, locked in their private thoughts as the moving service for Maris continued in the state's largest Catholic church.

Roger Maris, Jr., the first son, read from the scriptures and then said, "Though the just may die early, he should be at rest."

James Carvell, Pat Maris's brother, also read from the scriptures, Michael Joncas reprieved "On Eagles Wings," and Rev. Moore delivered the homily. A young niece, Tasha Carvell, and young grandson Steven Maris were gift bearers, and Rev. Moore proclaimed, "When we eat this bread and drink this cup, we proclaim your death, Lord Jesus, until you come in glory."

Bobby Richardson, always the most religious and most respected of Yankees, arose from his seat to deliver the eulogy. He talked of the baseball feats of Roger and then spoke of his humility. "He visited me in South Carolina a few years back," Richardson said, "and my son was playing in an American Legion game. A line drive was hit right to him and it went right through him. 'He's been watching me too much.' Roger said. I think some of his problems started with the press. That might keep Roger from the Hall of Fame. Roger is in God's Hall of Fame. In life, the honors are soon forgotten. God's Hall of Fame is for eternity."

Young Roger responded. "His number one priority was to live and see that he could give as much love as possible to his family and friends."

There was a communion reflection and then the recessional before the casket was wheeled down the aisle of the church. Pat Maris, stoic on the arms of two of her sons, followed close by the casket. The pallbearers, without coats in that bitter cold, lifted the casket containing the remains of their fallen teammate to a waiting hearse.

The cars collected now and drove north to the cemetery. The prayer service was gentle and quick and the players once again walked back to the waiting cars.

They were scattering back to their own lives now, and when Bobby Richardson sat on that flight from Fargo to Minneapolis, where he would change planes for the trip south, he talked about his teammates. "Mickey said I did such a good job with Roger he wanted to sign me up for his funeral," said Richardson. The old Yankee second baseman, portly now, smiled as he remembered a day some twenty years ago. "I was retiring from baseball, and all the players on the Yankees chipped in to give me a beautiful, wooden gun case for my hunting weapons at my home in South Carolina," Richardson said. "I got one private gift from one player. It was a gold watch. I'm wearing it right now. It was from Roger Maris."

*  *  *

New York was aglow with Christmas. Fifth Avenue was filled with shoppers. It was December 23, 1985, and St. Patrick's Cathedral bustled with holiday worshipers. It was here, at 1:00 P.M. that day, that the people of the city of New York said farewell to Roger Maris.

President Richard Nixon, an inveterate baseball fan, sat in a front row seat next to New York City Mayor Edward Koch, limousine magnate Bill Fugazy, and Yankee owner George Steinbrenner, the man who had done so much for Maris in his last years. Baseball Commissioner Peter Ueberroth sat next to American League president Bobby Brown, the former Yankee. Behind them sat Bob Fishel, who had journeyed to Fargo and now was here again at St. Patrick's. There were other old Yankees—Jim Bouton, Phil Linz, Yogi Berra, Sparky Lyle, Joe Collins—and other baseball players: Ralph Branca (often also described as the man who...his description ends with the name of Bobby Thomson), Eddie Lopat, Neil Allen and Phil Rizzuto. Other members of the New York establishment included former Mayor Abe Beame, former Governor Hugh Carey, police commissioner Ben Ward, politician Stanley Steingut, former commissioner Bowie Kuhn, and more than 2,500 others crowded into the grand old church.

The program cover showed a young Roger Maris, blond and smiling in his Yankee uniform, during a spring training scene, with the number 9 and the NY logo of the Yankees broken by Yankee pinstripes. Roger Maris 1934-1985. On the back of the program was the memorial plaque created a little more than a year earlier and resting forever on the Stadium wall.

Inside the program the familiar stanzas from Ecclesiastes 3:1-8 read, "For everything there is a season and a time for every matter under heaven; a time to be born

and a time to die; a time to plant, and a time to pluck up
what is planted; a time to kill, and a time to heal; a time
to break down, and a time to build up; a time to weep,
and a time to laugh; a time to mourn and a time to dance,
a time to cast away stones together; a time to embrace and
a time to refrain from embracing; a time to seek and a
time to lose; a time to keep and a time to cast away; a
time to rend and time to sow; a time to keep silence and
a time to speak; a time to love, and a time to hate; a time
for war, and a time for peace."

John Cardinal O'Connor, the leader of New York's Cath-
olics, celebrated the Mass for Maris and began by addressing Pat Maris, seated between her two oldest sons
at a front row seat on the right side of the church.

In his gentle, soft, clear voice Cardinal O'Connor told
Pat, "Mary was also a widow as she raised the young Jesus.
I recognize the pain you are feeling, all of you in the
family, especially at this holiday time of season. It may
be a white Christmas here or in North Dakota but it will
be a blue Christmas in your heart."

Cardinal O'Connor thanked the Maris family for allowing this service in New York, where young Maris sprung
to fame. Only Babe Ruth and Vince Lombardi, among
sports heroes, had been equally honored with a St. Patrick's Mass. He spoke for many when he told a story of
his own experience regarding the 1961 record.

"I had grown up in Philadelphia but my father was a
Babe Ruth fan. When Ruth died in 1948, the Yankees
played their scheduled game that day and my father was
very upset. He would not go to another Yankee game. He
said there would be no Yankees without the Babe. Even
worse than that, Roger broke the record.

"My father talked of the length of the season and the
lively ball, and I could not convince him otherwise. My

father was my father. I finally got him to go to a Yankee game and he saw the young Maris and he said, 'I must admit he sure does look like a fine, young fellow.' That was high praise indeed from my father," Cardinal O'Connor said.

Cardinal O'Connor smiled as he told the story, and continued in a warm, conversational tone. "We are grateful the Maris family is here, and we thank Mr. Steinbrenner and Mr. Cosell for arranging this. Howard assured me if I make any theological errors, he would correct me."

After the Cardinal spoke, Roger Maris, Jr. responded for the family, extolling the virtues of his father and accepting that he was now at rest with God.

Phil Rizzuto, who had saved one of his most exuberant "Holy cows" for the 61st home run, offered up a prayer and the children, Susan, Kevin, Randy, Richard and Sandra, participated in the offertory procession.

Opera star Robert Merrill, a Yankee fan, a Maris fan, a close friend of Steinbrenner, stood in a shallow light behind the rostrum and sang The Lord's Prayer.

Now it was time for Cosell to speak. As he walked forward, many in the crowd whispered. This was one of the most famous faces in America, a controversial man, but a distinguished citizen who always seemed present at the best of times and the worst of times in sports. He talked of Roger's "courage, integrity, character and principle—the perfect equation for guts." He described how thrilled Maris was in 1984, when told his number 9 Yankee uniform would be officially retired and that he would be part of the Yankee Memorial park.

The organist played and the cantor sang and Cardinal O'Connor moved forward once again to address the assemblage. He paused to look out over the crowd and then spoke softly of the departed baseball hero. "In closing,"

he said, "let us offer one last burst of applause for Roger
Maris." The noise, unusual at best in this house of God,
started slowly, timidly, with the gentle applause coming
from the first few rows. And then it grew louder and
louder and louder still, rolling in waves through the rows
of worshipers, a thunderous sound in the old church,
cracking against the windows and rushing back in inten-
sified volume. Pat Maris sat in her front row seat with her
hands clasped and her eyes fixed on the ground. The
children all stared straight ahead, lovingly, at the figure
of the Cardinal standing on the platform in front of them.
George Steinbrenner and Bill Fugazy and Ed Koch and
Richard Nixon applauded warmly. It engulfed all the people in the cavernous church, the old and the young, the
friends of Roger Maris and some of his foes, many who
knew him and most who never saw him, rolling on for
several minutes. It was as if, by this applause, the people
of New York were cleansing their own souls for errors of
the past, finally forgiving Roger Maris in death for the
effrontery he had committed in life—passing the beloved
Babe and beating the idolized Mickey in that summer of
1961.

As the noise finally abated, Cardinal O'Connor walked
from the platform to embrace Mrs. Maris. He patted the
head of young grandchild Steven. He shook hands with
each of the Maris children. The press, many of whom had
battled with Maris a quarter of a century earlier in clubhouses across America, now came forward to talk about
him with Steinbrenner, Cosell and Nixon. The former
President, at ease with the press a dozen years after Watergate, remembered evenings in the early 1960s he had
spent at Toots Shor's restaurant with Mantle and Maris
and Martin and Ford. He told how much he had admired
Maris and how he had cheered him on in 1961, a year he

experienced some of his own pain as a defeated Presidential candidate. He said he felt similarities between himself and Maris then, especially in their unfair treatment by the press and their supposed hard exterior. Then the former President, engulfed now by the media and urged to move on by security, began moving toward a side door. He was still talking as he walked slowly and, as he stood for an instant again in front of the first pew of the magnificent church, he said he remembered something he had once read from a philosopher in ancient times. "One must wait until the evening to see how splendid the day was."

It was as if, in death, Roger Maris had a day in New York more splendid than any he had ever experienced in life.

The family returned home to Gainesville for a sorrowful Christmas. They had been traveling from Franklin, Tennessee, to Houston to Fargo to New York for several weeks, and now they could resume their lives. Roger's brother Rudy returned to the business and plunged into the paperwork that had piled up these many weeks. The children knew it was time to move on with their lives and the young golfers, Roger Jr. and Kevin, would soon be out on the courses again in hopes of advancing their careers. The pain was most felt, of course, by Pat Maris who had stayed stoic in the face of all this anguish and now would be called upon to face her tasks as mother and grandmother and heir to the deeds of her husband.

There would be some tensions in the family, as there always is after so great a loss, and Roger's father, Rudy, would feel the loss of his son even more as he sat alone in his apartment in Florida.

"I wasn't even invited to the St. Patrick's event," he was

saying now some weeks later. "I don't know who was responsible for that. I wanted to be there. I should have been there. I just don't know why I wasn't asked."

In New York, George Steinbrenner was being congratulated for arranging such a noble event as the St. Patrick's service. Even that would not be without some controversy. Steinbrenner had fired his latest publicity director, Joe Safety, for failing to return from a California vacation to handle the press arrangements for the event. There never seemed anything involving Maris and the Yankees that would not lead to tensions.

Julie Isaacson had kept in touch with Pat in those weeks following the December events, and one day he said, "She's really down. She's having a tough time dealing with it. I don't think she'll ever get over it. How do you get over losing Roger Maris as a husband or a friend?"

# 14

# a place in history

EACH January there is a momentous day when the world of baseball pauses to look back at its history. In the Fiftieth anniversary year of the 1936 establishment of the Baseball Hall of Fame at Cooperstown, New York, the baseball writers of America elected one player, Willie McCovey, to the Hall of Fame. He had been a fine first baseman and a slugging left-handed hitter. Known as "Stretch" for his angular six-foot-four-inch reach, McCovey had smashed 521 home runs in twenty-two big league seasons with the San Francisco Giants, San Diego Padres and Oakland A's. He had never hit more than 45 home runs in any single season. It was a fact not lost on many sportswriters voting in this prestigious election. Roger Maris had hit 61 in 1961, and so many of the voters had agreed with Mickey Mantle's assertion that this was "the greatest single feat in sports history."

There had been some encouragement for the Maris family. Billy Williams had wound up four votes short for getting the needed 319 votes (or 75 per cent) of the ballots cast, with Catfish Hunter collecting 289 and Jim Bunning recording 279. Fifth in the voting with 177 votes, still some 142 away from the needed total for election, was the name of Roger Maris. Many sportswriters thought the Maris vote was a "sympathy" vote and predicted his vote total would slip back again in 1987. Others were convinced his true worth was finally being recognized and that Maris might still be included in the baseball shrine, his name welded into baseball history along with Mantle, Ford, Babe Ruth, Ted Williams, McCovey and the rest. Time would tell.

By March another spring training was moving forward again with young sluggers powering baseballs against the palm trees in Florida or sending them crashing against the cactus in Arizona. It was a rite of spring that had always captured the imagination of fans across the country as they studied those early baseball photographs of a new year or watched the television cameras record that ritual.

By April another championship baseball season would start and the public would be involved in that unexplainable, intense sensation of rooting for the home club, watching the Yankees fight to regain their spot on the top of the American League, or seeing the Mets challenge, or considering the possiblity of a repeat pennant for the Cardinals or the Royals.

There would certainly be some young slugger, Darryl Strawberry of the Mets perhaps or Don Mattingly of the Yankees, who would start the season going with a hot bat and have 15 or 20 or 25 homers early in June...and the name of Roger Maris would be in the sports pages again. As the sluggers faded, the Maris name would fade again unless some sportswriter paused to examine that spectacular season and see the numbers Maris recorded and relive that tension and that time.

"Every time somebody gets off hot," Maris once said, "a newspaper guy calls me and thinks he has a story about how easy hitting 60 or 61 was. I'm the only one who knows just how hard it was."

As the twenty-fifth anniversary of that feat approaches, it is certain no one on the current scene is capable of surpassing it—not Strawberry, not Mattingly, not any young slugger cracking baseballs over minor league fences at the moment. There is simply too much pressure, too much wear and tear on a young body, too many airplane rides, too many uncomfortable hotel beds, too many cold, late night meals.

"The two greatest feats in sports," says George Steinbrenner, "are the records of Joe DiMaggio and Roger Maris, hitting in 56 straight games and hitting 61 home runs."

On July 19, 1986, the teammates of Roger Maris will gather once again at Yankee Stadium—middle-aged men, some too heavy, many ailing, a few in financial trouble, too many of them admitting finally the pains of their lost youth—to reunite again for Old Timers Day. They will put on Yankee uniforms, look a bit garish in them, and parade out to the home plate area as their names are called and the attention focuses on them. It will be a celebration, a silver anniversary, of that 1961 season. And the man who made it possible will be missing. Current Yankees will wear black armbands in his memory.

The next morning many of them will board a plane at LaGuardia Airport for a flight to Minneapolis and then change planes for the last leg of that journey to Fargo. They will all play in the Roger Maris Memorial Golf tournament, and the funds raised will go for cancer research and to underwrite scholarships at Shanley High.

"Roger gave me that job, to keep the tournament going

and keep the guys coming out there," says Moose Sko-wron. "That's what I'll be doing. I'll be working with Pat on this and keep it going for Roger just like I promised him. It is a fun day, and that's how I will always think of Roger, as a guy I always had fun with."

Some seventy-two years after he first played a big league game, the name of Babe Ruth remains as recognizable and viable in American life as it did at its peak. His name is part of the language. A schoolboy will hit a long fly ball in a sandlot game, and a teammate will yell, "You think you're Babe Ruth, huh?" The name of Roger Maris is unlikely to enter the language.

It was hard to know Maris in life. It takes more study to appreciate him in death. For five seasons, 1960 through 1964, he was one of the most astounding players in the game, the most prolific home run hitter, a marvelous fielder, a skilled base runner, a man with a wonderful throwing arm, a winner. There were five Yankee pennants in his seven seasons in New York and two more in his two seasons in St. Louis—not a circumstantial coincidence.

The man had a hard shell but he also had a certain trait, uncommon in sports, uncommon in life: it was a devotion to honesty—brutal, unfeeling at times, but always necessary. Fame was bestowed on Roger Maris at the age of twenty-six, when he would have merely chosen success on the baseball field and quiet off it. He did not cope with it easily but, then again, he had very little help. He was thrown into a cauldron not of his own making—a cauldron in which the names of Ruth, Mantle and Frick swept over him like a roaring sea. The land he loved in North Dakota had toughened him and yet, he always seemed out of place, almost a foreigner in the hubbub of New York

City. His values were old-fashioned—hard work, dedication, love of family, pride, loyalty, grace—in a world that exploited pizzazz. In personality, he was colorless. In performance, he was thrilling. He could be passionate about the art of hitting a baseball and cantankerous about discussing it. He seemed closest, most comfortable, warmest, even funniest, with his trusted friends and tested teammates. He was loved by his family and grew to be appreciated by his fans.

Roger Maris would have mixed feelings about the public accolades that followed in the wake of his death, prideful in the attention his feats had finally earned, but somewhat bitter that the appreciation had come so many years after it mattered. Years from now, when some young slugger hits 40 or 45 or 50 home runs midway through a glorious baseball season, the deeds of Roger Maris will be reexamined. They will be considered remarkable until the worn clippings are brought out and his persona considered. There will be confusion, then, about the man who hit more home runs in one majestic season than anyone ever did before or is likely to again. Old teammates and old sportswriters will be sought out and, once again, the descriptions that Maris wore in his complex youth will be resurrected——"surly," "prickly," "abrasive."

Roger Maris never pretended to be anything other than what he was—a man who wanted nothing more than to excel at his chosen profession. He never asked to be famous. He only asked to be appreciated.

Then, 61 in '61——a feat unlike any other in the history of the game. Let them equal it if they can. There will only ever be one Roger Maris.

# Appendix

## ROGER MARIS'S CAREER PLAYING RECORD

Established major league records for most home runs, season
(61) (162-game season), 1961; combined with Mickey Mantle
to break Babe Ruth and Lou Gehrig's 1927 home run total of
115 in 1961. (112 in 154 decisions); longest doubleheader
with no chances offered (24 innings), August 6, 1961.

Tied major league mark for most home runs, six consecutive
games (7), August 11-12-13-13-15-16, 1961.

Established American League mark for most intentional bases
on ball in game (4), 12-inning game, May 22, 1962.

Tied American League standard for most home runs, doubleheader (4), July 25, 1961, hitting two in each game.

Led American League in slugging percentage with .581 in 1960;
led in total bases with 366 in 1961.

Named Most Valuable Player in American League, 1960–61.

Named Player of the Year by THE SPORTING NEWS, 1961.

Named "Sportsman of the Year" by SPORTS ILLUSTRATED,
1961.

Named "Man of the Year" by SPORT MAGAZINE, 1961.

Named as Outfielder on THE SPORTING NEWS' All-Star Major
League Team, 60–61.

Received American League Gold Glove for outfield play, 1960.

Winner of Hickok Belt as Top Professional Athlete of Year, 1961.

A.P. Professional Athlete of Year, 1961.

"Sultan of Swat" Award winner in 60–61.

Ranks 6th on the all-time Yankee slugging list (.515); 7th on the
Yanks all-time HR list (203); and 6th on all-time World Series
runs scored list (26).

## CAREER PLAYING RECORD (continued)

| YR | Club | AVG | G | AB | R | H | 2B | 3B | HR | RBI | BB | SO | SB |
|---|---|---|---|---|---|---|---|---|---|---|---|---|---|
| 1953 | Fargo-M'rhead | .325 | 114 | 418 | 74 | 136 | 18 | 13 | 9 | 80 | 76 | 62 | 14 |
| 1954 | Keokuk | .315 | 134 | 502 | 105 | 158 | 26 | 6 | 32 | 111 | 80 | 53 | 25 |
| 1955 | Tulsa | .233 | 25 | 90 | 9 | 21 | 1 | 0 | 1 | 9 | 15 | 18 | 2 |
| | Reading | .289 | 113 | 374 | 74 | 108 | 15 | 3 | 19 | 78 | 77 | 60 | 24 |
| 1956 | Indianapolis | .293 | 131 | 433 | 77 | 127 | 20 | 8 | 17 | 75 | 41 | 55 | 7 |
| 1957 | CLEVELAND | .235 | 116 | 358 | 61 | 84 | 9 | 5 | 14 | 60 | 60 | 79 | 4 |
| 1958 | CLEVELAND-a | .225 | 51 | 182 | 26 | 41 | 5 | 1 | 9 | 27 | 17 | 33 | 4 |
| | KANSAS CITY | .247 | 99 | 401 | 61 | 99 | 14 | 3 | 19 | 53 | 28 | 52 | 0 |
| | 1958 Totals | .240 | 150 | 583 | 87 | 140 | 19 | 4 | 28 | 80 | 45 | 85 | 4 |
| 1959 | KANSAS CITY-b | .273 | 122 | 433 | 69 | 118 | 21 | 7 | 16 | 72 | 58 | 53 | 2 |
| 1960 | YANKEES | .283 | 136 | 499 | 98 | 141 | 18 | 7 | 39 | 112* | 70 | 65 | 2 |
| 1961 | YANKEES | .269 | 161 | 590 | 132 | 159 | 16 | 4 | 61* | 142* | 94 | 67 | 0 |
| 1962 | YANKEES | .256 | 157 | 590 | 92 | 151 | 34 | 1 | 33 | 100 | 87 | 78 | 1 |
| 1963 | YANKEES | .269 | 90 | 312 | 53 | 84 | 14 | 1 | 23 | 53 | 35 | 40 | 1 |
| 1964 | YANKEES | .281 | 141 | 513 | 86 | 144 | 12 | 2 | 26 | 71 | 62 | 78 | 3 |
| 1965 | YANKEES | .239 | 46 | 155 | 22 | 37 | 7 | 0 | 8 | 27 | 29 | 29 | 0 |
| 1966 | YANKEES-c | .233 | 119 | 348 | 37 | 81 | 9 | 2 | 13 | 43 | 26 | 60 | 0 |
| 1967 | ST. LOUIS | .261 | 125 | 410 | 64 | 107 | 18 | 7 | 9 | 55 | 52 | 61 | 0 |
| 1968 | ST. LOUIS | .255 | 100 | 310 | 25 | 79 | 18 | 2 | 5 | 45 | 24 | 38 | 0 |
| **N.Y.Y. Totals** | | **.265** | **850** | **3007** | **520** | **797** | **110** | **17** | **203** | **548** | **413** | **417** | **7** |
| **A.L. Totals** | | **.260** | **1238** | **4381** | **737** | **1139** | **159** | **33** | **261** | **751** | **576** | **634** | **21** |
| **N.L. Totals** | | **.258** | **225** | **720** | **89** | **186** | **36** | **9** | **14** | **100** | **76** | **99** | **0** |
| **M.L. Totals** | | **.260** | **1463** | **5101** | **826** | **1325** | **195** | **42** | **275** | **851** | **652** | **733** | **21** |

a-Traded to Kansas City Athletics with Pitcher Dick Tomanek and Infielder Preston Ward for
   Infielder Vic Power and Infielder-Outfielder Woodie Held, June 15, 1958.
b-Traded to New York Yankees with First Baseman Kent Hadley and Shortstop Joe DeMaestri for
   Pitcher Don Larsen, First Baseman Marv Throneberry and Outfielders Hank Bauer and Norm
   Siebern, December 11, 1959.
c-Traded to St. Louis Cardinals for Third Baseman Charlie Smith, December 8, 1966.
*Led league

## NEW YORK YANKEES—1961 ROSTER (As of February 1, 1961)

| Uniform No. STAFF | Name | | | Ht. | Wt. | Date of Birth | Age |
|---|---|---|---|---|---|---|---|
| 35 | HOUK, Ralph (Manager) | | | 5:10 | 190 | Aug. 9, 1920 | (40) |
| 2 | CROSETTI, Frank (Coach) | | | 5:10 | 165 | Oct. 4, 1910 | (50) |
| 44 | HEGAN, Jim (Coach) | | | 6:02 | 195 | Aug. 3, 1920 | (40) |
| 36 | MOSES, Wally (Coach) | | | 5:10 | 161 | Oct. 8, 1910 | (50) |
| 31 | SAIN, Johnny (Coach) | | | 6:02 | 205 | Sept. 25, 1917 | (43) |

**PITCHERS (17)**      **Bats Throws**

| No. | Name | Bats | Throws | Ht. | Wt. | Date of Birth | Age |
|---|---|---|---|---|---|---|---|
| 47 | ARROYO, Luis | R | L | 5:08½ | 190 | Feb. 18, 1928 | (32) |
| 18 | BRONSTAD, Jim | R | R | 6:03 | 192 | June 22, 1936 | (24) |
| 39 | COATES, Jim | R | R | 6:04 | 180 | Aug. 4, 1932 | (28) |
| 28 | DITMAR, Art | R | R | 6:02 | 197 | Apr. 3, 1929 | (31) |
| 26 | DUREN, Ryne | R | R | 6:01½ | 198 | Feb. 22, 1929 | (31) |
| 16 | FORD, Whitey | L | L | 5:10 | 181 | Oct. 21, 1928 | (32) |
| 53 | JAMES, John | L | R | 5:10 | 163 | July 23, 1933 | (27) |
| 48 | HEINTZ, Gerald | R | R | 6:00 | 171 | Feb. 3, 1942 | (18) |
| 24 | McDEVITT, Dan | L | L | 5:10 | 175 | Nov. 18, 1932 | (28) |
| 49 | MEYER, Bob | L | L | 6:02 | 165 | Aug. 4, 1939 | (21) |
| 45 | SHELDON, Roland | R | R | 6:04 | 185 | Dec. 17, 1939 | (21) |
| 46 | SHORT, Billy | L | L | 5:09 | 178 | Nov. 27, 1937 | (23) |
| 22 | STAFFORD, Bill | R | R | 6:01 | 183 | Aug. 13, 1938 | (22) |
| 27 | STOWE, Harold | L | L | 6:00 | 170 | Aug. 29, 1937 | (23) |
| 23 | TERRY, Ralph | R | R | 6:03 | 190 | Jan. 9, 1936 | (24) |
| 19 | TURLEY, Bob | R | R | 6:02 | 212 | Sept. 19, 1930 | (30) |
| 21 | WIEAND, Ted | R | R | 6:02 | 195 | Apr. 4, 1933 | (27) |

**CATCHERS (5)**

| No. | Name | Bats | Throws | Ht. | Wt. | Date of Birth | Age |
|---|---|---|---|---|---|---|---|
| 8 | *BERRA, Yogi | L | R | 5:08 | 191 | May 12, 1925 | (35) |
| 38 | BLANCHARD, John | L | R | 6:01 | 197 | Feb. 26, 1933 | (27) |
| 25 | GONDER, Jesse | L | R | 5:10 | 190 | Jan. 20, 1936 | (25) |
| 40 | HALL, Alan | R | R | 6:01 | 185 | Aug. 31, 1938 | (22) |
| 32 | *HOWARD, Elston | R | R | 6:02 | 200 | Feb. 23, 1929 | (31) |

**INFIELDERS (7)**

| No. | Name | Bats | Throws | Ht. | Wt. | Date of Birth | Age |
|---|---|---|---|---|---|---|---|
| 34 | BOYER, Cletis | R | R | 6:00 | 180 | Feb. 8, 1937 | (23) |
| 42 | BRICKELL, Fritz | R | R | 5:05½ | 155 | Mar. 19, 1935 | (25) |
| 20 | DEMAESTRI, Joe | R | R | 6:00 | 178 | Dec. 9, 1928 | (32) |
| 6 | *JOHNSON, Deron | R | R | 6:02 | 200 | July 17, 1938 | (22) |
| 10 | *KUBEK, Tony | L | R | 6:03 | 190 | Oct. 12, 1936 | (24) |
| 1 | RICHARDSON, Bobby | R | R | 5:09 | 169 | Aug. 19, 1935 | (25) |
| 14 | SKOWRON, Bill | R | R | 6:00 | 200 | Dec. 18, 1931 | (29) |

**OUTFIELDERS (4)**

| No. | Name | Bats | Throws | Ht. | Wt. | Date of Birth | Age |
|---|---|---|---|---|---|---|---|
| 11 | LOPEZ, Hector | R | R | 6:00 | 177 | July 8, 1932 | (28) |
| 7 | MANTLE, Mickey | L-R | R | 6:00 | 198 | Oct. 20, 1931 | (29) |
| 9 | MARIS, Roger | L | R | 6:00 | 200 | Sept. 10, 1934 | (26) |
| 17 | THOMAS, Leroy | L | R | 6:02 | 192 | Feb. 5, 1936 | (24) |

Traveling Secretary—Bruce Henry
Team Physician—Dr. Sidney S. Gaynor
Trainers—Gus Mauch and Joe Soares

*Also OF

| Place of Birth | Winter Residence | Marital Status | No. Children |
|---|---|---|---|
| Lawrence, Kans. | Saddle River, N.J. | M | 3 |
| San Francisco, Cal. | Stockton, Cal. | M | 2 |
| Lynn, Mass. | Lakewood, Ohio | M | 2 |
| Uvalda, Ga. | Philadelphia, Pa. | M | 1 |
| Havana, Ark. | Walnut Ridge, Ark. | M | 4 |

| Place of Birth | Winter Residence | Marital Status | No. Children | 1960 Club | IP | W | L | ERA |
|---|---|---|---|---|---|---|---|---|
| Penuelas, Puerto Rico | Ponce, Puerto Rico | M | 5 | Jersey City | 95 | 9 | 7 | 2.46 |
|  |  |  |  | New York | 41 | 5 | 1 | 2.85 |
| Ft. Worth, Tex. | Ft. Worth, Tex. | M | 1 | Richmond | 200 | 9 | 13 | 3.11 |
| Farnham, Va. | Village, Va. | M | 2 | New York | 148 | 13 | 3 | 4.20 |
| Winthrop, Mass. | Springfield, Mass. | M | 2 | New York | 200 | 15 | 9 | 3.06 |
| Cazenovia, Wisc. | San Antonio, Tex. | M | 1 | New York | 48 | 3 | 4 | 4.88 |
| New York, N.Y. | Lake Success, N.Y. | M | 3 | New York | 194 | 12 | 9 | 3.08 |
| Bonners Ferry, Ida. | Pac. Palisades, Cal. | S | — | New York | 43 | 5 | 1 | 4.40 |
|  |  |  |  | Richmond | 35 | 3 | 2 | 5.67 |
| Belleville, Ill. | St. Libory, Ill. | S | — | Auburn | 50 | 3 | 4 | 5.40 |
| New York, N.Y. | Greenwood, Miss. | M | 0 | Los Angeles | 53 | 0 | 4 | 4.25 |
| Toledo, Ohio | Toledo, Ohio | S | — | Modesto | 144 | 8 | 9 | 5.75 |
| Putnam, Conn. | Woodstock, Conn. | S | — | Auburn | 150 | 15 | 1 | 2.88 |
| Kingston, N.Y. | Newburgh, N.Y. | M | 0 | New York | 47 | 3 | 5 | 4.79 |
|  |  |  |  | Richmond | 79 | 6 | 2 | 2.50 |
| Catskill, N.Y. | Athens, N.Y. | M | 0 | Richmond | 144 | 11 | 7 | 2.00 |
|  |  |  |  | New York | 61 | 3 | 1 | 2.21 |
| Gastonia, N.C. | Gastonia, N.C. | M | 1 | Amarillo | 209 | 12 | 12 | 4.35 |
| Chelsea, Okla. | Kansas City, Mo. | M | 0 | New York | 167 | 10 | 8 | 3.50 |
| Troy, Ill. | Lutherville, Md. | M | 2 | New York | 173 | 9 | 3 | 3.28 |
| Walnutsport, Pa. | Slatington, Pa. | M | 3 | Seattle | 109 | 8 | 7 | 3.63 |

| Place of Birth | Winter Residence | Marital Status | No. Children | Club 1960 | G | HR | RBI | BA |
|---|---|---|---|---|---|---|---|---|
| St. Louis, Mo. | Montclair, N.J. | M | 3 | New York | 120 | 15 | 62 | .276 |
| Minneapolis, Minn. | Minneapolis, Minn. | M | 1 | New York | 53 | 4 | 14 | .242 |
| Monticello, Ark. | Oakland, Cal. | M | 1 | Richmond | 109 | 13 | 44 | .327 |
|  |  |  |  | New York | 7 | 1 | 3 | .286 |
| San Diego, Cal. | Tucson, Ariz. | M | 0 | Binghamton | 34 | 3 | 18 | .164 |
| St. Louis, Mo. | Teaneck, N.J. | M | 3 | New York | 107 | 6 | 39 | .245 |
| Cossville, Mo. | Webb City, Mo. | M | 2 | New York | 124 | 14 | 45 | .242 |
| Wichita, Kans. | Wichita, Kans. | M | 2 | Richmond | 94 | 9 | 38 | .258 |
| San Francisco, Cal. | San Anselmo, Cal. | M | 3 | New York | 49 | 0 | 2 | .222 |
| San Diego, Cal. | San Diego, Cal. | S | — | Richmond | 127 | 27 | 92 | .245 |
| Milwaukee, Wisc. | Milwaukee, Wisc. | S | — | New York | 147 | 14 | 62 | .273 |
| Sumter, S.C. | Sumter, S.C. | M | 3 | New York | 150 | 1 | 26 | .252 |
| Chicago, Ill. | Hillsdale, N.J. | M | 2 | New York | 146 | 26 | 91 | .309 |
| Christobal, Pana. | Colon, Panama | M | 0 | New York | 131 | 9 | 42 | .284 |
| Spavinaw, Okla. | Dallas, Texas | M | 3 | New York | 153 | 40 | 94 | .276 |
| Hibbing, Minn. | Raytown, Mo. | M | 3 | New York | 136 | 39 | 112 | .283 |
| St. Louis, Mo. | Peoria, Ill. | S | — | Amarillo | 61 | 17 | 76 | .390 |
|  |  |  |  | Richmond | 50 | 9 | 31 | .246 |

## ROGER MARIS'S WORLD SERIES RECORD

Tied World Series records for most consecutive series played (5), 1960–1964 and most putouts, inning, center fielder (3), October 11, 1964, third inning. Homered in first World Series at-bat, October 5, 1960.

| YR | Club, Opp. | AVG | G | AB | R | H | 2B | 3B | HR | RBI | BB | SO | SB |
|---|---|---|---|---|---|---|---|---|---|---|---|---|---|
| 1960 | N.Y. vs. Pit. | .267 | 7 | 30 | 6 | 6 | 1 | 0 | 2 | 2 | 3 | 4 | 0 |
| 1961 | N.Y. vs. Cin. | .105 | 5 | 19 | 4 | 2 | 1 | 0 | 1 | 2 | 4 | 6 | 0 |
| 1962 | N.Y. vs. S.F. | .174 | 7 | 23 | 4 | 4 | 1 | 0 | 1 | 5 | 5 | 2 | 0 |
| 1963 | N.Y. vs. L.A. | .000 | 2 | 5 | 0 | 0 | 0 | 0 | 0 | 0 | 0 | 1 | 0 |
| 1964 | N.Y. vs. StL. | .200 | 7 | 30 | 4 | 6 | 0 | 0 | 1 | 1 | 1 | 4 | 0 |
| 1967 | StL. vs Bos. | .385 | 7 | 26 | 3 | 10 | 1 | 0 | 1 | 7 | 1 | 3 | 0 |
| 1968 | StL. vs Det. | .158 | 6 | 19 | 5 | 3 | 1 | 0 | 0 | 1 | 3 | 3 | 0 |
| **W.S. Totals** | | **.217** | **41** | **152** | **26** | **33** | **5** | **0** | **6** | **18** | **18** | **21** | **0** |

## ROGER MARIS'S ALL-STAR GAME RECORD

| YR | Club, Site | AVG | G | AB | R | H | 2B | 3B | HR | RBI | BB | SO | SB |
|---|---|---|---|---|---|---|---|---|---|---|---|---|---|
| 1959 | A.L., L.S.-N. | .000 | 1 | 2 | 0 | 0 | 0 | 0 | 0 | 0 | 0 | 1 | 0 |
| 1960 | A.L., K.C., N.Y.-A | .000 | 2 | 6 | 0 | 0 | 0 | 0 | 0 | 0 | 0 | 1 | 0 |
| 1961 | A.L., S.F., Bos. | .200 | 2 | 5 | 0 | 1 | 0 | 0 | 0 | 0 | 1 | 2 | 0 |
| 1962 | A.L., Was., Chi-N. | .167 | 2 | 6 | 2 | 1 | 1 | 0 | 0 | 2 | 1 | 1 | 0 |
| **A.S. Totals** | | **.105** | **7** | **19** | **2** | **2** | **1** | **0** | **0** | **2** | **2** | **5** | **0** |

# INDEX

263